Transcendent
Sex

Transcendent Sex

When Lovemaking Opens the Veil

Jenny Wade, Ph.D.

PARAVIEW POCKET BOOKS

New York   London   Toronto   Sydney

PARAVIEW
191 Seventh Avenue, New York, NY 10011

POCKET BOOKS, a division of Simon & Schuster, Inc.
1230 Avenue of the Americas, New York, NY 10020

ISBN: 0-7434-8217-4

First Paraview Pocket Books trade paperback edition April 2004

10 9 8 7 6 5 4 3 2 1

POCKET and colophon are registered trademarks of
Simon & Schuster, Inc.

Manufactured in the United States of America

For information regarding special discounts for bulk purchases,
please contact Simon & Schuster Special Sales at 1-800-456-6798
or business@simonandschuster.com.

Contents

Foreword

WHY DO PEOPLE JOKE ABOUT SEX? Is it because sex is . . . what? Too embarrassing? Too "dirty," vulgar, raw? Anything that rabbits and weasels can do simply can't be that great, and hence is worth at most a snicker or two? Is sex too intimate?—such that public discussion is met with giggles? Or is sex too real, too close to the truth, the hidden truth, of what we are?

When Jenny Wade first began her research on sexual experiences, we happened to be having the first meetings of Integral Institute (which is devoted to an "integral" or comprehensive approach to reality), which Jenny and I attended. One of the best things about all those meetings was that, at the end of each, Jenny would make an announcement about her research, something like, "I am doing a phenomenological study of mystical, spiritual, or transcendent experiences during sex. Anybody interested in being a part of this study, please contact me."

Yes, the best thing about those meetings was listening to what everybody said after that announcement. On bathroom walls across the country, we could imagine what was being written: "For a good time, call Heidi. For a *really* good time, call Jenny."

Still, why do we laugh at that? Surely the correct answer is that it is really funny. But philosophers, of which I am one, make a nonliving out of asking incredibly stupid questions, over and over and over again, until we get an answer so obscure and inherently ridiculous that the average person is forced to assume that it is really profound and . . . well, philosophical. So here goes.

I think we laugh at sex because it can kill us.

Okay, that is not as completely ridiculous as, say, deconstruction, but bear with me. Almost all major psychologists (who are people involved in a marginally less silly profession than philosophy) have at some point examined the meaning and function of laughter (perhaps most famously, Freud in "Wit and Its Relation to the Unconscious"). They all reached somewhat different conclusions, except that all of them agreed that we only laugh at something that is unnervingly significant. Even something as silly as, say, somebody slipping on a banana peel, is funny because it touches on the fact that anybody can, without warning and at any time, fall from the dignity of being an upstanding human to being a pathetic and total klutz.

Which is funny if it happens to that guy, not me. Aristotle (not known for his wit) once nevertheless managed to comment, "Luck is what happens when the arrow hits the guy next to you." It's often the same with humor: a horrible experience is really funny when it happens to the guy next to you. Somehow we have to be removed from the incident in order for it to be funny, which is why it is often said that "tragedy plus time is humor." Well, Woody Allen said that in *Crimes and Misdemeanors*, but I think he knows more about the subject than, say, Freud or Aristotle (ever seen a picture of either of them smiling?).

Sex is unnervingly significant, so we laugh. What is so important about Jenny's research, however, is that it shows that whatever danger we thought sex held for us, it is even worse. Sex really can kill you, if by "you" is meant the ordinary you, the everyday you, the skin-encapsulated ego of your everyday persona. It's not just that sex can be "mind-blowing"; it's that sex can show you the face of God, the smile of the Goddess, the radiance of Spirit—and more unnerving still, not as a force or presence out there, but as your own deepest self and nature.

Welcome to the world of transcendent sex. As you will see in the following pages, spiritual experiences during sex are not confined to tantric yogis or mystical Taoists, but happen with astonishing regularity to all varieties of people—true believers and atheists alike, males and females, hetero and homo and bi—and with such general similarities that one can't help but draw several far-reaching conclusions.

The first is that, despite what some religious authorities maintain, sex and spirit are not opposites but more like two dimensions of a single reality. Or perhaps different colors in the same rainbow of the miracle of existence. Sex might not be conducive to certain religious *beliefs*, but it is definitely conducive to religious *experience*, spiritual experience, direct apprehensions of a living, luminous, radiant, unqualifiable reality that is what there is and all there is, a reality that can be—and is—often elicited in sexual activity.

The second is that, no matter how frequent or earthshaking a transcendent sexual experience might be, it is seldom talked about. An astonishing 80 percent of the respondents in Jenny's study reported that they never told a single person—not even their partner—about the experience.

I'm sure they thought that if they did, their partner would laugh, yes?

To me, the enormous service that Jenny's work offers is that it can help the untold number of individuals who have had these types of experiences begin to come to terms with them; to understand that they are not abnormal or pathological; that they contain in many cases what even Aristotle would call the *summum bonum*, the supreme good of life—namely, contemplation of (or even identification with) the Divine; but, nonetheless, these experiences are not to be sought casually or recklessly—they are dynamite, in every sense of the word.

As Jenny's research shows, these sexual/mystical experiences come in almost all varieties, and parallel in many cases the types of spiritual experiences available through other means—including experiences of God or Goddess, oneness with an all-embracing Reality or Light, identification with plants or animals, past-life visions, a sense of the sacredness of all Life, and so on. Like any altered state or peak experience, even a brief glimmer can be an earth-shattering, life-changing, reality-altering experience. The altered state itself might pass, but the meaning it brought lingers, a fine perfume in the air, reminding the person that Spirit is all and one, here and everywhere, even now, even here, in this body, on this earth, everlastingly. "And all shall be well, and all shall be well, and all manner of things shall be well," as St. Julian of Norwich would say.

Jenny Wade is herself a developmental psychologist (see, e.g., her superb *Changes of Mind*), which means she specializes in the study of various stages of consciousness that people demonstrate as they grow and evolve. The question naturally arises: What is the relation of those *stages* of consciousness to the *states* of consciousness such as the peak experiences in transcendent sex? It's an important question in that Jenny's research touches on a central issue in spiritual studies, namely, whether "genuine spirituality" involves brief and intense experiences, or whether it involves arduous and prolonged practice. The answer is almost certainly that it can involve both, and perhaps ideally ought to involve both. Experiences such as transcendent sex are authentic and genuine spiritual experiences, but in order to convert those *temporary states* into *permanent traits*, extended spiritual practice is usually required (such as that offered by meditation, contemplation, yoga, genuine tantric practice, integral transformative practice, and so on).

In short, a more integral spirituality would involve both states and stages. We have a fair amount of research on exactly that topic, research that suggests that the net effect of altered states or peak experiences is that they accelerate development through various stages of growth. There is no evidence that altered states will allow one to skip stages of growth, but they do accelerate their unfolding. The upshot of all that research is simply that the more often one is dunked into the Divine via altered states (such as transcendent sex), the more likely one will grow and evolve to a point where one can maintain that awareness of the Divine in a more permanent and enduring fashion. Combine states with stages and you are on the fast path to Spirit.

That is why sex can kill you. As the simplest, most accessible, most here-and-now transcendent experience that anybody can have, it is the most common doorway to the Divine, the most ordinary (in the best sense of the word) altered state that accelerates the stages of spiritual realization. The more one is plunged into the ocean of Spirit, into the ocean of infinite ease, the more one dies to one's smaller self, dies to one's ego, that finite and contracted and mortal coil, and finds instead one's own Original Face, one's own Godhead, one's own True Nature, prior to but not other to the entire manifest world.

And discovering *That*, we laugh—and laugh and laugh and laugh. It is truly the ultimate inside joke: You are That. In the deepest, highest, wildest part of yourself, you intersect Infinity, you are one with the radiant Divine, you are the luminescent Essence of everything that exists, the blazing realization of which brings such a shattering relief that henceforth you might never stop laughing. Or crying—at that point, they mean pretty much the same thing. But the ultimate cosmic joke is simply that *You're It*.

So I think we laugh for all those reasons.

And therefore, if you want a *really* good time, call Jenny. Or simply read the following pages, where your guide will take you through this extraordinary thing called sex, this extraordinarily ordinary thing called sex, and you might, rather literally, never be the same again. And you might never, *never*, stop laughing.

KEN WILBER

Discovering Transcendent Sex

This sexual experience is so much greater than anything I'd conceptualized before. This can blow the doors off normal, waking reality and normal sexual interactions. Even a week afterward, I was still thinking, "Wow! Did that really happen?"
—Austin

I would describe regular sex as two-dimensional, whereas this elevated sexual experience is multicolored, holographic.
—Elaine

This is kicking it up to the next level. If going to the store or tying your shoe is a level-one activity, just a mindless thing your body automatically does, and ordinary sex is a level 10, this is a whole other order of magnitude.
—Muntu

THERE REALLY IS SOMETHING better than sex—by orders of magnitude. And it doesn't leave sex behind. It's lovemaking that shatters reality, opens new dimensions, rips the veil between the worlds, and produces ecstasies a thousand times more powerful than the most exquisite orgasm. It's lovemaking so spectacular that it literally *is* a religious experience.

This is not a book about Tantra, the Hindu sexual path of realization through deliberate manipulation of the body's sacred life-energy. It's about one of the best-kept secrets in human history: the fact that ordinary people, the kind we pass on the street every day without a second glance—people just like us—can suddenly, without any warning or preparation, find themselves in otherworldly realms when making love as though God's lightning bolt of grace had illuminated the bedroom, transforming everything. Nothing is ever the same again.

The fact is, sex—all by itself—can trigger states identical to those attained by spiritual adepts of all traditions: the animal possession and otherworldly travels of shamans, the bodily fireworks of kundalini yoga, the past-life revelations of reincarnation religions, the Void of Buddhism, and the *unio mystica* described by Western saints. These are real spiritual experiences, the kind that change people's lives (but not the kind that make people take up celibacy or otherwise forgo the delights of the flesh). They've happened to countless thousands of people regardless of their background, to hairdressers, investment managers, nurses, lawyers, retailers, and executives. They've surprised people whose religions take different views of sex—Baptists, Catholics, Presbyterians, Jews, atheists, Mormons—as well as people with no religious beliefs at all. It makes no difference. Transcendent sex occurs regardless of skill in the bedroom. In fact, it has sometimes been the ultimate blessing to people who have never been able to enjoy sex before because they were abused. Like other spiritual awakenings, these transcendent sexual episodes change people's lives for the better. They produce healing, fulfillment, joy and insight. They also can leave miraculous gifts in their wake.

Oddly enough, transcendent sex really isn't anything new. The ancients knew far more about it than we do today. The oldest document in the world, the *Epic of Gilgamesh*, contains a description of transcendent sex and its transformative powers. It was inscribed about 3,000 years ago from a much older oral tradition about a historical king of Uruk in Mesopotamia who lived about 2700 B.C.E. Enkidu, a central character in the epic, is a wild man, more animal than human. His body is covered with shaggy fur. He lives in the wild, eating grass with the other animals and shouldering them aside for space at the watering hole. One day, a goddess commanded Shamhat, a priestess of sacred sex, to leave the temple and go make love to Enkidu in the wilderness. They enjoyed a lusty weeklong sex bout that resulted in Enkidu's evolution to a higher life-form:

> Shamhat unclutched her bosom, exposed her sex, and he
>   took in her voluptuousness.
> She was not restrained, but took his energy.
> She spread out her robe and he lay upon her. . . .
> His lust groaned over her;
> for six days and seven nights, Enkidu stayed aroused,
> and had intercourse with the [sacred] harlot
> until he was sated with her charms.
> But when he turned his attention to his animals,
> the gazelles saw Enkidu and darted off,
> the wild animals distanced themselves from his body. . . .
> But then he drew himself up, for his understanding had
>   broadened. . . .
> The [sacred] harlot said to Enkidu:
> "You are beautiful, Enkidu, you are become like a god."[1]

Enkidu lost his bestial ways, began to walk upright like a human being, increased in intelligence, and became partly divine—all through the power of sacred sex. *This story contains all of the elements found in transcendent sex today.* Transcendent sex can bring about miraculous personal transformations that elevate people's understanding, insight, and way of being in the world, including rendering them more "godly" in terms of spiritual attainment and orientation.

Unfortunately, the ancient world's legacy of sacred sex was lost as the institutionalization of religion eventually monopolized spirituality. Private, personal revelations—however they occurred—weren't legitimate unless they were scrutinized and then approved by religious authorities.[2] At the same time these authorities were ratifying spiritual openings, they were beginning to circumscribe sex, too. Today we have religions that dictate almost everything about lovemaking: what kinds of partners people may select; what the nature of their relationship must be; what sorts of acts they may perform; when they can couple, including which days, times of day, and how often; what their motivations must be; and how much enjoyment they may have. Furthermore, in most traditions, *really* serious aspirants must abstain from sex altogether. It would be hard to imagine a greater split between sex and Spirit.

The Divorce of Sex from Spirit

It's a popular notion that Eastern religions have always embraced sex, while Western ones have banned it, but this really isn't true. In all institutionalized religions, the pleasurable powers of sex gradually changed from a celebration of divine forces to a distraction from the spiritual path—and from a distraction to a hazard. For some, it was only a small step from a hazard to a sin.

Despite stories of divine couples in Hinduism, such as the god Shiva and goddess Shakti, and Krishna and Radha, whose relationships are primarily sexual, carnal desire is to be avoided at all costs because it chains humanity to the world of illusion.[3] Similarly in Buddhism, classic texts, such as the *Visuddhimagga*, deny worldly pleasures to aspirants. Serious seekers were, and are, expected to be celibate, if not actually ascetic. In fact, the cessation of sexual desires is considered one of the marks of the adept, the natural outgrowth of effective spiritual practice.[4] Tantra, Vajrayana Buddhism, and Taoism aren't the straightforwardly "pro-sex" paths many people think. Tantra is a yogic practice that began as a countercultural movement of "reverse spirituality"—that is, doing the opposite of religious conventions—in a kind of "crazy wisdom" in which eating forbidden food, drinking forbidden drinks, violating taboos, and engaging in sex could be ritualized into a path for realization.[5] Even in Tantra, actual sex is given up as quickly as possible. Vajrayana Buddhism incorporates ancient indigenous Tibetan and Indian traditions. It requires high levels of attainment before initiates can participate in sexual practices that have more to do with meditation than lovemaking.[6] Taoist sex is a rigorously disciplined form that is less about enjoyment and more about practices that will produce health and longevity. It can involve methods that resemble austerities.[7]

In the West, sex retained a place in religion, though it was never considered the way to salvation. Sex played a much greater role in Judaism than in Christianity or Islam. Married Jews obeyed the commandment in Genesis (1:28) to be fruitful and multiply, and in Kabbalic Judaism, a mystical branch that emerged in the Middle Ages, sexual intercourse became a powerful spiritual act that enabled spouses to participate in the male and female aspects of God sustaining the cosmos.[8] Even though sex is expected for married couples on most holy days, there is ambivalence about experiencing too much pleasure.[9] Christianity took a different tack from its inception. Jesus shocked his Jewish contemporaries by condoning practices that would limit procreation, such as forbidding divorce for any reason, including the wife's infertility (Matthew 19:4–6), as well as connecting celibacy with eternal life (Luke 20:34–36).[10] Augustine, probably the single most influential voice on Christian thinking about sex, believed that God had condemned humanity to eternal damnation through Adam's sexual act.[11] Abstinence and asceticism became hallmarks of the early Christian era, casting a shadow on sexuality still felt today. Although Gnostic and mystical sects have always incorporated sexual imagery, most of them were persecuted out of existence.[12] Finally, sexuality is consecrated in the Qu'ran, and its mystical forms are rife with a feminine principle and a sacralization of intercourse. But mainstream Islam became conservative about sex and today widely regards women as a chaotic element in Moslem society.[13]

But no matter how hard societies tried to stamp it out, the divine play of sex and Spirit didn't disappear. It was just driven underground. The ghostly imprint of sacred sex can still be discerned in every mainstream religion today.[14] It can't be eradicated from the pool of human experience, and it keeps popping up randomly and irrepressibly. Transcendent sex is going on behind closed doors this very moment, just as it always has. Transcendent sex has been a well-kept secret, but like any secret, it leaks out. Research studies on sex routinely turn up episodes of Spirit. And research studies on spirituality regularly turn up sex. Anyone can have it, and it can happen at any time. So why hasn't anyone really talked about it before now?

What's a Nice Girl like You . . .?

I actually wasn't going to talk about it either. But two things happened. One day, out of the blue, after a lifetime of ordinary sex, it happened to me. I kept silent. It was only years later, in the course of my work, that I rebelled against the assumptions of colleagues and friends, many of them prominent in contemporary spirituality, who maintained that "real" spiritual seeking involves only certain recognized disciplines, practices, and lineages. I began a research project to see whether I was alone in having some of my most transformative moments occur adventitiously in the bedroom.

I discovered more reports of transcendent sexual experiences than I ever could have imagined. But I also discovered that virtually nobody talked about them, even to their lovers. None of us had had the courage to admit that we have been profoundly changed by events that, had they happened on a *prie-Dieu* or a meditation cushion instead of in a bed, would have been celebrated.

People always want to know my story, but it's not nearly so dramatic as those I've gathered from others. I'm a developmental psychologist who researches different types of consciousness, from the ones considered normal to those considered altered states (such as prenatal memories, trance, etc.). That may sound esoteric but as an organization development consultant, I actually apply a lot of my expertise concerning "normal" states to very practical, real-world business situations.

Nothing in my life really prepared me for ecstatic sex. I'm not a spiritual adept, and I'm certainly not a love goddess. I was brought up in a conservative Methodist and Southern Baptist home. I became Episcopalian with contemplative leanings. As a baby boomer coming of age in the early 1970s, my attitude about sex is relatively liberal, and I've had a number of partners over the years. I don't consider myself a particularly gifted or sophisticated lover.

On this occasion, I went to bed, as I had countless times before, with a man with whom I was deeply in love and with whom sex was always terrific but not in any way unusual. To my surprise, the room we were in began to change. Its right-angled white walls dissolved into a round, pink chamber with a silver Greek-key border around the ceiling. The next thing I knew, I was no longer in that room but looking out over sparkling, ultramarine ocean waves from a sunny shore. Then I found myself surrounded by sea creatures. I thought at first I had been drawn from the beach into the ocean's depths, but then I realized the sea creatures weren't real. Instead they were fantastic *pictures* of all sorts of fish and octopi on the pale greenish-blue walls of yet another and very different room. The pictures were painted in the distinctive style of ancient Crete, a culture about which I know almost nothing. The greatest peace, wonder, delight, and bliss pervaded me.

Gradually I found myself back in the real world, making love with no idea where the vision had come from or how long it had lasted. My partner seemed unaware that anything unusual had occurred, and I felt it would be tactless to mention that my attention had strayed so far from him. Besides, it was also just a little too weird, probably some temporary aberration that would never happen again. Or so I reasoned.

That wasn't the end of it, though. I never saw that particular vision again, but there were others. And then I had an episode that was too big to contain. The whole world disappeared in a wash of white light that became clear, and then nothingness, nonduality, the Void—what Zen Buddhists call *kensho* or what is popularly known as nirvana or samadhi. My understanding of reality was forever altered. When I came back to normal consciousness, I was awestruck, jubilant. Suddenly, I *got* it—*this* is what the saints and sages were talking about, *this* is what is true. I was bubbling over with the profundity and blessed absurdity of it all, including amusement at having a Buddhist experience rather than a Christian one (this is not uncommon, as I found out later). My lover wondered why I had such a dazed look on my face and was laughing so hard. Fortunately, he was sympathetic. I learned that very few people tell their partners for fear of being ridiculed, another reason sacred sex has remained a secret.

It took a while, but the episode definitely changed my life, including creating a desire to learn more about such experiences and make them public.[15] In my research, I uncovered marvelous tales of love, adventure, insight, ecstasy and transformation, stories equal to any in the annals of spiritual discovery. I wanted to share this incredibly beautiful facet of human potential with others who may benefit from it, just as near-death experiences, which have impacted so many people's lives, were finally made public in a way that has given hope and comfort to many. Sex may not be so dramatic or universal as death, but it offers many more chances for deep spiritual openings and healing, even for those who have been most damaged by it through abuse or incest. I also wanted to provide a helpful context in which to understand such events because transcendent experiences, especially when they occur spontaneously, can be unsettling, challenging our assumptions about reality or even our own sanity. Many of the people I talked to were delighted but confused by their experiences, and they felt they had nowhere to turn for a sympathetic hearing, least of all to their lovers or spiritual advisers.

The Research

This book is based on the narratives of ninety-one ordinary people who stumbled into extraordinary experiences during sex (see Appendix for details of the research). The information, however sensational or controversial it may appear, is grounded in actual experiences independently reported by a number of individuals. Some people have only one type of experience, such as an out-of-body episode, which may have occurred only once in their lives, or repeatedly. Others have several different types of experience. A lucky few only seldom have "ordinary sex."

I wanted to conduct my research in a way that would be as free from bias as possible, so I deliberately chose people who had had nonordinary experiences triggered by sex but who *did not have a ready-made framework of explanation for what had happened to them from a spiritual ideology*. Thus I selected people who said they had been overcome by *spontaneous* "nonordinary," "altered," "mystical," or "transcendent" states of consciousness when they were making love. I eliminated those who might have been deliberately trying to create an altered state by using psychotropic drugs or practicing esoteric sexual techniques designed to bring about or influence what happened, as well as their interpretation of the experience. I wanted "naïve" participants whose interpretations were completely their own.

I was lucky enough to find many of them. In fact, probably about one in twenty people has had a spontaneous transcendent episode during sex.[16] Participants in my study came from the Americas, mostly the United States, representing different races, religions, ages, cultures, and sexual preferences. They are courageous and articulate people who trusted me with the most intimate and sacred events in their lives, for which I am deeply, humbly grateful. Their lives are like ours; their stories tell of events that just might happen to any one of us. They exalt the body and heart as well as the spirit potentially available to all of us.

Just What *Is* Transcendent Sex?

What distinguishes transcendent sex from the most intense regular sex? People who have had a transcendent experience making love *know* it. It is so far removed from ordinary sex that there is no mistaking it. Something changes radically, taking lovers out of their normal sense of themselves and out of the here and now. Their senses may be altered, or their body may seem changed. They may not feel like themselves, but like someone else—or even a host of others. Their lover may become someone else—or even something else. They may be here, but not now, or now, but not here. Or the world may vanish entirely as they plunge into the heart of God.

For instance, here's how "Blake" (all names are pseudonyms), a retired Jewish schoolteacher, talks about transcendent sex, which began for him in his sixties:

> This love you call transcendent . . . begins in sensuality and ends in God. . . . I feel as if my body is made of filaments and radiating enormous energy. Pure feeling, a kind of primordial bliss, is streaming through it. There is only a fragment of my own personal consciousness left because I feel as if I am entering God, or God is entering me, that I am blazing with the energy of God and pouring that energy back into my lover, and worshiping her and God at the same time. And then thoughts spin out and there is *only That*—the utterly inexpressible, the union with the Source of all, and a kind of divine annihilation.

Blake is describing one type of transcendent episode, the only kind he experiences. There are many different kinds, and some individuals may experience several types. But his example serves to illustrate three features that define the way the term transcendent sex is used in this book.

1. Transcendent sex involves altered states that seem to come out of nowhere and overcome one or both of the lovers. The term "transcendent sex" comes from the sense of transcending (going beyond or breaking through) the usual constraints

of space, time, or self that constitute normal, waking consciousness. For instance, a person might suddenly be out of body, hovering over the bed, traveling back in time to a past life, or expanding to include the consciousness of all living creatures.

2. In transcendent sex, there is a pervasive sense that these events participate in, or come from, a supernatural force, which people usually associate with Spirit, however understood. Whether it's stepping into another reality, seeing visions, being possessed by an animal power or imploding into the utter emptiness of the Void, most people attribute a numinous quality to the events, even if they consider themselves atheists or agnostics.

3. Transcendent sex involves relationship. It is rooted in the ground created by the lovers, even when one person is taken so far beyond reality that the partner and the lovemaking recede into infinity. Or, in some cases, even when the partner is not human.[17]

The accounts in this book roughly progress from the least transcendent to the most transcendent, though this is not meant to suggest a progression or hierarchy of these sexual altered states. The book begins with the experiences that are most like "normal reality" or "normal consciousness," where events may seem very odd, even hallucinatory, but occur in the recognizable here and now, and the participants feel they are completely themselves. The first section, The Magical Mystery Tour, covers episodes in which lovers experience dimensions of reality commonly associated with visions and enchantment. They find themselves in a version of ordinary reality that seems much more vibrant and to be populated with far more wondrous lifeforms than they ever realized. The experiences in the second section, Loosening the Boundaries of Reality, dissolve the boundaries of self, space, and other. People may no longer recognize themselves or their lovers. They may be possessed by another entity, or transported to another location. In the third section, The Shattering of the Vessels, a name taken from the Kabbalic tradition of mystical Judaism, even time melts away. Individuals may find themselves and their lovers sucked into past lives as different people in remote times and places. Here reality collapses completely, resulting in what is popularly known as enlightenment in the East or the Kingdom of Heaven (*unio mystica*) in the West. The last section, Using the Knowledge of Transcendent Sex, presents the dark side of transcendent sex, gives precautions and instructions for engaging in it, and discusses the transformative effects it produces.

What Causes It:
Common Sense and the Seeds of Controversy

When I began this study, I had several ideas about what might be causing transcendent sex. Virtually every one of them was shattered in my research. I mention them here because most people have the same preconceptions about the topic. Transcendent sex can't be explained—or explained away—through common sense. It also isn't limited to the practices or relationships approved by some religions and cultures.

1. Transcendent episodes have little or nothing to do with sexual mechanics or technique. They can occur within the general context of lovemaking no matter what the couple is doing. Some people are swept away even before they touch. Since mechanics are not a factor, people engaging in a wide variety of behaviors have transcendent experiences—whether or not those behaviors conform to religious or social

norms. My study includes people who were having heterosexual, gay, and lesbian relations in ways that might be considered mainstream, as well as ways that might be considered
exotic (such as bondage, cross-dressing, and the like). This
book focuses on the experience, not the sex play itself.

2. Transcendent sex is not related to physiological differences
associated with male and female arousal. The arousal curve
spiking at the single orgasm typical for most men and the
ability of some women to be multiorgasmic or to "chain"
orgasms almost indefinitely make no difference in either the
ability to have a transcendent experience during sex, nor in
the kind of transcendent experience produced. Men and
women can and do have the same kinds of transcendent
episodes.[18]

3. Orgasm is not a causal factor. An orgasm may occur before,
during, or after the transcendent state as a discrete, uncon-
nected event. For most people, climaxing was completely
overshadowed by the pleasures of the transcendent events.
Climax was irrelevant, or even a nuisance that detracted
from more compelling delights. Often, the transcendent
episodes were so powerful some lovers had no idea whether
they climaxed or not. Some try to avoid it entirely because it
shatters or diminishes the ecstasy.

4. Sexual abuse is not a causal factor. Although early sexual
abuse has been associated with a susceptibility to altered-
state experiences, especially a proneness to escape into
altered states during sex, these transcendent experiences
had no discernible relationship to the dynamics researchers
have reported concerning abuse. In the first place, only
seven out of ninety-one participants had a history of sexual
abuse. In the second place, the abuse had made having consensual sex extremely difficult for participants. The states
they went into to avoid "being present" during sex involved

a shutting down of bodily sensations, psychological and physical numbness, and dissociation from the body and from sex. These previously abused participants reported transcendent sex episodes that were quite different: joyous, sensual, here-and-now events. Furthermore, the transcendent episodes helped them heal psychologically so that the tendency to dissociate during sex or shut the body down was subsequently markedly reduced.

5. Transcendent sex isn't limited to certain relationships. It can happen under any circumstances, even after years with the same person or during a one-night stand. People have reported it in relationships of high trust, like long-term monogamous commitments, but that isn't a prerequisite. Transcendent sex is not limited to "true love," nor is it a sign of it. It's also not a function of high-intensity infatuations, such as falling in love or a sudden hot connection. It has even occurred, against every expectation, when the participants felt they were doing something morally wrong (such as having sex with a partner they didn't love, engaging in a same-sex liaison or having an adulterous affair).

6. The transcendent states produced have no discernible relationship to a person's spiritual beliefs or practices. Atheists and agnostics may see God. Zen meditators may have shamanic journeys. Jews and Presbyterians who have never meditated a day in their lives may glimpse *satori*. Roman Catholics may activate kundalini energy. Long-term meditators may not have very unusual sexual altered states, while someone who has never followed a practice designed to bring about altered states may have a full-blown, nondualistic experience of the Void. Most contemplative traditions suggest a fairly fixed progression of altered states along the path to the ultimate goal, but I found no relationship between states attained during a contemplative practice (or

even indigenous spiritual practices) and those that occurred during sex.[19]

Clearly some of these findings challenge common sense, norms regarding what constitutes moral sexual behavior, and conventions too numerous to mention. But, as the stories here will show, such events can and do happen, regardless of our circumstances, readiness, or beliefs.

So What?

These findings allow us to rediscover the perfection in the material world. They remind us that Spirit is everywhere, especially in the places we never think to look. I think they indicate that grace infuses every part of the human experience—even sex—whether we're doing it "right" or doing it "wrong." It isn't about the activity, the attitude, or even the partner. It's about *us*. These narratives show that people were transformed. They broke out of constricting patterns into more expansive, more fulfilling, and more altruistic ways of being as a result of strange events that happened when they were making love. Remarkably, even individuals who had been sexually abused were capable of incredibly healing experiences that, although they did not obviate the abuse, opened doors to enjoyment and wholeness beyond their wildest dreams.

I am writing this book in the hope that we who have had mystical sex will recognize ourselves in the stories of others and feel affirmed. Other people know what we know. And they know some other things, too. No single individual I've spoken to has had the entire range of experiences, or even imagined what they involve.

Perhaps even more important, this book is written for those

of us who never imagined that sex and Spirit could be intertwined. Spirit is no less pure when it wears a human face, or a human body. Sex can be—is—much more than we ever imagined. And it's never too late to find out. Not one person in this book expected it to happen, yet it did. For some, it came after scores of partners, after true love had been lost, after disillusionment and routine. For others, it came after the unimaginable suffering of incest and rape. The vision these stories hold of healing seems little short of miraculous.

As Colleen, a victim of incest who converted to Tibetan Buddhism from having been reared Baptist, says of her transcendent sexual experience:

> Sex is absolutely sacred, absolutely holy. There's nothing dirty about it, nothing bad. It's something to be awestruck about. I have the feeling of being able to see beyond death to how beautiful and holy it all is, what the universe is really all about.

> I've had a lot of sexual experiences that seem so holy that they protected me from feeling so bad about myself when I remembered what had happened to me before. They left me feeling so joyous, so blessed, absolutely beautiful and overflowing with love.

Still, a word of caution is in order. I am not an advocate for transcendent sex; it is enough to acknowledge its reality and its power. Learning about the full celebration of sexual love enriches all of us, but it should *never* become a standard by which to measure personal prowess. The narratives in this book are not about some sexual Olympics for more and better orgasms or spiritual elitism.

Nobody "should" have altered-state experiences during sex. The body is not the way for everyone. Transcendent sex is only one of many ways Spirit enters our lives. It is good to know that this path exists, but for many, perhaps, it may wisely remain the road not taken.

In any case, it's not the heights of exaltation that are important, any more than it's the number of years spent on the meditation cushion or kneeling in prayer. The spiritual journey is about transformation. Apprehending the Absolute, or at least the greater reality, through sex changes people, just as it does in more established practices. We come to understand the world in a different way, a way that leaves us forever changed.

The Magical Mystery Tour

Reality is not this little thing we think it is. This [sexual experi-ence] showed me that there is more, so much more. This left me with a sense of wonderment, and a sense of confirmation.
—Esteban

CHAPTER I

Fireworks, Energy, and Light: Experiencing the Body Electric

Like on Star Trek when they get into the transporter and they sort of dissolve, I have that feeling of light going through me and a fire that goes down, the feeling that my body has been burned away to ash and there's nothing left, but I've been transported elsewhere. —Lucky

I've felt my cells literally get lit up . . . like those little fiber-optic things. It's pervasive, not just on the surface of me, but through my whole system . . . and that would sometimes last for days. —Shaka

It's like liquid fireworks. It's like sparks that come out in liquid form. —Adele

I MET SUZETTE, a vivacious, petite redhead, when she was in her fifties. She is a pragmatic, no-nonsense woman whose career had been spent in nursing and public health administration. She had been brought up in a conventional Midwestern home without knowledge of spiritual traditions outside the mainstream Christianity and Judaism of 1950s Middle America. She had never considered herself religious, but she came to me with a story that represents how transcendent sex transforms. She is the "everyman" and "everywoman" we all are. As we settled down to coffee in my office, she began to tell me about something that had happened many years ago with a man she'd only dated a few times. "I guess we've known each other more than twenty-five years now. We've had an on-and-off relationship because we live far apart," she explained. "When we've gotten together, many times we've had sex, and many times we've not. He's been a good friend."

They were business acquaintances living in different states whose professional activities brought them together periodically. They were just beginning to explore a more romantic connection when they had an opportunity to go to San Francisco together. "This trip was our first time to have sex," she confided, adding that it was enjoyable, that she was a little more nervous and excited than usual, but that nothing unusual had happened, until:

> I had my eyes closed, and I began to see light, and light moving. It was just so incredibly powerful. It could even have been a different dimension. It felt very unusual.

> The light was just going through me. I didn't know what it was part of, but it was definitely a physical feeling going through me and shooting out of the top of my head. I had feelings of white lights shooting out of the top of my head. The lights were really brilliant. The brightness of the lights was incredible. You think of sunlight or lightning, but *nothing* like *this!* It was radiant white light brighter than anything I'd seen in nature.

> And then it also affected me emotionally in a way, and I started crying because it was overwhelming, an emotional effect like "Oh, my God, I'm coming home. I got home." A feeling that I'd

been separated for a long time, like coming together, and finally being home.

I'm mainly a thinker, not emotional, but it was as if someone had taken a finger and pushed that incredible emotion button, and I really didn't know what hit me. I was so happy. It was a wonderful, peaceful feeling. Total peace, a feeling of great love and connection, and of going home.

Suzette was stunned. Nothing remotely like this had ever happened in her practical, down-to-earth life. Furthermore, such happenings did not mesh with her scientific knowledge or beliefs. She made some attempt to communicate what had occurred to her partner, but said, smiling ruefully, "I don't think he was aware of what was going on. I remember trying to tell him, and I think he laughed. He was a real stud, and we were in our early twenties, so it wasn't like he took it really seriously."

Suzette and her lover continued to see each other. Sex was always good, but it never reached those heights again for her. The liaison drifted into a friendship, and she eventually married someone else. Her marriage didn't work out, something she attributes to her ineptitude in the bedroom.

"I was just so naïve about sex," she commented, shaking her head. "My sex life with my husband was *so bad*. He was into black fringe and nudity, and I was into my flannel nightgown. The poor guy! I feel sorry for him now when I think of it."

They eventually divorced. Weary of prolonged celibacy during the years raising her son alone and wanting to "get some experience," Suzette began to date the relative of a good friend. There was some affection but no real chemistry between them. To her surprise, after having sex with him on a few occasions, she had another experience of transcendence.

I had the lights again, the brilliant lights. It was all so amazing, that way of shooting lights out of my head. The only difference was that it was not as emotional as the first time. Still, it was intense.

I was sad when it was over because it was really an exciting, thrilling experience. I wasn't aware of anything else when the lights were going. I wasn't seeing anything else, had no sense of time. . . . The whole world was gone away, so I wouldn't have had a clue.

And then it just kind of eased off. I felt a little shaky afterward. The first time, I cried more, probably because the chemistry seemed better so that I felt more melded to [the first lover], but not enough that I picked him and decided to be his partner.

This time, I was surprised, especially since I didn't really like him. . . . I've had wonderful sex since then with other people, but it happened just those two times. It was such a beautiful, wonderful experience. What would it be like to have it with someone you were really loving and wanting to have a relationship with?

As moving as these two incidents were, they had little impact on her life at the time. She mused, "I'd have thought that after having that experience, I'd have been more interested in spirituality and sexuality, but no. I was struggling to have my career and raise my child."

Still the seed took root. When I met her, her son was grown and Suzette had laid aside her health-care career to undertake several years of spiritual exploration, a quest she attributed to those two episodes. She had become a practitioner of Transcendental Meditation and yoga. Both gave Suzette a way to understand her experiences, though she was never able to replicate them nor have comparable experiences through meditation or yoga. Groping for words to describe how she understood the sexual episodes, she said, "[They] seemed spiritual because there was a feeling of unity and because of the brilliance of the lights. I don't know if it was God or Buddha or something like that, but it was such a positive feeling that it had to be a higher power of some kind." She continued, moving to discuss how these events had changed her:

It made me have more confidence in myself. . . . I do feel like a special person now. It gave me hope. It made me curious . . . I'm starting to look back at my life, and there's a part of my life I've really neglected. I'm working on spirituality now.

Having this kind of experience makes me believe that there is so much more than I ever realized there could be . . . more than I was seeing in the world. And it amuses me that it happened through a sexual experience. That wouldn't have been a predictable thing for me to guess!

So when I could, I started looking at other ways of living and thinking. I would have bet you money that I wouldn't be here [in the religious community where I interviewed her], but now look at me.

To have an experience like this gave me hope that there's guidance in my life, and in other peoples' lives. That there's more of a plan. It's like you're being pulled by Spirit, which—I don't know—but that experience gave me hope that such a thing might be possible.

Suzette's story, in a way, is like all the other stories in this book. The experiences follow a clear pattern:

- Individuals are surprised and dazzled by bedroom events that reveal a reality entirely foreign to their usual way of thinking. The events confound a religious person's beliefs or the disbelief of agnostics and atheists.
- The experience can occur regardless of how much "in love" or sexually skillful a person is.
- Most often, but not always, the experience involves only one member of the couple. The other party is frequently unaware that something earth-shattering is happening to the lover. Sadly, most people are reluctant to share these sacred, unsettling moments with partners because they fear a response that will be skeptical, mocking, or belittling. Over 80 percent of the people I talked to had never told another person what had happened to them.
- Depending on the nature of the episode—and Suzette's experience is actually one of the most "normal" or least strange—the person may feel euphoric, omniscient, dazed, disturbed, or frightened. Their foundations are shaken in ways that may seem life-affirming or threatening.
- The events may be hidden, but they are never forgotten. Like the near-death experiences that people kept secret before they became an acceptable part of public discourse, transcendent sexual episodes were recalled with extraordinarily vivid detail, even if they occurred long ago. Participants were relieved to be able to tell someone who was appreciative and nonjudgmental about some of the most significant things that had ever happened to them.
- Like more recognized spiritual openings, these experiences were life-changing events. The most skeptical agnostics and atheists were reluctant to ascribe a spiritual meaning to what had happened, but even they admitted that their understanding of the world had been radically altered and that they could not explain what had happened to them (the

sample includes physicists, physicians, and other "hard" scientists). However the vast majority, regardless of their former religious beliefs or disbelief, eventually went on to take up some form of spiritual quest in an attempt to understand what had transpired. Of those, many began an active spiritual practice or vocation, attributing their interest to the "awakening" they had had during sex.

Transcendent episodes during sex, however bizarre, resemble those recognized in the world's major spiritual traditions. In fact, except for the context (making love as opposed to meditating, praying, ingesting sacred medicine, or participating in ritual ceremonies), transcendent sexual experiences have exact counterparts in the shamanism of indigenous religions as well as in the mysticism of Christianity, Judaism, Islam, Hinduism, Buddhism, and Taoism. The chapters in this section cross many different spiritual traditions, but they all include recognized altered states in which people access greater dimensions of the natural world than are part of "normal, walking-around reality."

Heat and Light

Even when a person's sense of self and reality remain "normal," some people report strange energies coursing through the body. Sometimes it starts with a sense that the sexual charge normally rooted in the genitals is spreading throughout the entire body, lighting it up with crackling power and fireworks, shooting arcs, sparks, flashes of light and color. Two very different descriptions of what can happen come from Jorge, a professor, author, and lecturer, and Nell, a housewife and accomplished Buddhist meditator.

Jorge's experience began while just caressing his partner;

actual intercourse never occurred. Despite the fact that he had neither an erection nor an orgasm, he described it as a "very sexual experience." "I'm not that familiar with [Tantra]," he began, "but the movement of energy was very clear . . . from the genital area, spreading through the body, through the arms and legs, reaching the areas of the hands and mouth that were extremely charged and then moving them to my partner . . . energy going through my arms, my legs, her arms, her legs, our mouths." As his body vibrated with sexual electricity, it seemed to break free of its usual constraints:

> I felt a tremendous openness, and at some point, almost the emergence of a different body coming out, with a different breathing pattern, almost a different vibrational pattern, and more energy to it. I can't relate it to an astral body—who knows? But it was a very clear, tangible experience of this emerging body. . . . That body was very sexual, very sexual. I was still in my own body, but there was still this other body coming out. . . . It's extremely exhilarating—Beethoven's Ninth Symphony comes to mind, one of those big crescendos.

Nell, in contrast, began to dislike climaxing because her transcendent experiences were so much more thrilling. "Ordinary sex isn't interesting anymore," she said. "It's kind of boring and stupid to have this little spasm. [A] genital orgasm is a distraction now because it foreshortens or throws the switch on what can happen otherwise." She described the "otherwise" this way:

> There's a very strong genital aspect to it, but it's more a sort of dance that brings one into a kind of luminous state where nectars are flowing and everything is light both internally and externally.

It is totally circulating, totally energizing. I never feel more totally awake, more totally alive than then. It's electric, really light-oriented, very much upwardly oriented. It enlightens the whole body. You have the subjective experience of all the molecules of your body, all the cells of your body lightening and separating so that each one becomes like a lightbulb. You become a light being totally embodied.

Still other people have experiences that clearly involve sexual energy but in ways that are much less direct. Some report being immersed in brilliant emerald, purple, blue, or golden light. Whether involving strong charges of heat and light, or quieter, more melting sensations, these experiences produce an amazing range of energetic perceptions. The strange perceptions and sensations are not merely odd, like a mild electric shock or an optical illusion, rather they are always accompanied by blissful emotions that seemed to elevate the participants to sublime realizations, especially a sense of heightened love and peace. Here are a few examples.

Austin, a social services professional, describes a night of love while he was in graduate school:

I started noticing what I would call a field of energy around our bodies, what in my mind's eye I would have called "red," and a sense that I was expanding outward. My sense of self extended five or six feet all around us and outward. My body was tingling all over, and there was a feeling of heat that went with the energy and the redness. The tingling was as intense as when your foot falls asleep but there wasn't the numbness.

It was completely pleasurable, blissful. I was filled with an amazing sense of love for my wife, myself, and for us as a unity, a whole. Definitely above and beyond the normal feelings of love.

It was as much generated by her as by me or our situation. We filled the room with this red energy and heat . . . so that I felt I could reach out and touch all the corners.

Gloria, an agnostic who owns a retail business, talks about her connection with her lover:

The warmth and tingling starts in my toes, an electrical feeling that moves up my body and just goes out my eyes. When it's intense, it's almost blinding. There is an element of heat, but it's more the brightness of the light that's somewhat shocking.

But always this great sense of peace. I feel like it's the Universe's way of reassuring me that everything is right, as if I were a dog lying in front of a fireplace, and this giant, gentle hand is patting me, it just feels so good and comfortable. I'm connected with an energy level we don't usually connect to the everyday experience. I wouldn't necessarily say it's God, but maybe whatever the life force is. One day I may call it God.

Reginald, a self-employed businessman who lives on the East Coast describes an almost psychedelic experience:

I'm aware of energy, patterns, and electric colors, golden, white, or blue. . . . It's like there's pure crackling, surging, grinding, burning energy.

Boundaries will tend to expand, and as the energy gets up into the head, it's like the top of the head gets blasted off. The farther the energy goes up the spine, the more intense it gets.

Opal, a former Roman Catholic and business manager of a computer company, thought the house was on fire:

When we were making love it seemed as though there was almost a ribbon of yellow, golden light streaming between us and around us in the room. I could see it visually but feel it as well. Afterward, we had fallen asleep, and I got up to go to the bathroom and saw this fire. I thought the loft was truly on fire, it was that vivid. There was a lot of golden light and fire shooting up. It was as though the whole downstairs was filled with these huge, gigantic flames.

But when I got downstairs, it wasn't there, even though I could see it from the loft. I realized then it wasn't actually a *physical* fire, but an *essential* one that was golden and quite beautiful. It didn't feel erratic, but calm, steady, not hot. Even as I'm talking about it to you, I can feel the flames in my heart like some passionate quality that was manifesting. I can feel it in the cells of my body, just this relaxation everywhere, this sweet love.

I can always come back to that place with my husband in one way or another even when we go through difficult things, I'm critical of him, he's driving me crazy or even when I hate him . . . this heart opening . . . never really closes back, as though the golden fire is always burning there to some degree.

The Snake Lady and the Divine Hermaphrodite

Every one of the lovers above described experiences that are typical of Tantra, a centuries-old spiritual path. Yet none of them knew anything about Tantra, except Nell, who said her Vajrayana Buddhist community leaders had forbidden it as too powerful a practice for all but the most advanced initiates. So what is going on here?

Tantra is a Hindu and Buddhist tradition that cultivates sexual energy as a path to enlightenment (Taoism does, as well[1]). Yogic Tantra is based on the premise that Spirit exists even in the profane and can be accessed through the most forbidden acts.[2] It was a revolutionary movement originally aimed at breaking the class system and violating taboos by using "reverse" spirituality, in other words, achieving enlightenment by doing the very things most forbidden by religious authorities. (Classic Tantra includes the ritual eating of meat, for instance, and other taboo substances, as well as glorifying sex.)

In Tantra, enlightenment is achieved through increasingly subtle participation in the mantrum, *Om mani padme om* (popularly translated as "the jewel is in the lotus"), a sexual metaphor that encodes the route for dissolution of the individual's soul into the World Soul (Atman). Although the World Soul is inexpressible, it is symbolized by the god Shiva and the goddess Shakti, whose eternal sexual embrace sustains reality. Shiva is all-powerful but passive. Shakti's sexual energy is the enlivening spiritual force of the cosmos. The World Soul arises from their interpenetrating union.[3] Tantric aspirants are taught to emulate this divine union in their own bodies by becoming one with the Goddess and at the same time uniting with the God. In other words, they must become both male and female themselves.

Classic Tantric training involved actual sexual intercourse. Over time, though, physical lovemaking between men and women was gradually eliminated. Soon men were the only acceptable initiates, and women were invited primarily as Goddess surrogates to assist the initiates' spiritual advancement until the men could activate their sexual arousal just by meditating on Shakti. The men would learn to move genital excitement, a form of holy energy, into other parts of the body without intercourse.

This holy energy is thought to reside in every human body. It is symbolized by a female snake named Kundalini coiled at the base of the spine. Spiritual practices involve "awakening" the Snake Lady, and learning to move her sacred life force upward from the sexual organs and anus to higher levels in the body. Kundalini awakenings in historic and contemporary records describe exactly the same altered perceptions reported by people having spontaneous transcendent sex experiences. Kundalini normally ascends through the body's primary energy centers (chakras) until it bursts from the top of the head (the crown chakra)—as Suzette's did. This energetic phenomenon is widely recognized as a sign of spirituality. In fact, in Eastern and Western sacred art, saints and sages are shown with luminosity streaming from the crown chakra in the form of halos or tongues of fire surrounding the head.

When fully activated, the Snake Lady is said to course through two channels identified as the male and female meridians in the human body. She first makes a complete circuit linking the masculine and feminine meridians within the person's body (and in contemporary Tantric practice, connecting with the male and female meridians in the lover's body to complete a circuit). Then, when the aspirant can move this energy from both male and female meridians up through the crown chakra, she completes the circuit with the male and female aspects of the World Soul. Adepts, regardless of their biological sex, are said to have transcended the polarities of male and female to achieve nonduality, the bliss of nirvana. In a spiritual sense reflected in their energetic transcendence of masculine and feminine, they are a microcosm of the Divine Hermaphrodite that is the World Soul, the One from which all sexual duality in creation emanates.

The Divine Hermaphrodite may be the most universally recognized symbol of Spirit. Virtually every theistic religion starts with an Original Being who embodies both male and female principles[4]. These deities—and other holy avatars, when they appear to mortals—are incandescent. They are represented as having energetic forms of blinding radiance. They are Beings of Light, variously portrayed in Tibetan *tankas*, described in the Bible in the afterglow of Moses' face from his encounter with God and in the transfiguration of Jesus, and repeatedly mentioned in contemporary near-death experiences, sightings of the Virgin Mary and other spiritual visitations. They reside in celestial realms of jeweled light, the land of eternal day.

Jorge, Nell, Austin, Gloria, Reginald and Opal all seem to have glimpsed these glorious possibilities. Perhaps they somehow jostled the Snake Lady, shifting her coils and unleashing enough of her powerful force within their bodies to pierce the veil. Since Tantra (and Taoist sex, too) involves controlling and redirecting genital excitement as well as withholding male ejaculation for the longest possible period of interpenetration, it's not surprising that some lovers discover the gifts of these practices on their own, without any formal tutoring in erotic technique. Some of the gifts can be startling, though, especially to the unprepared.

Amateur Night

Sexual energy is nothing to play with, and in fact, many Westerners who write books and lead workshops purporting to be Tantric actually focus more on relationship issues and achieving more and better orgasms, than on activating powerful and unpredictable forces for spiritual purposes. It's safer. Indeed, some individuals, seeking to enhance their sexual performance, have been discomfited by forces that can be difficult to channel without expert guidance. For example, a man I know who began to experiment with prolonged penetration after reading a book on Tantra developed such a tingling, buzzing sensation in his hands and feet that he was unable to sleep or be comfortable for weeks until it finally wore off. A woman, attempting to channel her sexual energy into her partner unbeknownst to him, caused him to have mild hallucinations for several hours.

It's good to have an idea of what *can* occur even when there is no deliberate attempt to manipulate or increase sexual energy. A number of people I interviewed wished they had had some way to understand what was happening to them because the effects were sometimes disturbing, especially those physical effects that seemed out of their control. But no matter how strange or out of place the behaviors they reported might be in an American bedroom, in every case these behaviors have been recognized as signs of spiritual attainment in different religious traditions.

For instance, some respondents reported generating great heat in their bodies far in excess of regular sexual flushing. They were hot to the touch and sweating copiously. One man's body temperature rose to about 105 degrees for several hours, yet he was certain he was not ill. As it happens, the ability to control the body's temperature at will, especially to elevate it, is a sign of spiritual mastery in yogic and Buddhist traditions. Tibetan monks may swathe themselves in wet clothing and then spend the night in the snow in *tumo,* an exercise to demonstrate their powers. Their ability not only to survive but also dry their clothing and melt the snow around them with their body heat is a sign of their spiritual attainment.

Other participants found that the energy streaming through their bodies caused them to move in unaccustomed and uncontrollable ways. According to one woman, "I could really distinguish between my voluntary movements and this energy that would move me. My lover could tell that it was different, too. It would be almost a convulsive energy. He called it flopping like a fish out of water, which kind of took the beauty out of it." She laughed, but went on to say, "This happened almost every time I made love for a year."

Such motions aren't laughing matters in most religions. Spontaneous gestures and postures (known respectively as *kriyas* and *mudras*) are standard features of yogic and other contemplative traditions, where they are considered signs of sublime realization.[5] In sacred art, many of these distinctive gestures are used to distinguish divinities from other beings, for example, through the way the fingers are displayed in the sign of blessing.

In my study, one woman was startled when she and her lover began speaking in tongues (glossolalia), a phenomenon associated with a visitation by the Holy Spirit and fairly common in charismatic Christian circles, but definitely not part of her Midwestern High-Church Episcopalian background.

> We would spontaneously start speaking in tongues. At first I felt kind of embarrassed about that, like, "What *is* this?" . . . It sometimes felt like I was just praising him [her lover]. It came out in these series of sounds, but they sounded like language, and sometimes they were the same sounds repeated again and again and again. I don't know if they're language or not, but sometimes they sound a little bit Asian or African to me.

> Either he would start speaking in tongues, or I would, and it was another signal that this wave of energy is coming over us, through the different movements of my tongue or different hand gestures.

Another couple was surprised by an event virtually unknown outside esoteric sexual practice. Lilah, a cosmopolitan jet-setter, and her lover were shocked when so much watery fluid gushed from them during lovemaking that their first thought was of lost bladder control:

> And at first, it was like, "Oh, my God, did you *pee?*" We both asked each other that. Eventually we realized I was ejaculating, and it would happen every time I was in orgasm.

> At first we were just freaked out at the massive quantities of it. One time it shot four feet into the air, and since I'd have forty orgasms or so, we had a soaking-wet bed, through and through and through. We had to laugh, it was so funny. We learned to get towels and blankets to put around us when we made love.

What was happening to Lilah is actually a commonplace occurrence in Tantric sex known as *amrita*, the profuse production of female ejaculate.

As odd—or even grotesque—as such manifestations may sound, when they occur they are accompanied by such intense bliss and insight that lovers are unconcerned about appearances, and totally convinced that these signs are beatific manifestations of Spirit. Lilah spoke for virtually all of the people I interviewed, when she said: "Even though these things would have looked strange to an observer . . . nothing was too way out there. The only thing you're really aware of is the intensity of this Divine Love and what's happening with this energy in your body. . . . We just had this experience of God and love that was like nothing anybody had ever seen."

Yet despite the fact that almost all the individuals in this study were positively transformed by events they ascribed to grace, such powerful openings can be destabilizing in the short term. The hazards associated with the deliberate pursuit of altered states along the spiritual path have been long recognized, one reason some practices are forbidden to aspirants until they have demonstrated certain levels of mastery. Accidental openings can happen to anyone, and those characterized by strong physical symptoms can sometimes convince experiencers and the people around them that they are going crazy or have become very ill.[6] The relatively large number of accidental openings in the United States in the 1970s spawned a crisis service for "spiritual emergencies" as an alternative to institutionalization.[7] Chapter 10 discusses some of the dangers associated with transcendent sex and ways to guard against them.

The Laughter of God

Yet no matter how strange, or even insignificant, changes in bodily sensation may seem to us—especially ones that happen during sex, of all things—the people who experience them regard them as profoundly moving events, an evaluation supported by the esteemed status these signs have in different spiritual traditions. Something as "simple" as seeing the light may, in fact, mean *literally seeing the Light,* as one woman attests: "The only thing in my life that equaled the feeling of seeing those lights was giving birth. Yes. It felt *that* significant and *that* emotional and *that* all-encompassing, and *that* creative and *that* fulfilling."

For Lilah, who was moved to tears while she was recounting what had happened to her, there is no question that she had a spiritual experience of the greatest magnitude, "because at some level it's only the Energy so that your body is not quite present. I'm aware of the heart chakra being as big as the universe—huge and infinitely loving. I equate that with Christ-consciousness, with Buddha-consciousness. It's one with everything."

And even for Jorge, whose liaison, like Suzette's, didn't occur within the venue of a meaningful relationship, there is no question that the events had a joyfully sacred quality that eventually changed the entire orientation of his professional interests:

> You have this sense of being present, of an openness to life energies that are sacred, like an ecstasy that my mind associates with spirituality. You're in the middle of it, and the sense of Divinity becomes very playful. You're filled with emotions, but you're not taking yourself so seriously. There's something about it, almost of humor, like the laughter of God.

Another participant voiced the universal response to such openings: "There were times where there was somebody inside me shouting yes, yes, yes. Not just my little voice, but much bigger than me. That whole cosmic YES, YES, YES."

In the next chapter, the presence of God—and the gods—is not confined to subtle or even dramatic sensations, but manifests as outward visitations in the bedroom.

CHAPTER 2

The Good Gods and Grace: It Was a Religious Experience

I've always had a fear of snakes, nightmares about snakes. It's always been a terrifying thing. And I've never had visions, like people I know who see auras. We think we know what's possible, and then we have an experience like seeing the Rainbow Serpent. It has generated a dream of hope for all that is possible for me. —Natasha

It's not like God is somewhere else, on Cloud Nine directing traffic. When we were . . . making love, God was the Third Being present. —Lilah

SOMETHING ABOUT THE MOST private moments making love draws others to us, beings from the other realms. This chapter and several others discuss the strange adventures that arise from such encounters. Some visitors are frightening and over-whelming, shunting the partners aside and possessing them utterly. But the ones in this chapter are beneficent, spreading blessings and love, even when the mystery surrounding them is impenetrable and their presence at first is disturbing. Among the benign visitors are angels, long forgotten gods from ancient days, and an alchemical Presence arising from the lovers' union known as the Third. All these visitations occur rather quietly, as though the gods and their heralds sneak up on lovers in the here and now. Yet somehow the very ordinariness of the setting provides the perfect backdrop for sacred encounters.

The Messengers of Spirit

Angels frequently herald holy events in Judaism, Christianity and Islam. Angels have predicted the births of spiritual leaders and divine avatars, such as Samson, John the Baptist, and Jesus.[1] Angels foreshadowed other significant encounters, such as persuading a suicidal Elijah to gather strength for a pilgrimage in which God appeared to him, telling Mary Magdalene that the resurrected Jesus would appear to his disciples, and Gabriel's first calling to Mohammed, immortalized as his Night of Power.[2] Sometimes, in similar ways, Spirit sends messengers to lovers to presage a beatific event. For instance, Yolanda, a hairdresser who now inclines to Eastern religions, on occasion sees angels hovering around the ceiling of her bedroom. They form a ring, with their wings just touching. Their heads are bowed. They never speak, but she believes that their rare presence signifies a benediction. "I have been told that when angels present themselves," she offers, "we see what we individually need to see." When they are present, she believes her lovemaking is amplified by a sweeter energy and deeper responsiveness in an affirmation that manifest, physical love can transform the collective consciousness.

Armand, who is proud of his French-Canadian and Native American heritage, saw his deceased sister during transcendent sex. Visitations by his sister's spirit had always prefigured breakthrough realizations in Armand's practice of prayer and meditation. He was therefore surprised when she appeared while he was making love. "I felt my little sister . . . who died when I was ten and she was six . . . in the room right then. To me that's always been an indicator [that some spiritual revelation was about to occur]," he explains, noting that he had always regarded his little sister as something of an angelic being:

> When I was growing up, she was really close to God because she was dying the whole time she was growing up. I felt . . . as if she came from God. So as an adult . . . I would see her, and it always seemed to mean something about divine Presence: *she's* close to God, so *I'm* coming close to God. So I see her, and in this instance, I remember feeling her presence real close.

During the experience, Armand's reality was shattered in a total union with God (described in Chapter 9).

Most people believe that loving relatives who have "gone before" are now partakers in the heavenly realms of the afterlife, and that they therefore exist in a more spiritual plane. In deathbed visions and near-death experiences, for instance, the spirits of predeceased loved ones appear as comforters and guides to the celestial realm where an individual may meet divine avatars, such as the Blessed Mother, Beings of Light, or the Light itself.[3] The dying report much the same sense of familiarity, recognition and comfort that characterize Armand's account when the spirit of a dead loved one appears. For example, a woman who had suffered a heart attack lay comatose at home, undiscovered for three days before being brought to a hospital where she had another cardiac arrest.[4] During this time she had a near-death experience in which she saw her mother, who had died years before. Her mother greeted her in Hungarian (her mother's native tongue), saying that she and her father had been waiting for the daughter and were going to help her. Her homeliness, humor, and love gave the woman tremendous happiness and comfort. Her mother then led her to the farther reaches of the other world before she was returned to resume her earthly life.

These divine messengers seem to be the bearers of good news and comforting insights, whether they are evoked during sex or some other activity. They work in the same way, whatever events impel them into human lives.

Strangers in the Night

Angels and their messages are one thing. Gods who drop in unannounced are another, especially when they're not the ones we know, but utter strangers. These gods are seen rather than felt, yet they are still so terrible in their majesty that their faces always remain hidden from direct human gaze. They are the ancient, mysterious ones whose temples on earth have crumbled and whose names are barely remembered. Their visits first inspire awe and only later produce a sense of their grace.

Natasha is of northern European descent, and she has had a lifelong phobia of snakes. Yet a snake god appeared to her one memorable weekend. The room where she was making love darkened into pitch blackness, and then with an unimaginable groaning clap the entire world split open, revealing the primordial sea. Swimming in it was a gigantic iridescent snake, a god whose proper name she didn't even know. It was Quetzalcoatl, the Toltec deity who left the earth centuries ago for the enchanted place where sea and sky come together, never to die, but one day to return. On this day, Natasha glimpsed one brief flash of his mighty head before it plunged into the sea. "I heard this horrible roar. I didn't know what it was," she recounts, then, "All of a sudden a huge serpent came out of the water, the Rainbow Serpent, and he dived back in."

She could see its long body flowing in and out of the water. "It was so *huge*, though. I don't know what an earthquake sounds like, but there was this primordial *cracking*, like the earth was opening up, as though the belly of the world was making a deep groaning, almost crying out," she says, adding with hushed reverence, "It felt very, very *old*."

Quetzalcoatl was impressive, but oddly enough, not frightening to Natasha, despite her usual terror of snakes. Divine visitations can, however, be disturbing, especially when the old gods represent forces that centuries of mainstream Judaism and Christianity have labeled dangerous, if not evil. Most of the ancient deities who manifest during lovemaking were the lords and ladies of fertility. Even in olden times, humans regarded them with a mixture of fear and reverence.

The experience of Zebediah, as he wished to be called, shows how these dynamics play out uneasily in the present. A gay man condemned by his Irish Catholic family and religion, he has struggled mightily to come to terms with his homosexuality. He never shared his family's pride in their Irish heritage, and had left the Church a long time ago.

Zebediah lives alone in the Pacific Northwest, in a secluded house at the top of a hill surrounded by a wilderness. When he arrived home after a hard day's work, he walked out on his deck to enjoy the distant view of Puget Sound. While he was relaxing, someone came up behind him, and without thinking, he leaned back slightly into a friendly embrace. It felt so natural, and he was so preoccupied that it took Zebediah a few moments to realize that no one was there. He was actually still alone. He laughed at himself, but had to acknowledge that he had indeed felt a distinct, comforting touch. It was so real that, after mulling it over, he finally decided that the presence must have been the spirit of his brother who had died not long ago. "It put me in a fairly tender, joyful place from having been hugged," he remarks, talking about how his brother had been the only family member to accept his homosexuality. He wasn't sure why his brother's spirit might have manifested in that way or at that particular time, but he felt a rush of gratitude for this mysterious blessing.

Another visitation occurred that same night, perhaps from the same presence. If so, it was definitely *not* his brother. Hours after Zebediah had gone to bed, he groggily became aware of a blacker density in the room. A hand grasped his thigh. He could perceive a frightful, shadowy shape, half-man, half-beast, crowned with a huge rack of antlers. The next thing Zebediah knew, he was being penetrated. His recollections were visually indistinct, yet the presence was definitely three-dimensional and left strong tactile impressions.

"When I sort of came to after that, he was gone," he states, but some mild bruising indicated that "this wasn't simply a mind experience, but the body had experienced it as well." Zebediah confesses:

> I got a little spooked. . . . I was elated and confused and anxious, troubled because I half wanted to believe what had happened and was half afraid that it *had* happened and what it might mean to my sense of reality, which really didn't include visitations by other beings.

> And if I *did* have to admit of such visitations, the only context I could find for it in my belief system was to make it evil. I couldn't think of it as divine, or if I did, I couldn't believe it.

His first thought was that the figure was Cernonnus, a Celtic hunting deity, about whom Zebediah knew very little and for whom he had even less affinity. "I have no experience with hunting, and the stag-headed god maybe came out of the fairy tales I'd read. I don't know where it was coming from because I'd been rejecting my Celtic background because my family is so *obsessed* with the Irish," he explains. "I just knew there was this god of the hunt that had a rack of antlers. He's the Lord of the Forest, and my association with him was that scary, unpredictable things can happen in the woods. The forest was never a friendly place for me."

The more he thought about it, the more anxious he became until Cernonnus became a surrogate for Satan in his mind: "I wasn't panicked, but I was definitely edgy about this. My Catholic upbringing, of course, recognized the Devil with those horns."

In fact, the episode was so unnerving, Zebediah was unable to remain in bed but determined that he needed to distance himself from the experience completely. It had been so mysterious in a weirdly sacralized way that the only thing that seemed appropriate to Zebediah was to rid himself of it through a ritual act of some sort. He felt guilty, as a man, accepting this sexual act. He determined to expiate himself (naïvely, as he later reflected) by offering the visitation back to Cernonnus's feminine consort, which he imagined to be the moon. Extremely fearful of being in the woods at night as a rule, he nevertheless bundled up against the cold and ventured into the forest to a place where he could see the moon clearly. "It happened to be a full moon that night, a crystal clear night, and this was about three in the morning," he says. As soon as he made his ceremonial gesture of offering, out of the stillness came " three claps of thunder from this clear sky in the middle of the night. *What was that?*"

The noise was so loud, startling, and seeming to come from nowhere that it completely unsettled him. Feeling as though he had "evoked rather than invoked something much larger" and potentially more dangerous than he could cope with, Zebediah scrambled back to his house in fear. But he couldn't get rid of his memories so easily. In the days following he began research-ing this ancient god:

> All I could find out was that he was a stag-headed god associ-ated with the hunt, and that he also presided over a sort of rit-ual trial associated with the underworld, in which initiates must face up to their fear of death, and in a sense die, and be reborn. Cernonnus presided over that stage of their initiations. I think the betrayal of trust and murder is the degree of anxiety I had around this figure.

This information was more explanatory than comforting, but as time passed, another visitation from the Lord of the Forest took place, albeit in a very different and much less dramatic way. Zebediah began to identify more with his homosexuality and during a partly social, partly political event demonstrating gay solidarity, he had an encounter with a powerful man, well respected in the gay community and a devout spiritual seeker in one of the major Western religions.

Although it had begun as a normal sexual event, suddenly Zebediah felt an incredible rush of energy, as his partner's hands and breath passed lightly over his body, and "it felt like every one of my chakras opened up, and I swooned; I practically fell." Other portions of Zebediah's experience with this lover didn't match the criteria for my study, so they have been omit-ted from discussion here, but this encounter completely changed his worldview, brief though it was. Everything about their meeting seemed sacred and healing. Before they parted, Zebediah happened to catch sight of a medallion around his partner's neck. Instead of its depicting an image from this man's faith, it was, of all things, a representation of an obscure Celtic god: Cernonnus. Zebediah felt that, in a way, this man, who was so comfortable with his sexuality and his spiritual seeking, represented another holy visitation.

Zebediah found that he could not quite embrace his lover's way of life, so they never became a couple, but the example alone and the confluence of these two visitations forever altered Zebediah's life. He decided that the visitations, whatever they were, represented a significant step in his personal journey. They helped him heal at multiple levels that are still unfolding. Speaking of his first, frightening encounter, which seemed to demonize Cernonnus, just as Christians had demonized the resurrection and fertility deities of the cultures they colonized, Zebediah goes on to reveal how his ability to accept himself as a gay man has evolved through the second, more human visitation by the god:

> This opened the doors to me to understand where the Devil emerges in my own life, where I was cast out, declared bad and evil, feared, disenfranchised as a gay man. . . . It's like, the first time the Devil appears, he grabs you. The second time, he comes as a god and embraces you. . . . [Cernonnus is] definitely mixed up with all the resurrected gods like Bacchus, the Fisher King, and Pan.

> I was held first in the doorway, and then taken by the god. My interactions with [the man with the medallion] were so loving that it has healed the fear I had and hatred of being gay and being loved by a man, and all the thoughts I had about God the Father as remote and very unpredictable. . . .

> As a human being relating to Spirit, it's a doorway to knowing my legacy as a gay human being. Cernonnus for me now is the guardian of nature. As I can now relate to him with less fear, I

can walk in the woods at night. My home on the earth becomes so much bigger. . . .

I don't believe that the god Cernonnus exists in fact, but that there is a spirit, which speaks in my need. We experience, somehow, what we need to experience, and we see what we need to see when we're able to. . . . It could be described as an epiphany.

The Third

In contrast to the gods who can be seen, even indistinctly, are those whose presence is merely felt. The subtlest visitations during lovemaking arise as an autonomous field or force, as an intelligence separate from the lovers, one that can't be reduced to them nor to their relationship. Jungian John R. Haule distilled this phenomenon he calls the Third from Western spiritual and philosophical sources in his book *Divine Madness: Archetypes of Romantic Love*. It is a Presence cocreated by the lovers' union, but impervious to deliberate manipulation by either partner.

Unlike the old gods who come calling, the Third doesn't draw attention to itself. It focuses on the lovers like a warm spotlight. The particular gift of this Presence is its ability to move in an atmosphere of miracles, transforming the most mundane acts, partners, and settings with divine love. In fact, that *is* the miracle: the senses may perceive no change, but for the heart everything is different. The world is transformed in the wake of that Presence. A beautiful reference to this alchemical process comes from the Sufi poet Rumi, paraphrasing the Bible in reference to two loving friends, which could also apply to lovers:

To watch and listen to these two
is to understand how, as it's written,
sometimes when two beings come together,
Christ becomes visible.[5]

Awareness of the Third comes in different ways. At its most anthropomorphic, the Third seems like God personified. At its most ephemeral, the Third seems like a state of grace. In between those extremes, the Third resembles a sacred space or field lovers may enter.

Signs and Portents

Many people infer the Third's presence from signs. The Third may not have a discernible persona but still act as an agent of messages or means that benefit the partners.[6] A beautiful, vibrant woman named Leona received a direct message during sex she attributes to the Third. She had met the love of her life, she began telling me, as I snuggled more deeply into the pillows of her sofa in her rather chilly apartment. This man was perfect, she declared: brilliant, charming, handsome, unselfish, visionary. I might have dismissed her words as a lover's hyperbole, but in this case I was independently acquainted with the man in question, and he is universally esteemed for all those qualities. She was head over heels in love. They had talked of marriage, and she was planning to mold her own professional aspirations to augment his in complementary altruistic careers.

Nevertheless, their relationship was difficult, especially in the bedroom. Leona had been sexually molested in childhood by a family member, causing severe vaginismus, a condition in which the vagina and cervix contract with tension, effectively blocking entrance to the body. This makes penetration extremely painful for both partners, if not impossible. She was unable to unlock—much less experience real pleasure—despite her lover's tender and patient attentions. For a variety of reasons, the man eventually broke off the relationship. She was devastated.

Leona tried valiantly to redirect her life. She began a course of therapies to release the sexual trauma from her body. She searched for an independent source of meaning and purpose in the absence of what had been a defining relationship for her. She tried to recover from her grief at the loss of a partner so superlative she thought she would never meet his equal again. Her faith, sometimes shaky, sustained her through the ordeal. At one point, she bought a special candle for affirmation. She burned it on her home altar when she needed a way to anchor her prayers and remain hopeful in the darkest days. "It was a very difficult time of transition for me," Leona comments, "And I said to myself, 'When this candle burns down, I'll be in a very different place.' I had that candle for several years."

To date Leona has not found an equivalent love, but at one point, she was in a primary relationship with a man named Jim who was not available as a life partner for reasons they both accepted. They were unusually well matched sexually. Leona continued to have difficulties experiencing orgasm, but therapy had made her more at home in her body. In fact, she and Jim actively explored a spiritual approach and attitude toward love-making. After acknowledging that she still frequently had problems reaching climax, Leona began to tell about a particular time when she and Jim were both feeling expansive and she began to feel confident she would have an orgasm. In fact, her state of peaceful relaxation was so great that she was able to just let go and enjoy herself fully.

So here I was in the middle of having—in some ways I could laugh and say the orgasm of my *life!*—a very, very, very expansive feeling of waves throughout my body and heat and just a total surrender when I heard this crackling and smelled smoke.

I turned to look at my altar, and that candle had burned all the way through! I mean *all* the way. *The entire bottom of my altar was on fire!*

I remembered then what I'd said several years ago when I dedicated that candle to the hope I needed to get through that time of despair, and I just felt like the Universe was saying, "Something's burning through. You're done with that. You've moved on now."

Leona *had* moved on, from the blocked, resistant, heartbroken lover to one who was open, joyful, and a believer in the goodness and sacredness of physical love. She believes the Third was there in the special—and dramatic!—sign she had asked for from the nadir of her life. Her prayers had been answered.

Yet in My Flesh Shall I See God

The Third remains mysterious, however. Partners can invite the Third to be present, but it originates outside themselves as a gift of Spirit, not something that can be willed. A lawyer who asked to be called Cougar describes how this intangible Presence arises:

There's the experience of another conscious, evolutionary Intelligence that is a pathway to God, is the key to God, *is* God.

I don't seem to have a lot of control over it. However this Energy manifests is perfect for *when* it does *what* it does.

Being aware of it brings a sense of bliss, a wholeness where there is no you, no I, but there is still the Watcher. It's sort of a paradox. There's that sense of a divine Being that's a part of me, of my lover, really a part of everybody.

To be in the presence of Spirit is enough; nothing else is required. According to one woman, "A corner is turned, and I know I'm close to, for lack of a better word, the Light. What that feels like internally is that a door has opened . . . the world just sloughs off. It's totally spiritual. It's transcendent. It represents the experience of being in the presence of God. There's the experience of just being totally *bathed* in it." The Third manifests as the sanctity of everything, certainly of the lovers, their union, and the act of sex.

Of course, the concept of a divine but evanescent Third is central to Christianity as the Holy Spirit of the Trinity. In fact, the subtle ways in which the Third functions as a loving but independent transformational agency is very much in keeping with contemporary understandings of the Holy Spirit. For example, Laura, who is Jewish, always thinks of the Third in those terms when the Presence manifests during lovemaking:

Yeah, the two becomes three becomes One. That's when we expand, the expansion. The Holy Spirit to me is when the energy current becomes very strong, when we become three.

There's also a sense of being in a womb, a cosmic womb with God holding us. If I could paint this, I would paint two hands cupped, and the couple in there with God holding them. This activates the heart in both of us that is God.

Perhaps the best illustration of the extraordinary transformational powers of the Third comes from Ellen, a middle-aged marriage and family counselor. She had a strong spiritual bond with her lover at the time, even though they weren't well suited physically. As she tells it,

> I must have been about twenty-four, and I had a sexual experience with a man I loved deeply and also felt very, very, very, very connected with at a spiritual level. But we weren't in a relationship.
>
> The actual sexual experience I don't even remember very well, but I know that the feeling that it was holy *wasn't* because it was the best sex in the physical sense that I've ever had, which is so interesting to me.
>
> While we were making love, it was just transcendent. We would just feel we were immersed in Divinity after a while. That sense would just grow and grow and grow. There was no leaving-the-body feeling. It was very much two lovers just being connected in our eyes and in our making love.
>
> I felt so much love. I felt *so much* love and joy. Just complete openness and connection and beauty. It felt very timeless.

Ellen's lover had the same experience: "We both talked about it then, and for both of us, it was just transcendent." Ellen is definite that her feeling of a visitation bore no resemblance to the more ordinary intoxication of infatuation.

> I've been *very* infatuated, quite a number of times. The experience was much bigger than infatuation. I don't remember feeling it was coming to me from him. It wasn't like I was

experiencing anything that was really *mine*. It was not all about *him* or *wanting* him or *needing* him or anything like that.

This thing would sort of descend on us, but it was happening *through* him and *through* our connection. It was more like we were just steeped in Divinity, and it was all One. And the feeling of love was just tremendous . . . just being imbued with something Other, something Divine.

It altered Ellen in remarkable ways. The sense of the Third stayed with her, conferring extraordinary capabilities on her, including enhancing her *own* presence.

I hardly needed to sleep. I remember staying up until four in the morning cleaning stuff, cleaning my entire life out. It was like having some greater energy. I was staying up for twenty-four hours at a time. I was really imbued with something not of my ordinary self in this experience.

It just had this quality of mental clarity, and I keep coming back to the word *presence*. I was just full of energy and clarity. A real, real mental clarity. And peace. And just presence.

I really felt less fear as a result of the experience, and that's a part of me that affects *my* presence. People I was working with at the time would want to check things with me [in a way that they had not before], and their comments were, "You're just really clear, outspoken."

I had a sense of being *with*, with that third Presence, and then being by myself later. That was really my own presence being infused with that Other, that divine Other, but as expressed through me and *my* presence.

The Gifts of Spirit

Divine visitations in all spiritual traditions are known to produce dramatic aftereffects, ranging from a change of heart to
supernatural capabilities. Some of these are the result of dedicated practice, such as the *siddhis* of Hinduism or charisms of
Christianity. Both refer to the miraculous or paranormal capabilities considered signs of spiritual attainment, such as
clairsentience (preternatural ways of knowing things, such as
an ability to view events remote in time and space), telekinesis
(the ability to move objects without touching them), spontaneous healing, and levitation. Other transformations may be
the effects of a single unsolicited encounter with Spirit, such as
the conversion of St. Paul on the road to Damascus,[7] the sudden enlightenment of Ramana Maharshi, or the metamorphosis of ordinary people as they enter the Light during near-death
experiences.

Ellen's transformation was perhaps not so dramatic, but just
as real. Although the effects she talked about gradually diminished over time, they revived once she met her lover again.

> Many years later, we saw each other again and made love. And
> the same thing happened. He and I both recognized it. He said,
> "*Wow*, I haven't made love like this in a long time!"

> It just felt like making love to the Divine. It just kind of came
> from nowhere, and for some reason it always occurred with this
> person.

> There was a similar transforming experience. I don't think it
> had quite the same lasting effect, but the experience was very
> much the same.

There was an overlay of that Presence and my presence. I remember people asking me the next day at work, "What happened to *you? Wow!*" They were picking up that Presence, energy, light, and joy.

Ellen perceived what living an awakened life might be. "I think of [those experiences] as gifts that were and are windows into a level of consciousness and a way of being and experiencing that I believe is possible," she avers. "The clarity and energy and peace that I experienced are like something that people develop through spiritual and meditative practices. They're like touchstones and counterbalances to the stress and constriction and difficulty of ordinary life."

Ultimately, perhaps, the Third can become a state of mind. It retains its own recognizable and autonomous integrity, resembling a new realm lovers can walk into or that is given to them, a realm of infinitely renewing loving-kindness. It is the state of mind attributed to saints, whether it is called *agape*, compassion, dharma, Buddha mind, Christ consciousness, or a state of grace.

Though some participants in this study engage in meditative practices, many do not. Meditation apparently had no effect on their ability to have a transcendent episode during sex. One woman who doesn't meditate speaks of first encountering the Third in lovemaking. Then it became a state of mind she could access at other times, just as meditators learn to make the stillness of contemplation part of their daily lives:

There's our relationship and what we call OneLove because it subsumes us completely, and yet it's not us. Our relationship occurs in the ordinary world. I don't know if we created OneLove or it created us.

It came about, I suppose, from the way we have sex. We have a way of falling into each other, in which neither of us is lost, but we become one Whole. It is the most perfect way to feel, way to be with each other. It is as if that is who we *really* are, not our personalities, but this one thing that is nothing but love.

But of course, our life is not always like that. It's real life. He does things that drive me nuts, and I'm cross and impatient, and I do things that irritate him. It ain't always pretty. When we quarrel, we can sometimes step back into OneLove by really *seeing* each other. When we can behold each other—that's an interesting word, *behold*, because we are *being* and *holding*, not just looking—we can step back into that OneLove again.

There we exist eternally outside of time and the vagaries of our relationship in a perfected love. In a way, how we are there has nothing to do with how we are in this world, and it's completely unaffected by it. It's more like our true natures, and the nature of our love. *This* is what is real, not what seems passing at the moment. All we have to do is remember. OneLove is what is true.

CHAPTER 3

The Spirit of Gaia: Supernatural Connections with Earthly Life

I was losing my definition . . . [into] the life energy in the forces of nature. I was not subsumed by [my lover] so much as by the sap in the trees and the leaves . . . and the blades of grass. When I'm in that consciousness, I'm very expansive. I'm aware of the crickets in the grass—and the cows that step on them and squish them. I'm aware of the gorgeous sea—and the fish eating each other under it.   —John

We had been making love, and it came as a vision, almost an in-body-out-of-body experience. I was in a canyon and aware of a form above me in the shape of an eagle. I was both myself and very powerful, but in a submissive posture to this Being, which is not typical for me. Later that weekend I was walking in a field, and as I turned to go back to the house, a huge golden eagle came and landed between me and the house. I had that same incredible sense of the power that lay there between us, and the awe. . . . I've had several other experiences in real life with eagles since then, but I'd never seen an eagle before that day.   —Eagle

MOTHER NATURE IS FAMOUS for inspiring transcendental states. Who has not been moved by the majesty of towering forests, the endlessness of the sea, the eternity of mountains, and the vast vault of the night sky? It's no wonder that the ancients practiced what we now call nature magic and preferred stunning outdoor sites, such as hilltops and groves, for their temples and altars. Nature's perfection and perfect indifference invite awe. Indigenous cultures have never moved far from these roots.[1] Native peoples in tribal cultures not only live in greater harmony with nature than people in civilizations, they also cultivate special relationships with the flora and fauna around them. They possess special sensitivities to natural forces, siting their ceremonial locations near geomagnetic vortices, unusual mineral formations, or geothermal activity. As ecological appreciation grows, more and more city dwellers are becoming reacquainted with the remnants of indigenous traditions that have survived into the present day: Pele, the volcano goddess of the Hawaiian islands; Coyote, a totem animal of Native American cultures; the sun god of hundreds of names and cultures; nameless spirits of trees, springs, and plants; and even the crocodile, ibis, vulture, bull, cow, and jackal deities of ancient Egypt.

The oldest belief systems are characterized by an appreciation for the sacredness of all life and a reverent study of each animal's attributes. Virtually the entire range of earthly creatures has a respected heritage in the spiritual life of humans.[2] A Native American shaman, contrasting the traditional orientation to power animals with the fanciful associations dreamed up by New Age neo-shamanic practitioners, remarks:

> They pick you. They are preordained. You don't think, "I would really like to have a wolf [for my power animal] because I think that it would be really keen." It doesn't happen that way. It has

to be an animal that somehow has a connection with you. There is no way to rationalize it. If it is a day-to-day thing for me, it will be a magpie. If something really heavy is going to happen, it will be a kestrel.[3]

Plants and animals may function as spiritual guides or tutelary deities to lovers, just as totem and power animals do with native peoples. During sex, people—even if they are indoors and not in any discernible way connected with the world outside the bedroom—can suddenly find that Gaia, the enchanted and enchanting goddess of nature, has restructured their relationship with the rest of creation. Lovers remain in the here and now, yet find that their connection with the natural world operates very differently from what they previously knew as "normal reality." This usually takes the form of mysterious interactions that weave humans and the life force more tightly together. Lovers become aware of their own participation in creation, in elemental forces, in the ancient and perpetual rhythms that animate nature, even the earth herself.

Animal, Vegetable, Mineral

Roland, a man with an unusually rich history of transcendent sex, told me about the following experience one foggy morning over some hot tea and oranges. One afternoon he and his partner had begun to make love in a peculiarly languid fashion, "as though we were in slow motion." He had a premonition that it would be a magical time.

Our caressing and touching was slow and languorous, and we were moving very slowly together. There was a real sense of connectedness to each other. We were looking into each other's eyes a lot, and I started feeling as if our boundaries were melting. . . .

We had an orgasm together which was lovely, really lovely. We were both kind of trembling in that moment.

And then the bed started to shake.

And then the whole room started to vibrate. So right at the moment that we were having this intense climactic, orgasmic experience, suddenly the whole world was shaking.

There was an earthquake!

Climaxing at the exact moment the earth convulses, if it happened once in my small sample, would have been an interesting coincidence. But two other people reported the same, precise confluence of earth tremors and mutual orgasm, though neither reported any premonition, nor did they alter the usual tempo of their lovemaking. They and the earth had moved at the same moment.

Retrospectively, Roland recalled that animals can sense changes in the earth before an earthquake starts and ventured that at some level he and his partner may have tuned in to the planet's geomagnetic field. "I wondered if somehow we were participating in that . . . energetic force that was happening. It was a heck of a lot bigger than us having sex," he chuckled. "It was really about us merging together with all these other energies coming together. It was very powerful, *very* powerful."

At other times, people make magical connections with a plant or an animal. Roland likes to make love outdoors, where he's had several unusual experiences. On one occasion, just as he and his lover finished making love, they became aware of a deer only fifteen feet away looking at them for some time. It was as if "a spirit had come to watch over us and be with us, something magical, very spiritual and profound." He added that their lovemaking seemed to be "a reaffirmation of creation in the natural world all the time. The deer was just saying it, too."

According to Roland, when he and his lover were coupling under a stand of towering oaks on another occasion,

> I had the sense that the tree was starting to send out its branches in a protective way. When I first had that sense, I sort of stopped and looked because the feeling was, "There's a presence here."
>
> I'd never had that feeling before, that a tree had that presence, so I said to myself, "Oh, it's just the tree. It's just standing there." I was sort of comforted by it.
>
> But [then] as we were . . . in our passion more, I had the sense that the tree was reaching out and protecting us in a way, that it was there to hold us, especially to hold us in this sacred place while we were outdoors.
>
> Afterward, my partner said, "I really feel safe lying here."
>
> I said, "What makes you say that?"
>
> And she said, "It's just being near this tree. I don't know, just something about that."

Only then did Roland tell her about his own sense that the tree had somehow reached out to embrace them. He is certain this event was no fantasy. In fact, it was so convincing that he began to study traditions about tree spirits. "Afterward, I found out that the Celtic and Druidic renewal ceremonies were about making love, and that oak trees were considered sacred specifically for that purpose," he says, adding that he is now gathering information on "tree experiences" as part of his work with Native Americans and people of Celtic ancestry.

Oddly enough, in an interview I conducted months later with Vivian, a woman unknown to Roland, she seemed to present a version of the *tree's* side of such an episode. Vivian introduced the subject by talking about a psychedelic episode years before in which she "became" a tree deep in the jungle. Her identification was complete. She was vitally aware of the sap running under her bark, the insects boring into her, her roots penetrating the soil and drawing up water, and animals climbing along her branches. As interesting as her description was, I wondered where all of this was going since I had made it clear that my study was not about drug trips, past or present. It turned out that she had had sex with her lover the night before she was to meet me, and while they were making love, she had been catapulted back into her "tree awareness" for the first and only time since she had taken drugs years ago. But this time was different. She seemed to be in two places at the same time. Her awareness was more concentrated in the tree, but as the tree, her attention was focused on herself and her partner making love, just as Roland's tree seemed to be blessing and holding the lovers. As she put it, "That reversal, that shift, it wasn't just being *me*. The tree was being *us*, the two of us making love there. . . . I really connected with that tree, and the tree experiencing us making love. I felt totally connected with all life on the planet."

High-Tech Cosmos

Plant and animal experiences aren't always so subtle. Max is a former secret agent who now makes his living as an inventor. He sidled up to me at a buffet line after hearing about my research, whispering that he had a story to tell me, provided I would consider an experience with a dolphin rather than a human partner. Almost dropping my plate of shrimp puffs in confusion, I dumbly nodded, and we made an appointment to talk.

Max's experience occurred more than twenty years ago, long before swimming with dolphins was a popular undertaking, and it was one that, he said, had provided the basis for many of his technological discoveries.

Friends who knew some of the early dolphin researchers had encouraged Max to go for a swim with the dolphins at a nearby research facility. Max, always up for new experiences, went over one day and stepped into the shallow end of a pool containing two dolphins, Joe and Rosie. His friends had given him instructions about how to play with the dolphins he wasn't sure he understood. Joe, the male, lurked around the bottom of the tank while Rosie swam right up to Max and began rubbing herself across his thigh.

"I thought [she] was just being playful," Max smiles, "So I got on the mask and dove on in. She flips over on her back in the water, and I just started rubbing the length of her body."

After a time, Max, who was alone at the facility, began to feel that he had taken on more than he realized: "I'm starting to think this isn't like playing with a dog or a cat. Here I am, a species in *their* natural element, and well, this is not like having pets. This is a whole different order."

He began to be aware of the dolphins' incredible intelligence and to regard them as powerful, sensitive beings whose ways of relating to him resembled human peer interactions. It was as though there were three humans in the tank, not a human and two beings of an inferior (or even different) species. His interaction with the female now seemed to create an odd relationship triangle with sexual overtones. Although Max to this day isn't sure to what degree anything he did with Rosie was actually sexual in dolphin terms, he is convinced that, however naïve he was, the experience was sexual for her—and that it seemed sexual to Joe—because of the way in which Rosie thanked him for a good time.

I'm becoming very aware of the intelligence that's going on in this zone. It's off the charts.

Rosie was like this really out-there liberated woman, the type who would say, "I want to go to bed with you," and you'd say, "All *right*." She was out there!

All this touching and swimming, Rosie and I must have played—or foreplayed without my knowing what it was—for an hour. Joe was always at the bottom of the tank. You could sense this real neurotic quality to him.

I'm getting exhausted. She's wearing me down. I'd be resting, and she comes up and rubs me again, and we start swimming again.

Anyway, I'm tired, so I just think, well, this was the experience. So I got up on land, pull the mask up on the top of my head, and I'm standing there at the edge of the tank, just resting and taking it in.

Rosie pops her head up out of the water three feet from me. Her head's bobbing, and she's looking at me, and *it happened*.

If they were making a movie of it, you'd see this stupid red beam coming out of her forehead, and it went *bam!* Right there to the pineal gland [Max pointed to the center of his forehead where the pineal gland, associated with the Third Eye of mysticism, is located].

It was like *wow!* Suddenly this whole quick-time movie that was stored somewhere in me or in her began, like a DVD of all the evolution of this planet, the unfoldment of all life: all the structures, the elements of it, the species, the birth and death of species, the whole thing.

I saw it as if on fast-forward, in full-color, in more than three dimensions in high resolution. It was like taking a film that would run six billion years and speeding it up to run in fifteen seconds so that you got the patterns, the codes. It was only a fifteen- to twenty-second experience, and when it stopped, she went under.

Wow! God! Just the *intelligence* of it all, the sheer brilliance of evolution itself, and the way these animals here could communicate in these high bandwidths. I took it as her way of saying thanks. It was that casual for *her,* but for *me,* it was like wow, pretty goddam *awesome.*

Max goes on to explain that it wasn't so much the "movie" that had electrified him as much as the way it was transmitted that fired his inventor's mind. "You've got to realize this was *sixteen* years before the internet, *years* before humans started languaging things like that in the culture," he says, jumping off his chair to gaze out over the bay into the far distance. "We didn't have even *words* for high bandwidth, fast transmission rates, streaming video. It was as if I got a virtual-transmission implant that could code a 60 gigahertz, 60-bit DVD ROM streaming video that portrayed all of evolution. It was *off the charts* in terms of communication! And it was stored in this species. That's how they communicate."

Turning back to me with a derisive gesture, he grins and adds, "Look at you and me here doing this interview with two hours of time and a RadioShack tape recorder, bumbling along in these lifetimes for seventy-five years or so. With them, all of that was eliminated. That's what was amazing—the purity of it. The absolute purity and brilliance of it."

Seduced by Gaia

Some nature connections are more diffuse yet at the same time more profound, as though everything that keeps humans somehow standing apart from the rest of nature—perhaps our observing minds—disintegrates. Lovers say they dissolve into the throbbing, humming, teeming ocean of life. In these experiences, they neither identify with specific creatures nor communicate with them because the boundaries separating "us" from "them" break down. During sex, some individuals have a direct experience of their participation in the oneness of all creation. They become one with Gaia herself as the once invisible background of life transforms into the whole fabric of awareness. When this occurs, lovers not only lose their sense of separateness, they also blaze with vitality as life energy surges through them. Vivian describes it this way:

> I'm aware of all the vibrant energy and the "sound of silence" in the air, loud and pulsating and buzzing with the subtle sounds of nature, especially the energy of all life, vegetation as well as microbes and insects. These are sounds that I've never heard.

It's not just sound but a *feeling* that penetrates every fiber of my being. I feel incredibly, vibrantly alive, passively aroused and totally connected with all of nature—vital and actively alive in what would outwardly appear to be a quiet, almost sleepy moment.

Terry, a writer who lives in Florida, says it is as if her self-boundaries become "porous," so that all living creatures flow into her and she into them, something that happens only during sex, never during meditation or yoga. "In the sexual experience, I get more of a sense of connection with the earthly, for obvious reasons," she muses. "There's a connection with the universe that happens. I sense a connection with the flora and fauna, all the other animals in the world. . . . We're really connected, all of us with each other for all time and all space. And there's a sense of *how vast the universe!*"

She believes that meditation seems to be a vertical path to increasingly subtle and etheric realms, whereas sexual experiences seem to expand her horizontally along the earthly plane. "I feel like that old Helen Reddy song, "I Am Woman." Woman in all capital letters," Terry declares, "and by that I mean vibrant, alive, whole, complete, using and participating in all of who I am. A sense of pleasure in being alive, in being a woman engaging in this life-affirming act and living with my whole body and being."

Reverence for all life and connectedness with it is essential to indigenous spirituality all over the world, especially in hunting cultures where sacred rituals surround the killing of animals for food. Hunters participate in preparatory rituals uniting themselves with their prey in a respectful, sacred dance. Indigenous and other early agrarian societies revered the forces of nature and the plants on which their survival depended. Sacred ceremonies and sacrifices exist up to the present day honoring vegetation gods and goddesses, such as the taro goddess of Oceana, the maize goddess Chicomecohuatl of South America, the rice goddesses of the Orient, and the wheat, rye, and barley gods of Europe.[4] Even when the contemplative practices of civilized religions seem antithetical to such practices, an appreciation for nature can still be discerned, especially in Taoism. Francis of Assisi and other saints and avatars in various religions embody supernatural connections with nature.

According to Terry and others, sex can produce revelations of rediscovery about the nature of reality or being in the world. It can enlarge our appreciation for "the way things really are" in a world infused with Spirit as a breathing, pulsing ever-present life force. It can blast apart our sterile, civilized, scientific worldviews with messy, raw vitality. And it can do it in a way so beautifully wild that our civilized ways no longer make sense.

This happened to Keith, a physician, self-described pragmatic and hard-core materialist who dismissed spirituality as just so much wishful thinking and claptrap. He only trusted what his senses or science could demonstrate was real—until his experience, which occurred once his life had unraveled. Although Keith was successful, he no longer found his profession fulfilling or meaningful. His personal life was a shambles: he was a middle-aged, divorced, single parent, and the long-term relationship he had been in had just failed. He decided that vacationing alone in the Caribbean might give him time to lick his wounds and make some sense out of his life.

As Keith sat in dejection on the beach by himself one misty evening during the rainy season, a light in the sky caught his attention. It outshone the stars, and as he watched it, it began to change color and shape. Unable to believe his eyes, Keith's first thought was that something must be wrong with his contact lenses. He blinked, squinted, and rubbed his eyes, but instead of ridding himself of the illusion, it overcame him. Keith was engulfed and bedazzled.

> I found myself transfixed by the Light and experiencing what I can only describe as a Force that instantaneously shattered all perceptions I had previously had as to what was real and unreal. I felt that I had just awoken from a dream that . . . had been so realistic that I had never before realized that all my previous memories were merely an illusion of wakefulness.

> I had never felt so alive before. . . . I remember saying to myself that all those Bible stories were correct and there really is a God. . . .

> Wherever and whatever I gazed upon was alive. I could see the life energy of the water in front of me, and looking at the moving waves [I] couldn't believe that I was unable previously to have appreciated this. The stars, the sand—everywhere I looked I saw and felt God. I felt the universe's connection to my own life force.

There was an erotic quality to the experience, so, although the entire beach was deserted that damp evening, he nevertheless walked down to an area reserved for nude bathing, and, in a gesture of the greatest respect, removed his clothing, which seemed to be a more appropriate and natural way of being in the Light. He was drawn to enter the water as a way of merging more completely with the web of life energy created by the Light. After an indeterminate time, he returned to his lounge chair. It began to rain, but still he sat peacefully. After the rain stopped, the mosquitoes came out and feasted on him, but still he didn't stir. Wordless insights flooded his being. "Though I didn't know it at the time, I was in a state of spiritual ecstasy," he says.

The next day he somehow went through the regular motions of living. He felt as if he were wrapped in a dream. That night, he went back down to the beach again in the hope of recapturing the intense magic of the previous evening. This time, however, no stars shone. The sky was completely overcast, and the sound of the waves was drowned out by the noise of music piping from tinny stereo speakers. He sat and waited anyway.

Hours passed.

Nothing happened.

After a long time, Keith reluctantly gave up. Then, just as he was standing to leave, the clouds parted, and the Light once more brought him into ecstatic realization. He began to weep and wonder how he could possibly *not* have believed in Spirit. How he could have been such a fool!

Again he went to the isolated beach to disrobe so that he could feel "the majesty of the Universe" as closely and completely as possible. The only way he could relate to this exquisite, pulsating majesty of the life force was to make love to it. The vast aliveness of the world around him, its eroticism, its throbbing sense of love seemed naturally, and in a way, supernaturally, sexual to him, which evoked his own sexual response. He began to make love to the earth, and then, after a time, to a vision of a woman that appeared to him.

> I'm not a poet and can't come close to describing the way I felt. I looked at the sand, felt it under my feet, kneeled and rubbed it all over my naked body. I then found myself falling prone on the sand, making love to It. Before reaching orgasm, I stood up and

walked into the water. For the first time, I saw a vision, that of a beautiful [woman]. I climaxed.

Keith, on his return to the East Coast metropolis where he lived, immediately researched the source of the light he had dignified with a capital L. Technically, it was nothing but a nearby planet, larger and brighter than the stars he could see. "I've become an amateur astronomer [since then], and the Light that awakened me turned out to be the planet Venus," he notes somewhat prosaically, failing to connect the vision of the woman he saw with the planet's namesake, the goddess of love worshiped in many different Western traditions for thousands of years. Sounding like the medical scientist he is, he continues, "The changes in color and shape that I saw are easily explainable by the fact that the moist atmosphere transforms the appearance of a celestial object. That information I had within forty-eight hours after my return."

But, despite his bedrock materialism, he couldn't put the episode aside. It transformed his entire life, leaving questions he knew he'd never be able to answer with his old way of thinking and no longer caring:

But what about the rest? I knew there would be no scientific explanations. [Since then] I've studied accounts of peak and near-death experiences, glimpses and openings, awakenings and other forms of mystical expression. I understand what happened to me by now but have felt a need, as I grow older, to transmit some of this to others who suffer so much with their needless fears and doubts. . . .

I have a bad case of what Alan Watts labeled the "divine madness" and I never want to be cured. . . .

In some mysterious way, I was touched by God. . . . I'm embarrassed, but mostly I consider myself the luckiest man alive.

Gaia is not an ancient myth or modern-day ecological metaphor, but a lived experience. As one experiencer suggests, "Sex and the sacred and life are all dancing together, and we are both the dancers and the dance."

Loosening the Boundaries of Reality

I spent three years in Africa studying, I read all these books, and I went to the East to get a conscious understanding of spirituality. But the impact of this sexual event was huge, the biggest. I know now there are these whole other realms that are barely explored by most of us.

—Ranier

CHAPTER 4

The Many Faces of Love:
The Partner in Transformation,
Transfiguration, and Transcendence

I actually saw the eleven faces of my wife in a flash. It would
change into all these others, as though she had an extra face.
—Mike

I don't get lost in him or him in me, more like we just lose our
identities in each other, dissolving into a unity that is us. . . . I
can no longer tell what is happening. Events lose their edges, so
that we're nothing but lovemaking, and neither of us is doing it
so much as we're a unified field of love manifesting. It is always
somewhat startling and unpleasant to come out of it and
awaken once again to having a separate, and so much smaller,
more ordinary self.
—Gwen

IN THE PREVIOUS SECTION, all the events, strange as they may be,
took place in the identifiable natural world to lovers whose
identities remained intact. In this section, the boundaries that
usually define experience become plastic, stretching so thin
they almost—but not quite—dissolve. This chapter begins with
changes that appear, at first, to involve only sensory impres-

77

sions of the partner, but it builds to experiences that completely transfigure the partner in ways that allow the experiencer to transcend his or her own limits of heart and spirit. Changes in the other evoke changes in the self.

Trespassing Spirits

One of most intimate pleasures of lovemaking is gazing at the unique way the beloved's face softens, opens or grows fiercer in the heat of passion. These are a person's private, most secret faces, those only a few are ever privileged to see.

Imagine, then, a lover's feelings when the partner's features become those of a complete stranger. The familiar face changes into someone else's altogether. Instead of making love to a black woman in her forties, the partner is suddenly making love to a twenty-year-old white man! And then "he" becomes an old man with a beard. And then an old Asian woman.

It's as if someone else has taken over the remote control, rapidly changing the channels constituting the partner's face. Everything else remains the same, but the lover's face and head become a theater of images so vivid that the lover's actual features can no longer be discerned. People find themselves making love to persons who look repellent or attractive—all of them utter strangers.

Cougar describes it as "just an experience of a different face [being] suddenly there. . . . It may look old, it may look young, it may look like the same sex, or like a different sex. Sometimes the person's personality will shift along with the visage that I'm seeing, and sometimes not. At times the images will be there for five, six, even ten minutes. Other times, it's just like that [snapping his fingers several times rapidly], one to the next to the next to the next."

Some faces are so distinctive they may be recognized when they reappear over a period of months, such as those of a couple of "cute and sweet eighteen-year-olds" he has seen his lover become. Cougar, who is heterosexual, says that sometimes when he sees his partner's face change into that of a man, he also senses greater strength, more force, and a "masculine energy" in her, but typically only her face alters.

The new faces are clear, sharp, and opaque. They aren't the indistinct, ghostly outlines usually associated with apparitions. Only with concentrated effort can the lover's true face be discerned behind the new one. According to one woman, even when she squints and moves her head from side to side to change her focal length and angle, the illusion remains. "It's not like I've lost my sense of reality," she observes. "But it's almost as if I have to close my eyes for a while to get back with regular-quality vision and perspective."

The appearance of ghostly features can happen to one or both lovers, but the illusion is always in the eyes of the beholder. Cougar's face changes without his being aware of it, except on those occasions when he was positioned so that he could see a mirror and witness his own features disappear behind a stranger's.

The human faces that appear have a rather neutral expression, and, as a result, are somewhat fixed and masklike. At other times, though, the partner's face manifests the alien features of no known creature. These inhuman countenances are usually contorted with strong feelings. Smiling, laughing, or beaming expressions are taken to be benevolent spirits while fierce or angry ones are described as demonic. According to Cougar:

It may look like an angel, demonic, whatever. Not long ago I had this energy come to me. . . . All of a sudden, here's this energy talking to me. It felt like it wasn't my mind playing a game with me, but another energy there. It sat, throwing up a lot of ugly, mean, nasty faces. I just kind of looked at them, and said, "Okay, is that the best you can do? I'm not going to get freaked out because you're throwing these faces at me."

Cougar's decision was exactly right, according to the collective wisdom concerning beings who appear in altered states (they are regular manifestations in meditation, dreaming, guided imagery, shamanism, holotropic breathwork, trance, etc.). No matter how different traditions account for these images— whether they represent subconscious desires or spirits from another world—the advice is the same. Books ranging from Stephen LaBerge's *Lucid Dreaming* to Carl Jung's *Man and His Symbols* to the sacred text known as *The Tibetan Book of the Dead* adjure readers to gaze unflinchingly at the entity, just as Cougar did. While meeting the creature's eyes, the person should invite it to reveal its significance (or the lack of it), without either being seduced by its attractiveness or repelled by its loathsomeness.

Cougar tries to remain mindful and steady in seeing exactly—and only—what is presenting itself, without falling into interpretation or emotional response. "It's a waste of time and energy to attach a meaning to the fact that I just saw a very demonic expression on this person's face. I'd rather watch it and observe it than say, 'Oh, that's what this means,'" he says.

Ironically, a sustained gaze may be exactly what produces such imagery in the first place. A venerable exercise common to Tibetan, Sufi, and Western esoteric schools teaches initiates to stare unblinkingly into each other's eyes for extended periods. This practice produces *trespasso*, the ability to see spirits "trespassing" into the human realm or the partner's body. None of the lovers I interviewed was intentionally engaging in a *trespasso* practice, but of course, it's highly likely that *trespasso* could occur from unwittingly gazing deeply into the partner's eyes as a natural part of a romantic encounter.

The First Time Ever I Saw Your Face

In the beatific visions of Western spirituality, the veils of ordinary perception are drawn aside, and for a moment, a glimpse is permitted of the greater reality. When people perceive the radiant beauty and perfection of other human beings, regardless of their solid, bodily encumbrance, they are said to be seeing with the eyes of God. It can happen during sex, and those descriptions are among the most moving odes to a partner's true glory.

Unlike *trespasso,* these changes don't obscure the partner's face, but instead transfigure it so that ordinary human features become idealized. The beloved appears in archetypal or divine form, recognizable but perfected.

One woman—who firmly rejected her Presbyterian upbringing to become a Vipassana Buddhist—was nonplussed to find the old theistic concepts of God staring her in the face when she saw her lover's transfiguration. "You have to understand, I forbade the word God to be used . . . [because of her conversion to a nontheistic religion] when I was married ten years ago, so it's very bizarre to me when these things come to mind, but I had that experience of seeing the face of God in my lover," she says, "We were kissing, and I pulled back slightly and am looking at this man and realizing I'm looking at the face of God in him."

Another woman, talking of a partner who was more a friend than a romantic interest, muses, "It wasn't like romantic love in which I regard my lover and think, 'Oh, he's so beautiful, and I love him, and we're so connected. . . .' It was like an archetypal love, in which I could see *all* of who he is, his struggles, his difficulties, his imperfections, and at the same time, his beauty, his soul. It's like giving someone pure nectar to drink, surrounding someone with such a love that there is no equal to it."

Blake, who did not even meet his lover until both of them were well into middle age, becomes enthralled with sacredness himself when he observes her transfiguration:

Sometimes when we make love, I see my lover's face grow young, and she looks twenty years old to me. She has that radiant, lit-up-from-within beauty, almost as if she is divine herself in a way, as if she becomes a perfect version of herself.

It's like looking at images in a church, or icons that can be suggestive of something beyond themselves. There's something transcendent even in the vision of her, like when great art gives rise to religious feeling. When she transforms before my eyes, I've been displaced to a different environment where everything has become radiant because *she's* my environment. I'm going into a holy place.

It's as if you lived in a closed-in world, and suddenly the veil that conceals the aperture is ripped away, and you shoot through that. It's not that you're going anywhere, but you have an awareness of God—I don't like to use the word God, but I don't know what word to use—of something vast beyond yourself.

I've had experiences of God in other ways, in nature and with drugs. But this is the way it comes to me in making love. . . . This is like making love with the Divine, so it's more than sex. You are aware of being more than you are.

The incandescent features of personal transfiguration are well known in the religions of the Book, where such radiance signifies an intimate encounter with God or other holy avatars. Familiar examples include Moses' blazing countenance when he returned from the mountain with the tablets of the Ten Commandments after communing with Yahweh and Jesus' illuminated features when he appeared to his disciples in the company of Elijah and Moses.[1] Blake's words closely echo C. S. Lewis's moving contemporary description of how the dead appear in heaven when their spirits shine through the recognizable bodies they had on earth:

Because they were bright I saw them while they were still very distant, and at first I did not know they were people at all. . . . No one in that company struck me as being of any particular age. One gets glimpses, even in our country [earth], of that which is ageless—heavy thought in the face of an infant, and frolic childhood in that of a very old man. Here it was all like that. . . .[2]

I cannot now remember whether she was naked or clothed. If she were naked, then it must have been the almost visible penumbra of her courtesy and joy which produces in my memory the illusion of a great and shining train that followed her. . . . If she were clothed, then the illusion of nakedness is doubtless due to the clarity with which her inmost spirit shone through the clothes. For clothes in that country are not a disguise: the spiritual body lives along each thread and turns them into living organs. . . .

But I have forgotten. And only partly do I remember the unbearable beauty of her face.[3]

The Two Shall Become One Flesh

At other times, it is not merely the lover who changes, but the self. People fuse with their partners. As commonplace as this may sound to people in love, it actually involves the beginnings of dissolution of the self as the sense of being contained and restricted by the body melts and begins to include the lover. The hard shell of the ego is pierced to let the other in. Such accounts rank among the most affecting in the literature on love.

Merging involves a sense of being totally fused with another person while still retaining individual awareness. It is a transpersonal state ("trans" meaning to go beyond the usual state of the individual, or personal, sense of the self). States of fusion are relatively common in secular as well as spiritual settings. They occur, for instance, between twins, between parents and very young children, and between spiritual teachers and their disciples.[4] When they occur during sex, their simultaneous self-expansion and self-dissolution produce a sense of the numinous.

Kyle, a conference planner who described himself as "a typical Type-A personality," merged with his lover in the single most sacred event of his thirtysomething life. It occurred after a six-weeks'-long backpacking trip one summer. The caldron of twenty-four-hour-a-day togetherness without the relief or distraction of other companionship had engendered closeness as well as conflict.

"There was something about that whittling or wearing away of the barriers, of the defenses between us that may well have helped to open us up on another level," he muses. "We had some difficult times working through issues, and we also had some really beautiful, tender, emotional lovemaking. . . . But there was something that really shifted this particular time. Perhaps it was having just to be really quiet."

Kyle is not referring to mental quiet, but literally to making love without a sound. At the end of their trek, he and his partner were overnight guests of her former boyfriend. The boyfriend's house was small, so they were sleeping in the living room. They wanted to make love, but also to avoid discovery to save embarrassment all around. Constraint heightened awareness.

It was very tender. We just gradually started to make the first unplanned motions. It was as if our bodies were moving autonomously in a way. There was a sense of no control, no doer-ship, just kind of moving together, sort of dancing gently and quietly.

Then any sense of separateness between us dissolved. I couldn't even tell whether I was making love to her or being made love to. I can hardly even tell you what our physical bodies were doing because it was like our bodies were part of the flow and ebb of all this energy and Spirit body. We were all mixed together in this mysterious, melting dance. Body awareness merged with all the other levels. It wasn't that we weren't aware of the body at all, but it was like transcending the gross level of the body in a way and feeling an enormous tactile delight.

That delight was clearly beyond the body as well. I was both very aware and totally beyond. It really wasn't a sense of me touching her or her touching me. We were one moving, touching mass of energy and awareness, not two separate poles of consciousness.

I sort of felt like a woman *and* a man, and beyond that, all sorts of things at the same time. No sense of two separate beings, as though we were both absorbed into a higher unity.

It was this enormously ecstatic state. Not ecstatic in a manic way, but like this really powerful dissolving into a sacred soup or something. An unboundaried place where all we were was one being, one love, kind of a melting together . . . into something greater than us.

As Kyle's story shows, merging occurs at multiple levels. One of the most fundamental is the physical, when people are no longer confined by the skin boundary that normally separates the sense of self from other.

Nanette, a Nordic-looking blonde, referring to herself and her lover, says, "It's more that we're just in a bubble or something, and there's this nervous system in this bubble, and it doesn't have the boundaries of our skin or even of the two of our skins together. I'm still in my body, aware of my body, but I'm moving and responding from a place that's not purely within my body, which seems like a paradox. My space is beyond my skin, but I'm still very much in the physical realm."

Her partner began to experience kundalini energy moving up her body "like shock waves" that produced spontaneous, involuntary movements recognized in yogic traditions as *kriyas*. Nanette, who has trained as a body worker, is familiar with subtle body energies, so she wasn't frightened, even when her lover's more violent movements sometimes looked as though she were having convulsions. In fact, Nanette "caught the wave," too:

She'll have a *kriya*, and my body will react. I'll feel it almost like my spine is a radar dish or something. Her spine is sending out this wave, and my spine catches it and responds based on what's going on with my physiology. And sometimes vice versa. I'll be having movement, and she'll respond.

Bonding wears off all too soon for lovers who usually hate returning to their own bodies in the usual way. One man regrets, "After some of these cosmic moments, it's very hard and disorienting to disengage physically. I've had the experience that our cells had actually merged and interwoven so that coming apart can be very painful. It's a very deep sense of loss or amputation. It's true that we've become one being here."

One with the Beloved

Dissolving into the partner usually happens only where deep love exists, not in casual encounters. However, in one extraordinary case, a woman named Margot, who works as a surrogate partner for people who have difficulty with sexual functioning, reported an amazing fusion with a client whom she found quite repellent. In the first place, the client was female, and Margot is heterosexual. In the second place, the client was physically unprepossessing: old, obese, deformed, and unhygienic. Margot shrank from the contact, but she was committed to expressing unconditional love, regardless. She steeled herself for the ordeal, and was completely taken by surprise when she felt they were "each filling up with the other's energy. It was a fusion. It was a merging . . . almost like a magnetic pull. . . . It was sacred, like a gift. We were healing each other," she marvels. At a later session, the client reflected Margot's own feelings in recalling that time:

> She used almost exactly the same words that I just described: "an energetic fusion," "this transcendent gift."

> She said that as she was lying there Jesus' words came to her: "Take and eat. This is my body, this is my body which is given for

you." And she said she understood, *really understood*, what that meant. Jesus meant that to share in that, in the body, is sacred. It was quite profound.

Such miracles more commonly occur in married couples. The following story reveals how differently two devoted partners may experience the same events. It shows how lovers can transform each other, even if they don't appear to be "equals" at ordinary or transcendent sex, for the woman had been abused and was only marginally functional sexually when their relationship began.

At the time she participated in the study, Eve was a graduate student. She had been reared in a Christian household but currently did not identify with any particular spiritual path. She recalls a single episode of transcendent sex that occurred long ago at Christmas, a time associated with miracles. To set the stage, she stated matter-of-factly, "I am an incest survivor, and I had just come out of a bad first marriage, so most of my sexual encounters were just physical sensation. Nothing emotional (or very little) ever happened." Then she begins,

I can't tell you how it happened. It was Christmas Eve , and I was newly in love with Hamilton. We had been living together less than a month at that point. He and I were visiting my mother and had just left her house for our hotel after attending midnight mass. For the first time in my adult life I was excited about Christmas and about the prospect of a life with this new man.

We got into bed and made the most physically sensual love I had ever experienced. It was more intense because it was the first time I felt mind-body integration. During most previous sex, my mind went almost blank except for wishing it would end, and my body's involvement was reflexive. This time I *felt* both with my body and with my mind.

Remarkable as it was for Eve to experience the pleasure of a deep and integral sexual union, she transcended these heights for a greater exaltation.

> While we were making love, I felt the most incredible spiritual awakening. I felt like I had actually attained a higher plane, feeling one with—and satisfied with—the whole universe. My partner was an extension of my physical being. I felt like I had received a gift from God in the form of this experience.

> I felt like I had truly made love for the first time in my life. It made me sure I was with the right person, and that we were blessed in our union.

Eve and Hamilton married. Eve continues to have uplifting relations, though she has never had another transcendent episode. She remarks, "Many of my lovemaking experiences with Hamilton, who is now my husband, are spiritual in nature as we share our mutual affection through our bodies, but this Christmas Eve encounter was extremely intense in comparison."

The healing of the holiday experience remains. Although the trauma she suffered as a child sometimes still haunts her, sex for her is now a beautiful spiritual union.

> My perspective on sex changed dramatically. It wasn't a chore or something I had to do to satisfy biological urges. It became more of a chance to commune with my husband's soul and feel like I had a body for the first time. I learned it was okay to relax and just let the good feelings happen, both cognitively and physically.

Sometimes it is still very hard for me to achieve this relaxed state and trust myself, but now I know that if I can allow myself to open up and relax, there is a wonderful, warm, rich reward waiting for me in the soul as well as the body.

I have never forgotten it. This one [experience] still makes me feel wonderment and happiness when I reflect on it. It was both an emotional and cognitive experience. I felt bathed in a golden light, warm and contented emotionally, and I remember thinking that I was part of a greater good that was all around me. I felt open and ready to receive whatever the universe had to offer. That feeling has stayed with me since.

Hamilton's story is equally moving in an entirely different way. A consultant in the broadcasting industry, he feels his union with Eve has transformed his entire being, to the point that his life prior to their marriage now seems like an unreal and shadowy existence. Unlike his wife, Hamilton is inevitably transported into ecstatic fusion every time they make love. No other way of making love with her exists for him.

Nearly every time Eve and I make love, I naturally find myself becoming very quickly and entirely one with her as the rest of reality disappears. It's like hitting the "zoom" control on a video camera at full speed and all the way to capture an image very far away. Within seconds, my focus narrows and intensifies, so that my mental image, visual and auditory, is our closeness. So close it's impossible to tell whose body is whose, or to separate sensory input into "Eve's" or "mine."

Our oneness is the only thing I feel, and it's a more complete experience than mere feeling. Even while my eyes are open, I am completely unaware of what I'm seeing and hearing; I guess

I'm not seeing or hearing anything. It's definitely not blackness, not whiteness, not sound nor noise, just Eve-ness. All my senses join together to form a whole new sense, like touchfeelsmell-tastehearsee.

It's like the supercharged intensity of a laser. During lovemaking with Eve I seem to be receiving incredible amounts of psychic and physical energy from her, yet hers does not seem to be depleted by a like amount.

Travel to this state requires no effort on my part; in fact, if I wanted to, I'd be helpless to fight it. Nothing on earth, no drug or other experience, compares to this euphoric bonding. It's as *happy* and *in touch* as I *ever* feel.

For Hamilton, who was reared Jewish but has fallen away from any faith, these experiences with Eve have a compelling spirituality, uniting them in the sacred.

When Eve and I are making love, and even sometimes when we're just holding each other, I feel as close as I'll ever get to a worshipful experience. Eve becomes to me who others describe as God. It's my perception that my soul and Eve's soul (by soul I mean the essence of the experience of life itself) simply fuse.

Upon recovering from orgasm, perhaps ten to fifteen seconds, the oneness I feel with Eve almost instantly segues to the strongest possible feelings of gratitude, emotional restoration, absolute fulfillment, and a conscious need to remain physically bonded to her for as long as possible. This high state of awareness puts me as close as I ever get to understanding the meaning of life.

Just as her union with Hamilton transformed sex from an ordeal to a source of joy for Eve, his experience transformed sex from a mere biological urge to a spiritual connection that is now the ground of his being.

Frankly, this simultaneous emotional and physical convergence of souls bears no relationship at all to sex before Eve, with a partner or by myself. Before meeting Eve I never experienced lovemaking. Sex with a partner was no better than masturbation. That was purely physical, more like the release provided by a sneeze or relief from constipation. Lovemaking with Eve is better than any fantasy I could ever have. The connection is so multisensory it approaches overload.

I became a whole person the day Eve and I first touched in a literal sense. When I look at a video or snapshots of me taken before that day, I don't feel as if I'm looking at myself. My self-measurement, the way I saw myself as a person prior to that day, was almost purely career-based. As I look at myself in the days since [that date] in 1988, I'm more likely to take stock of how giving I've been as a husband, father, and son, and how I've become increasingly receptive to, and dependent on, love as the measure of life's quality.

It's really difficult for me to believe that anyone else is as perfectly mated as Eve and I are, or that any other man got as lucky as Hamilton Jones in this life.

CHAPTER 5

By Love Possessed:
Shapeshifting, Channeling,
and Possession

When she steps into that place, she gets rougher sexually. There's a rawness. She even smells different. And she said my eyes seemed a lot darker when I looked up. I have light hazel eyes, and she said they were so dark it was almost like black eyes. Her sense was that they weren't my eyes at all.   —Lynn

I'm not a God kind of person to throw that term around or to talk about Christ. These are not tip-of-the-tongue things. But my arms became the swords of Christ, giving unconditionally. I was guided by an energy that was not my own. It was a healing in an elevated state.   —Cindy

Being an ex-Catholic I'll label it demonic. There was a sense of the real deep Pan quality of life, the chaos, the sheer raw exuberance where you and the other person could tear each other to pieces and wind up eating each other, literally, that fecund quality of life, the generativity I associate with Dionysian energies.   —Max

AT TIMES WITH TRANSCENDENT SEX, it is not the partner who transforms, or the person's relationship to the partner. There may be a supernatural metamorphosis of the body known as shapeshifting or an invasion of the self known as channeling and possession. In both cases, the normal self is shunted aside while other powerful intelligences—animal, human, and divine—take over the body and the psyche. When such events occur, it is only afterward that the person comes back into himself or herself and is able to comprehend what took place. Even though time and space remain the same, the self, including the body, may be altered beyond all normal recognition.

Animal Possession
and the Art of Gods and Wizards

Shapeshifting occurs in the spiritual traditions of virtually every culture in the world. It is the special purview of deities and great magicians, such as the Greek god Proteus and the Norse god Odin, who is the prototype for most European wizards like Merlin. They can inflict transmogrification on others as a cursed enchantment, such as when the sorceress Circe turned Odysseus's crew into swine, and when some nameless magician turned the legendary prince into a frog. Just as often, though, gods and magicians deliberately change their own shapes into an animal form to acquire some desired advantage, such as the hawk's ability to fly or see from a great height. Even today, we express the desire to turn ourselves into a "fly on the wall" to spy unobtrusively on events we might otherwise miss.

Sometimes shapechangers' personalities remain the same, regardless of what their bodies do, so they retain their human reasoning and other qualities. In shamanic societies, though, people commonly want to become the animals whose shapes they assume, to be possessed by the animal's spirit, not merely its shape. Religious rituals are designed to bring about animal possession by donning skins and masks and fasting, chanting, dancing, drumming, or ingesting hallucinogens.[1] Present-day indigenous people still cultivate special relationships with power animals. Voluntary animal possession is the source of special gifts that can assist an individual's personal development or resolve troubles for the community at large.

The animal possession that occurs during sex, though, seems to be more about assuming the animal's qualities than progressing along the spiritual path or solving problems. At one level, it appears to be a liberating way to let go and be wild. For instance, a shy, bespectacled college professor who said his normal lovemaking style is gentle and caressing, told of becoming one of the big cats: "My partner and I became other animals. Like shapeshifting. We were tigers or something. There was fur, and strength like an animal strength. There was growling and snarling. I'm not sure we *were* growling and snarling, but there was a sense of that going on. We were animals, not thinking humans, but animals in that moment."

The feline feeling persisted after sex was over, when his partner was "lying there, purring. She didn't feel present in that moment to me as herself, but in another essence. I definitely had the sense of my body becoming another animal." Another man said that in a similar instance, when his shoulder began to cramp, instead of massaging it, his partner, who wordlessly sensed his discomfort, knocked him to the mattress and began chewing and biting the area gently, then licking it and rubbing it with her face, as the cougars they had become might have done.

Animal possession during lovemaking usually involves aggressive, rough sex play, a common, unremarkable occurrence we normally chalk up as fantasy. But the people I talked to were convinced that it wasn't a fantasy. They insisted that something supernatural overtook them and caused the fierceness, not the other way around. More than increased strength and bestial mannerisms—growling, snarling, scratching, biting, fighting, or wrestling—these individuals went into altered states where they felt possessed by an alien way of thinking and being. Curiously, unlike the wide range of animals revered in indigenous cultures as power animals—such as scorpions, vultures, weasels, grubs, salamanders, rats, spiders, lizards, etc.— sexual shapeshifting is more limited. Invariably people identified with the predatory mammals symbolizing strength, vigor, and domination in American culture: wolves, bears, and the big cats. This might be an indication that Americans revere animals that are culturally significant to them, just as other cultures do; however, it is also true that these are the animals most associated with shamans.[2]

A Modern-Day Shapechanger

But perhaps there is another reason such animals are most often associated with the altered states of sex. Kim's story is an intriguing example. I met her at a conference. She has a high-level sales position for a line of famous brand-name foods. Like other shapeshifters I interviewed, this humorous, heavyset woman has no idea what causes her transformation, though it is always accompanied by a surge in strength. In fact, she calls her shapechanging episodes "power shifts." Kim usually becomes either a wolf or a bear, but very occasionally she becomes a bird of prey, perhaps, she thinks, an eagle or hawk. The bird entity is less well defined. Kim has no control over when these "power shifts" occur, nor over which animal she will become.

Transformation starts with a sensation like electricity centered in her torso that spreads to her extremities. She can actually look down and see her arms becoming hairier and elongating, changing their proportions after the electrical charge begins to spread. Then, she says, "comes a power and a strength that makes me feel invincible, like [I] could run through the woods and jump over trees any time now. As if I could jump over a tree any second, but I'm just choosing not to at this moment. It's that kind of strength." She continues:

> If I'm the wolf, my hips and butt and legs, especially the tops of my legs where the quadriceps are, feel different. Definitely leaner, sinewy—God, I *wish* I were sinewy!—kind of like a haunch sort of a musculature so you could spring.

> When I'm a wolf, it seems easier to move and jump about, and when I'm a bear, it doesn't. As the bear, I feel the weight of the head, really, really big, and very, very heavy.

Kim's normal way of thinking alters. It becomes wordless, entirely without concepts. The bear's mental mode is distinct from the wolf's.

> I don't have the same kind of cognitive processing that I have normally. I feel the shapeshift coming, and it's that electric kind of charge. I remember feeling that, and then, as it changes, it's almost like *I am,* therefore why would I have to *change?*

> The change is kind of funny, and it's not like I go, "Oh, my God, I've turned into a wolf!" It's only afterward that I realize, "Oh, I think I was a wolf." When I'm a wolf, I'm not aware that I was a person before I was a wolf, but when I come back to being a person, then I realize I was a wolf. Same with the bear.

There are two different mindsets that come from those. The bear is more controlling and protective. It's more protective than aggressive, and pretty possessive. Like, this is mine, and if you get near me, I'll rip you to shreds with this little bear-claw hand I have. I think the bear tries to be reassuring to the part-ner that everything's all right, and that he's in control.

The wolf doesn't care about that stuff. The wolf just wants to get laid. The wolf has some kind of a freedom thing going on. It's about feeling that I can leave at any time, and you can't catch me if I did. Everything is about what I need for *me*, what I'm going to get for *me*, and that I'm going to leave now. I think the wolf is maybe a guy. He's got that attitude, you know?

Emotionally, when I'm a wolf, I feel very alone, more separated from the whole world than at other times. The wolf is a little bit meaner, more like it could tear you to pieces at any moment. It's about how I'm going to satisfy only physical things—hunger, thirst, sex—and not a lot of consideration for other people. [Even when it comes to my partner], I just don't care. I'd never hurt her, but I'm definitely more selfish right then and definitely only concerned about me for that time. The bear's not like that.

Kim's perception changes, too. Neither her hearing nor smell is enhanced, which might be expected when a human becomes an animal, but her vision changes in a surprising way: "Percep-tion of all things becomes a little distorted, maybe more—here's a technical term—squashed. Things actually become shorter and distorted, like the headboard will become shorter and a little bit blurry. Everything's distorted that way, like the imagery is surreal."

Even stranger, Kim swears that she can see herself from an out-of-body vantage point. She seems to enter the body of her partner, and from there, look back and see herself from her partner's eyes. Kim maintains this is another way she knows she has become an animal. It is her human essence, with its human cognition, that splits off and resides in her lover's body while Kim is embodying either the wolf or the bear.

> When I see the wolf from there [the vantage point in her lover's body], it's not like a picture that's sharp, more like a picture of a Sasquatch [Bigfoot]. You know, you can't really touch them or make them out. They are always far away and a little distorted. It's like that.

> But it's me, and I always know I'm in there. That's not confusing for me at all. The wolf and the bear are kind of external.

Few individuals associate their shapeshifting with spirituality, and Kim is no exception. She's more inclined to believe it reflects a way she escapes her inhibitions. "I'm very serious about my responsibilities and my commitments. I'm absolutely anal about doing everything absolutely the right way. Integrity and honor weigh heavy on me," she muses. "So this is breaking out of that. Like the wolf's attitude of 'Screw you. This is about *me* today. I'm just going to do what I want for my pleasure and I'm not going to worry about how anybody else feels.' "

The more elusive raptor possession provides even greater liberation. When she is flying, Kim says, "I have that overwhelming sense of freedom. It's very joyful, which sounds like a dorky word, but I'll use it. Liberating may be better than joyful . . . freedom from responsibility, especially the kind of responsibilities I take so seriously all the time. The bird is everything free."

I wasn't sure what to make of Kim's account. Naturalists would argue that, at a minimum, her sense of the wolf's being out for itself is contrary to the way this social animal behaves.

Except for rare outcasts, these successful, intelligent hunters are among the most collaborative group mammals. Was her vivid account nothing more than a fantasy?

Berserkers, Werewolves and Shamans

The wolf-bear-raptor combination, her oddly altered vision, and the weight of the bear's head suggest another interpretation: Kim may not have been possessed by the spirits of these animals,[3] but instead by the spirit of an ancient shaman, perhaps a special sort of shaman.

In the ancient Northern European societies that gave rise to the Viking and other cultures, elite warriors dedicated to Odin trained to become berserkers. Today the word is casually used to mean going crazy in a way that is dramatic, destructive, and angry. Its original meaning, though, referred to the cultivation of a trance that turned these warrior-shamans into invincible fighters. "Berserk" comes from the root for bear and sark (shirt),[4] probably referring to the ritual donning of ceremonial garments made of bearskins, a universal shamanic practice for identifying with an animal's spirit. When a shaman puts on the bear coat and, sometimes, a bear mask (or head), he metamorphoses into the archetypal Bear in a ceremony that produces an altered state, which may account for altered vision.

Berserkers were members of a religious warrior cult dedicated to Odin, the shaman-god of magic, battle, poetry, and death who was the most skillful shapeshifter of all. They became juggernauts in battle—fierce, with frighteningly distorted countenances, slashing and smiting anything in their way, impervious to their own wounds, and virtually impossible to stop until the state wore off by itself. Eyewitness accounts tell how these warrior-shamans had a magical immunity to weapons so that "iron could not bite into them."[5] Going berserk—*berserkergang*—was considered a divine madness that protected the warriors who had no recollection of what they had done until the state faded away—and sometimes only *then* would they die of wounds that should have been fatal hours before.

Berserkergang was strong magic indeed, for it not only affected the warrior-shaman, but also those around him. Berserkers didn't merely "feel like bears," *there are contemporary eyewitness accounts of berserkers actually looking like bears, not men, to their comrades and to their enemies.* And, significantly, berserkers were not always in their bodies, just as Kim has a sense of being in two places at once. Bjarki Bothvar, a famous berserker, appeared as a great bear in King Hrolf Kraki's army while his human body was seen miles away at his home, apparently asleep.[6]

Last, berserkers were shapeshifters who also became wolves (*ulfhednar*, which means wolf skins), and are perhaps the origins of our werewolf legends. In fact, these bear and wolf identities were interchangeable features of the same battle state, so that both the berserker and *ulfhednar* terms and descriptions are used, sometimes in the same sentence, to describe these warrior-shamans.[7] *Ulfhednar* are also closely associated with shapechangers who become birds by donning feather skins (*federhamo*), raptors being forms shamans favored.

Can all this be coincidence, or is it likely that Kim, rather than identifying with a random clutch of animal spirits that behave peculiarly for their species, somehow channels the shamans who identified with those animal spirits, so that she is actually at one remove from the animals? Clearly her experience has amazingly direct parallels to an ancient Northern European spiritual tradition whose particulars are unknown to most people today, including Kim.

Channeling the Hordes

Not all cases of possession involve shapechanging. When human entities intrude on the psyche during sex, they usually leave the body alone and take over only a portion of the person's awareness. Instead of full possession, the experience is more one of channeling.

Channeling today usually refers to episodes in which people claim to communicate messages given to them from supernatural beings, such as spirits or other nonphysical entities, frequently during a trance.[8] Channeling during sex works somewhat differently. It is as though the person becomes a radio antenna picking up a signal that's always in the air but usually unavailable because it's outside normal bandwidths. Rather than transmitting a specific message from a particular entity, channeling during sex involves the archetypal extremes of human emotion. Hordes of nameless people throughout history, rather than individuals, come pouring through.

Stanislav Grof, who first described these states in LSD research, gave the name "group identification" and "group consciousness" to a state in which subjects identify with a strong emotion shared by the human race as a whole.[9] This could be the despair and anguish felt by Third-World refugee mothers at being unable to feed their starving children or the rage of rapists, sadists, and murderers. Veterans of such experiences speak of unbearable agony.[10] In sex, such global emotions are felt strongly, yet they don't seem to belong to the individual. They have an anonymous quality.

One woman, recalling such an episode while we sat outdoors on my deck, observes, "It seemed to be rage, but it really didn't feel like *my* rage. It felt like I plugged into an emotional thing that goes beyond myself." To demonstrate, she threw her head back and, with corded throat, roared so loudly she sent the startled birds in the trees around us into flight, adding that, "Sounds would come out, using *my* voice.... When those emotions come around, there's a lot to let out, and I don't want the sirens coming [for me]."

Although most of Grof's LSD research reports negative group emotions, in lovemaking, people also channel collective joy. Rhonda, a broker's assistant in her thirties, feels surrounded by invisible others who resonate with the collective emotion that starts to course through her.

I'm feeling a tremendously strong amount of emotion. Sometimes it's tears of joy and laughing, and sometimes it's just sadness. . . .

It's not attached to any particular feeling of *mine,* not *my* feeling, in that moment. When it's joyful, it's a kind of joy that doesn't have to do with anything. It's not like having an ice-cream cone and being happy or buying something. It's not about orgasms or anything like that.

When I cry, it doesn't just feel like crying from my head. I'm not even sure where it starts, there is such a depth. . . .

I feel completely open and overcome. At times, I've even felt that I was not alone in the room. In fact, it feels like the room is full at that moment. I know there are others around me, and my skin prickles on the back of my neck. There's not anything I can hear with my ears, but there's a resonance I feel that fills the space with feeling. It's like I'm tapping into something else, like the world's emotion is coming through me.

Kristin, whose German Roman Catholic upbringing had been quite sexually repressive, felt liberated when she suddenly felt all women's experience flooding her during a sexual episode: "I identified as a woman, as women. . . . I am all women, now and back in time, and their state of mind. My identity falls away, and I'm all women. There's not a separation."

Lovers who have such experiences feel they are being called to express the mass emotions filling them, a sacred role to give voice to the experience of the anonymous hordes. They are compelled to yell, roar, cry, groan. Whether they become healed themselves, as Kristin did, or merely express the darkness of human experience, such encounters seem to bring them closer to Spirit. For instance, Rhonda, whose Irish and Italian Catholic family had taught her that sex was "tremendously bad and wrong, oh, God, *bad and wrong!*" now sees it as sacred. She had rebelled against her upbringing by becoming more promiscuous and experimental with sex, but as a result of her transcendent experiences, she now has a different attitude entirely. "It was being close to God, which is something I never would have considered with sex," she says, laughing. "I take sex a lot more seriously now because I believe it totally connects you with . . . everything in a way I wasn't aware of before. It's really a gift. It actually brings me back to myself more."

The Old Gods Laugh

The old gods, some associated with bacchanals and fertility, many now assigned by Christianity to the dark side, may also enter humans during sex. These ancient deities sweep aside the lovers' personalities the way the wind scatters dead leaves. The self remains, more as a bemused observer than anything else, displaced as savage energies play through the lovers' bodies. There is nothing gentle about it. It is as though Nature's immense powers of procreation and destruction combine to hurl people into a biological maelstrom of life and death. Women report being overtaken by Kali, the dark counterpart of Shakti, the Terrible One of many names who is forever birthing and destroying, who pours forth a river of blood and must have blood to drink, who is death but also bliss. Men report "lust, really hot lust, pure red, the most basic force in the cells, an experience of nothing *but* the physical."

It would be easy to dismiss such episodes as "the-devil-made-me-do-it" lapses—ones in which normally repressed people justify letting themselves go, just as the annual or biannual orgiastic rites of ancient cults ceremonially channeled and released such energies long before the days of modern psychology.[11] By taking no responsibility for their actions, people can have an abandoned romp and blame it on being overcome, somehow, by supernatural forces. Temporary insanity. There may be something to that argument, for one man in this study says:

> My experience was that something else was coming through me because at that age I was a bit of a control freak. Suddenly to be opened to the pure generative forces themselves was a shock to my system.

> I hadn't thought about it for twenty-seven years, but now if I had that same experience, I would see it as another gateway to the earth energies. We've got a tremendous amount of trepidation about the raw energies, the power of the material. My fear buttons go off when I'm dealing with the deepest energetic forces that make up the world, but it's the messy vitality you *have* to deal with in order to be fully alive.

Dion, another participant, is a sophisticated, worldly man, a professor of philosophy who considers himself agnostic. Rather than be interviewed, he wrote to me about a surprise visit his lover paid him at the university on the first warm day of spring. No sooner had they closed the door to his office, than something he could only describe as "possession" by ancient gods began. "Something had reached down and seized both of us at the same moment and was realizing itself through us, something vast and ultimate," the normally skeptical intellectual declares. For Dion, an almost legendary womanizer, there was no question of repression or buttoned-up attitudes to be discarded. He has always enjoyed a life of liberated sex. But he was no more prepared for what took place than anyone else.

> I turned the radio on to some top-forty pop hits station, and we started slow-dancing, and that's the last thing I clearly remember. Suddenly, abruptly, from nowhere, without knowing why, I found myself mashing her frantically, face first, against the wall, my hands digging into her sex, while she reached behind her, groaning, to find mine. We were both frenzied. It was overpoweringly sexual, but it wasn't sex in any way that I had ever known before, and in any conventional sense of the word, it wasn't sex at all.

> I wanted to ravish her, but here words cease to apply. It is absurd to use that or any other term, because none can possibly express what I wanted. Nor was the agent "I," because I wasn't any longer my I, and in any event whatever I had become was being acted upon, not acting autonomously. . . .

> I found myself—for lack of a better term—fuck-dancing her, but even that is simplistic, because it so far exceeded either fucking or dancing. . . . The pop tunes were the universe and I was the god of the spheres, the absolute Mover and Cause, improvising, infinite, spontaneous design. A cosmic Jackson

Pollock hovering over his canvas and improvising intricate, overlapping patterns on its waiting tension, absolute awareness and intention in every pitch of the paint, yet in the grip of a force far beyond this self. Balancing, composing, playing off curve against angle, violent against tender, theme against variation, retreating, advancing, superimposing layer upon layer of world.

I also found myself plying her with words, speaking in visionary images whose meaning lay beyond me, images from nowhere, each image linked to all the others before and to come and linked in turn to my dance, the lyrics of the dance, love lyrics as I had never heard them before. . . . They emerged endlessly from the core of whatever I had become as it merged into the core of what she was. Not to have spoken it would have diminished it, would have made it lacking in clarity and articulation. To be absolute it needed also to be uttered, even if incomprehensibly, and the words of it came to me in an endless stream, which I expressed as they came, and so did she her part.

We watched ourselves in ecstasy, living art beyond all museums or concert halls. Witnessed ourselves, because we were no longer ourselves. We were whirling furies of wind and air. We clashed and mingled against the walls, the bookcases, the filing cabinets, and writhed in unspeakable throes atop the desk. "How perfect!" we kept exclaiming. Still, from noon until six, the whole afternoon is a kaleidoscopic blur. I have no recollection of sequence of one event preceding or following another. Only isolated instants. . . . We were dying of thirst, but it seemed irrelevant, because it wasn't our thirst.

I insist that the lover, the artist, the dancer, wasn't me, wasn't my person, wasn't my transperson or my subperson or any form of a person. I had left mere personhood far behind—it was much too trivial and limited a way of being, something binding and merely finite. I had no identity for those six hours or so, but had instead become—here again, words are wholly inadequate—something akin to pure energy, to a physical force of nature itself. Not this living thing, naming itself, conjugating itself, like a Bach fugue. Shiva Nataraja. Dios Nysos. Revealing itself to itself in its true majesty, without reservation or the restriction of form, endlessly, "like the shining of shook foil". . . .

And then slowly, mysteriously, from we didn't know where, we started drifting back. Back to this mundane world, this fallenness again. Back to our selves, our persons, our identities. Back to words again. Back to the finite.

Sacred and Profane

These earthy forces don't conform to mainstream or mystical spiritual conventions. They may even seem obscene, especially to those who believe the sacred is only about subtle cerebral events and altruism. Sex, the life force and one of the first attributes of deities, has so long been relegated to the recesses of civilized life that only its ghostly imprint remains in what we now call the "major religions" and "perennial philosophies." Yet even in these, sex once was a holy quality of the Absolute (including the God of the Old Testament).[12] It is perhaps this uneasy balance between the rude, vernal urge of life and the self-sacrificing norms of civilized society and its religions that creates the human struggle.[13] What is striking in these episodes is that even the wildest experience produces personal transformation leading to spiritual insight, including a much greater vision of the human condition.

Regardless of the emotions these ancient powers evoke, the individuals they touch come away with a greater sense of Spirit, the rightness of the world, and humanity's place in it. Max, who has done his share of meditation and was also possessed by the old gods, said, in a philosophizing moment:

> We in our culture think we're on the leading edge when we say we're being present, especially in spiritual circles. But that's deluded. We're kidding ourselves. This paltry experience isn't being present.

> Being present is like that sexual experience, when your DNA, your chromosomes, your cells are all resonating with awareness, and you've totally embraced the body for the transformer and tuner that it is.

> We've *over*privileged those states that are purely mental because they're not embodied, and we've *under*privileged the ones that are hardest for us to deal with as human beings. We say, let's love each other, but we don't really mean the fucking *of* you *with* you, having the universe fucking *through* you in the orgy of awareness with life and its sheer raw suchness.

If Max's portrayal of the ancient life-force deities conveys the meaning too rudely for some, Rhonda captures the gifts of these same experiences in language more aligned with contemporary notions of spirituality when she says,

> I thought that in order to have a spiritual experience, I'd have to do a tremendous amount of work or meditate for years or have some special powers. . . . I thought in order to be spiritual, I wouldn't be able to be human. I would have to *not* be human.

Instead, it's really going into being totally and utterly human that I find my most profound moments, that being human is such a beautiful experience. I don't have to go far or work hard at it. The most profound is in the most mundane. I didn't used to know that because I was looking elsewhere for something harder.

And now I know I'm not alone, I'm not alone in the universe. I love life so much more now that I feel that to be true.

CHAPTER 6

Breaking Away:
Cosmic Journeys that
Leave the Body Behind

I felt her back in my hands and was aware of her hands on my back, and then . . . I could see us on the bed. I was floating above us and looking down. I could see the room, I could see the bed, I could see the floor. . . . It wasn't like a dream.

—Gordon

I was taken up beyond my body and the warmth of the sun on my skin and the clear blue sky until I went into that golden sunlight and cerulean blue. Then I shot out beyond it into the vastness of space where all was silence and blackness lit by stars. Everything there looked clear and beautiful and cold, yet I could feel the life pulsating through it, the fierce fires of the distant suns and burning stars. It was beauty and it was love and there I was in the middle of this universe stretching forever. I wanted to stay there always.

—Rachel

There was this sudden shift of the ocean and sky and me. In the film world, there are POVs (points of view), usually two of them. But in this experience, there were multiple, simultaneous

*POVs like the eyes in a peacock's tail, and I was seeing from all
of them at once: from the eyes of me making love, from the eyes
of me the ocean, from the eyes of me the stars, the eyes of me
the sky, me the air, me the land, me the multiples of all of these.
It was all the facets of this prismatic sense. I was everywhere,
and seeing everywhere all at once.* —Jason

SEX BINDS OUR AWARENESS to our bodies through high levels of
activity, sensation and arousal. Yet it can also send people into
transports, rapturous travels through space unconfined by the
body's limitations. Transcendent sex can bend and even break
the boundaries of normal spatial reality. Lovers in these situations are still themselves, but they are out of their bodies, in
another place, a psychic space of altered sensations, imagery
and bliss. In fact, the word one West African tribe uses for lovemaking literally means "going on a journey together," a phrase
that aptly captures the essence of these experiences.[1] Some of
them involve a comparatively short trip out of the body while
others send lovers traveling the three worlds of shamanism: the
underworld, the middle world (earth), and the celestial worlds.
Breaking the "natural laws" of location is an ancient spiritual
and magical art. Whether it's astral projection, shamanic jour-
neying, or making objects disappear from one location to reappear in another, escaping the usual rules governing spatial
placement has long been a sign of supernatural power.

Unfortunately, leaving the body also has a reputation in the
sexual arena, but in a highly negative context. Rape and sexual
abuse can trigger fantasy flights and out-of-body experiences—
anything to override the terrible events actually occurring. Clini-
cally called dissociation, this involuntary protective mechanism
helps an individual cope with unbearable psychological pain.
The structures of dissociation resemble those of ecstatic sexual
transports, but they differ in significant ways. Dissociation comes

from a need for distraction and diminishment. As a result, it is a somewhat flattened state in terms of emotion and realism.

Ecstatic transports, on the other hand, feature vividly heightened awareness, attunement to the intensely pleasurable feelings of the body, and rapturously shimmering joy. As a matter of fact, transports usually begin as sensation heightens, turning into a delicious hyperawareness in which everything associated with the body acquires greater pungency.[2]

Ming, whom I met after a victory for her company's softball team, is a bubbly editor for a national magazine with a large circulation. She speaks for the majority of my respondents when she describes how the process unfolds, "It's almost like I'm hyperaware. . . . I can feel the sheets against me more intensely, or whatever is around me. It's not distracting, but just *there*. I'm more a *part* of the world, but not *of* it at the same time, if that makes any sense. It's more sensation than anything else, physical sensation."

Lovers who start out grounded in exquisite pleasure slip at some point into incorporeal experiences as the transcendent journey begins. The body becomes the conveyance, supporting experience but no longer its focus, any more than you are paying attention now to the white space surrounding the black letters as you read this page. Or, as one woman, put it, "There's so much more space that you don't define the physical body in the same way. It's diffused. So you start getting a whole different kind of information, and you can translate that back into the body. You can feed it back, but you can no longer identify with the body as the respondent. It's doing a dance, and that dance is like a call."

Pleasure and Realization Without a Body

Some dislocated lovers never escape the bedroom's confines. They merely shed their bodies, but remain nearby.

Sexual out-of-body experiences (OBEs) resemble the OBEs reported in numerous other circumstances. Lovers are released from their usual interior vantage point and find themselves looking back at their bodies from a short distance away and above. OBEs typically occur during recovery just after an unusually intense climax.

Betty is a gorgeous, high-powered consultant to the computer industry who really didn't believe in paranormal events. Then one day,

> We had this simultaneous orgasm, and it was pretty intense. The experience of that moment was so physically different for me that I couldn't just dismiss it by saying, "Well, this is a different kind of orgasm," or "That's intense because it's happening to both of us at the same time." This state felt totally nonordinary; some whole other class of thing had happened to me.

> It was an experience of being both completely and totally aware of every cell in my body—and of every cell in my body vibrating at the same frequency—and yet not even *inhabiting* my body at exactly the same time.

> It was as though my physical body was still lying there, but I was also up here [gestures toward ceiling] floating, watching the room, but *not* just a sense of in-a-mind's-eye kind of thing as much as truly being somewhere else spatially.

> I was definitely in my body, *and* I was sort of floating, very much being in two places at once. It wasn't an out-of-body experience so much as it was as though there were a channel, a really high bandwidth connecting the physical body with me in it and this other sort of energetic being where I was so I could be in both places at once.

The sensation of being in two places at once is startling, especially since it may occur in an instant, even if it seems to begin in the ordinary way people change location. According to one woman, "I thought, 'I'm going to rise up' in the usual sense that my *body* is going to do that. And then the next thing I was aware of, I really was about two or three feet up off the bed and looking at me. It was as if my *brain* was rising up, and what I was seeing was my body and my partner on the bed. It was weird, really weird."

The sudden disorientation can be scary. Sandra is a devout Roman Catholic who normally has difficulty enjoying sex, especially coming to orgasm. After one of the most intensely pleasurable bouts of lovemaking she had ever experienced, she lost her body's moorings, which made her fear she was dead.

"I don't do drugs, don't drink, maybe just half a glass of wine, and that evening I hadn't had anything. But I more or less just floated out of my body. It was so weird at first I thought I was dreaming because it didn't seem like reality," she reports. "I was initially a little frightened because I didn't know. My God, am I *dying?* Am I floating up to heaven? I was panicking a little. But then I could see my body, that I was breathing and that everything was fine, that my boyfriend was holding me. So okay, I'm not dying, but in the back of my mind I was still thinking, why am I up *here?*"

The vivid realism convinces lovers that they are not dreaming. Not only do they have a bird's-eye view of themselves, but somehow leaving their bodies grants them greater objectivity and discernment than normal, sometimes with surprising—and touchingly human—results. When Sandra could look back at her naked body, she was dismayed by what she saw: "People always said, 'Oh, gosh, you're really thin,' and 'You should gain weight,' and 'You look anorexic' and that kind of thing. And then when I actually saw myself, I realized, oh my God, I really *am* thin. That was the first thing I noticed. In a mirror, it's different. But when you actually see yourself like this, you *really* see yourself." A man said, "Yeah, I could suddenly see [my lover's] back, and the way I was looking, I'm thinking, you know, you really ought to have that mole looked at."

Consequently people who have had OBEs may revise their beliefs about how the material world works, though it may take them years to face that realization and what it means. Dick, now in his forties, reflects on an incident from his college days:

> I really didn't know what to make of it. In later years, I was able to hear other people put into language what I'd experienced when they talked of out-of-body experiences. It affirmed what I had gone through.

> It did establish an openness in me to the possibility that we are really not our bodies, that we have abilities beyond our bodies, that reality might be different from what I believed about the physical world. I became more open to exploring those greater possibilities.

Betty alludes to the internal struggle she had to undergo because it drastically deconstructed her understanding of reality:

> My old belief system [was] that this body is a substantial object, and it doesn't actually travel through time, unless it's clock time, to get from one place to the other. And it doesn't dissolve and reappear in other places or exist at more than one place at one time.

> At that moment, those things weren't true. . . . If someone had come in and said at that moment, "We can teleport you to the twelfth century," I probably would have believed it.

It lent a credibility to the idea that tangible reality isn't all there is. I'm kind of slow about these things. It wasn't until five years later that I put some of this together.

Sandra's OBE actually confirmed and deepened her faith. "I've always been afraid of dying, but I'm not really afraid of death anymore. I realized that our spirits *do* live on, and that we can leave our bodies," she observes. "Even though that's the only time it's happened to me, there's a big spiritual realm out there we're not even aware of that I believe in because of what happened."

Psychics, Seers, and Oracles

Out-of-body experiences are one of the markers of near-death experiences. They also appear routinely as part of lucid dreams, meditation, the ingestion of certain drugs, trance dancing, and even normal, everyday activity.[3] Some of the circumstances surrounding OBEs—including sex and its aftermath—share qualities of muscular relaxation, exhaustion, monotonous sounds, and repetitive movements that may interfere with normal body awareness,[4] but theories accounting for OBEs are conflicting and inconclusive. The most conservative dismiss them as mere figments of the imagination. Others suggest that they are fantasies the psyche constructs to "fill in the gaps" when regular sensory processing breaks down. A third school of thought considers them access to an energetic body (popularly called an astral or etheric body) that extends from the physical body. Still others contend that OBEs are a type of extrasensory perception.

It is certainly true that telepathy can occur during sexual OBEs. Sandra, who had just reconnected with her partner after a breakup, states:

When I was up there, I could read his mind and what he was thinking. Not like I actually got inside his head, but I could read what he was thinking.

I didn't tell him what had happened right away because I didn't want him to think I was crazy. He's very straitlaced, very conservative, and I knew if I told him, he'd be laughing or whatever because he just wouldn't get it. But when I thought it over, there were things he was thinking about that I wanted to bring up with him. When I told him what I had felt, he said, 'Yes, I was thinking those things.'

I thought if I brought it up and they were right, then he would believe me [about having an out-of-body experience]. And they *were* right.

And that's when he got scared.

Telepathy is fairly common in close, loving relationships. Twins seem to know what each other is thinking. Mothers know which child is calling before they answer the telephone. Lovers can share thoughts or dreams at the same time over long distances. But love isn't necessary. People gifted at telepathy and out-of-body travel today may function as psychics and clairvoyants; in former times they were seers, oracles and prophets.

One man who makes no claim to being psychic had an extraordinary telepathic connection during sex—but not with his lover. Esteban had a traditional, Roman Catholic, Latino upbringing. A short, attractive man with a slight build and an engaging grin, he describes a never-to-be-repeated event that occurred when he was nineteen years old. It began when Esteban and his girlfriend at that time went to a wedding accompanied by Esteban's best friend, Tom. Esteban and his girlfriend slipped away from the festivities during the reception when everyone, including Tom, was too busy partying to notice their absence. They went to Esteban's car for a little romance. "We started kissing. One thing led to another, and we were becoming very intimate," Esteban looked at his hands for a moment, and then said that he seemed to drop his body and fall, without it, into a void:

I went into an emptiness, and in that emptiness an awareness came to me that Tom was in danger. It probably happened in an instant. I vividly recall the feeling of stopping, in the sense that all the emotion in my body just stopped, and I was aware of this void, but it seemed like a flash, an instant. And it was such *truth* that I *knew* he was in danger. I just *knew* it was so.

So I immediately came back into my body. I said, "Oh my God! Oh my God! Something's wrong with Tom!"

She said, "No, there's not. He's still at the reception. He's having a great time."

I said, "No, something's really wrong," and I got out of the car, and I started running down the street throwing on my clothes, trying to get my pants on.

Somehow, Esteban knew that he wouldn't find Tom in the reception hall. Unerringly, he made a beeline to Tom's exact location on a nearby street where a crowd had gathered. Esteban barreled through the crush. He found Tom being beaten by a "huge, Hell's Angels type of guy." Without any hesitation, Esteban launched into the fray. He was so small, he had to jump up in order to try to put the attacker in a headlock from behind. "I probably came up to his knee. It was kind of comical in that he just picked me up, plucked me off his neck and threw me against the wall, " Esteban says, smiling ruefully. He bounced off, and lunged at the brawler again and again, each time being thrown off and slammed into the brick building. He adds, "I was obviously not in my right mind. All I knew was that I had to protect Tom, and yet Tom is bigger than I am. He's got a lot better chance than I do of taking care of himself."

Esteban, despite his monomaniacal attempts to save his friend, is not clear on exactly how the fight was resolved. His supernatural courage and perseverance were perhaps not matched with superhuman strength, but the state he was in did render him miraculously immune from harm.

It wasn't until after everything had subsided and we had left that it hit me. This guy could have taken me out with his thumb, if he had wanted to, but I just had this tremendous energy, a strength that I don't have in the normal sense, so somewhere, somehow, it was being channeled in.

That evening, Tom said, "You should really be hurting." And I should have been because that was a brick wall he threw me against, *several* times. I was not bruised or in any kind of physical pain out of the experience, during it or afterward.

Something took over, and I was not me. I was reacting out of protection and love. I just felt this connection, and I had to acknowledge it as spiritual.

The Realms of Bliss

For some lovers, spatial dislocation is more than a trip within the immediate here and now. They may break away from their present location entirely to find themselves wandering in visionary landscapes. As in my own experience, a few respondents found themselves in beautiful palazzos, ancient villas, or courtyards belonging to other cultures and perhaps other times. But most people found themselves wandering far and wide in the air or under the sea. Without the sense of becoming birds, they nevertheless soared joyfully above the earth, gliding over immense canyons and deep green forests, suffused with tranquillity and a sense of the utter rightness of things. Without the sense of becoming fish, they found themselves far beneath the sea in beautiful coral reefs.

In fact, when lovers are transported to other venues, they usually go where humans can move freely in three dimensions: the depths of the ocean, the heights of the sky, the farthest reaches of outer space, as well as the microcosmic world. These mysterious horizons have beckoned human imagination from time immemorial.

Jill was swept into transcendent sex for the first time in her thirties, much against her will. She was married when she met a man with whom she had an undeniable and almost paranormal connection. She wanted to resist her illicit attraction. Additionally, her strict Lutheran upbringing and down-to-earth career as a statistician initially made her dismiss the signs of a preternatural attraction. She and this partner never did consummate their relationship, yet their kissing and holding hands was sufficient to transport Jill.

> In his presence I lost touch with sensory reality, and I got a lot of visual impressions, which were so unusual for me. . . . One of

the things that kept popping into my head was, "This is better than sex," and I kept thinking, "What could be better than sex?" Here we were, fully clothed, and all we were doing was touching our hands.

There was a time when we were like dolphins in the water. I saw other fish in the water, but I was more aware of us.

It feels total: really complete on all levels, as though spiritual, emotional, intellectual, and physical levels were all being accessed at the same time. It's almost like getting in touch with home—home being heaven. Getting to feel what it's like to be in heaven, it's just such an open, free, joyous experience, much greater than the regular falling in love or just the physical inter-action. It's a deeper, more complex, more intense feeling.

Another lover reported "being underwater and swimming with fish in just a peaceful, underwater scene. The water was blue, dark blue. . . . There were fish, colored fish, but not necessarily ones I'd remembered seeing in person. . . . It was so beautiful."

Wherever transports take people, the primary feeling is one of incomparable bliss. The fantastic nature of the surroundings doesn't seem at all like the stuff of dreams or daydreams. Of her trips into the microcosm, Donna says:

[These sexual states] are not at all like dreams. Things in dreams look a lot like real life with a fantasy element, but the only way I can describe it is to say that everything was *more*.

I'm accessing more dimensions or more modes of thought than I do normally, and things are not as solid as concrete forms and shapes. It's almost like a biologist or physicist looking at sub-atomic particles or things under the electron microscope, the basic patterns of energy that the universe is made of: forms of waves and rays and points and the interplay of expansion and contraction, progressions, and the experience of densities.

I'm having all kinds of visions and insights, the kind I imagine physicists have, where there's the confluence of energy and matter, the regeneration of life and death. This understanding of life, of the universe, in this profound way is so multidimensional that it could never fit into words. It's not at all like waking reality.

Microcosmic travels in which molecular and cellular structures become the planets and galaxies of another universe are closely paralleled by transports that rocket lovers at lightning speed through starry outer space. According to one man,

There are these wonderful possibilities, like shooting through the sky together. I'm suddenly flying, out in the stars. It's like going through the galaxies, traveling at amazing speeds. It's visual and physical. I've actually seen stars like galaxies rushing past and also have a physical sense of my body rushing along, or maybe *our* bodies rushing along.

The beauty and wonder of intergalactic travels is ravishing, according to another respondent. "There was a lot of space between what was out there, blackness with points of lights, stars . . . like in the solar system with solid planets and gaseous planets present and around me," according to a woman who added, "I felt utterly full and empty and as though some very profound spiritual energy filled me . . . with this deepest, deepest sense of peace."

Cosmic travels appear in all manner of altered states— dreams, trance, psychedelic trips, holotropic breathwork, meditation, free association—where they have powerful archetypal meaning. Usually, these are symbols with many-layered messages specific to the individual and his or her life circumstances. The underworld, including the ocean's depths, is variously the realm of the dead, of the past, of the unconscious, of creatures both natural and supernatural (such as mermaids and dwarfs), of buried treasure. The celestial realms are the residence of natural and supernatural airborne creatures, of fate and the future, of the gods and their messengers, and of infinite expansion and possibility. These worlds are regularly visited by shamans and spiritual adepts seeking knowledge normally outside human awareness that can be brought back to the "middle world" of earthly existence.

Otherworldly visitations during sex, though, don't appear to convey symbolic messages to lovers in the same way they do for shamans, meditators, or depth-psychology explorers. In place of highly personalized insights, lovers return with a sense of expansion, connection, and awe.[5] They enjoy belonging in the world in a way they didn't formerly understand or appreciate. Donna's response is representative: "There's a feeling of joy, love, warmth, lightness, ease, and peace. It's like really being cradled in the universe, a feeling that the universe is *me*. There's no good or bad, certainly nothing evil. Nothing for me to be afraid of, nothing to concern myself about."

As simple or odd as the displacement to other worlds may appear, it has, in fact, the potential for spiritual realization, especially for those of a materialistic turn of mind. Transports convince lovers that they are part of a much greater, much more mysterious reality than they ever dreamed possible. According to Aurelia,

There's a part of me that deals with the world, and then another part of me that transcends the world and has access to—I don't know—something beyond me. That part isn't limited the way my physical, conscious being is. That part of me is vast and interconnected and very deep. The feeling I have [during these sexual experiences] is that a door opens up, and that that other me and that other world become available, and a lot of things travel freely across that barrier because the door is open.

Such unintentional violations of "natural laws" made by lovers resemble the way seers of old often had their normal awareness interrupted by visions outside their control, just as some psychics have unsolicited "breakthroughs" of disturbing, remote events. Accidental dislocation or activation of a subtle energy body is considered a mark of spirituality around the world. Sometimes it is a sign that a person is divinely chosen to become a seer or shaman. Shamanic training then involves learning to enhance such gifts and make them more intentional. The adept can visit other worlds at will to carry out specific missions in order to improve local conditions. The early stages of meditation may also be also marked by otherworldly experiences and OBEs, but most contemplative traditions advise practitioners to ignore such powers as distractions from the path of true realization. Nevertheless, some gurus report using their astral bodies to travel to subtle planes.

Whether they involve otherworldly visits or merely momentary escapes of the body's domicile, sexual dislocations are profoundly moving, even when they appear to be banal. Their beauty, and the awe with which they inspire lovers to recognize the greater reality, convince them that the material world is not all there is. At the same time, they return to this world with a renewed sense of the fitness of it and their place within it. One woman sums it up this way:

I have my eyes open, and I can see, but it's almost as if what I'm seeing is not real, and the sounds that I hear are not real, and the world around me is not real. It's not like a vision exactly, but a state of consciousness. In Hindu terms, it's as if I've become aware of the *maya*. I'm aware of the dream within the dream, and what we call the real world is seen as a dream. There is the truth.

It's a place of true bliss, just such a warm, yummy feeling that I hold those moments as truly enlightening states that allow me to come back with a sense of well-being and groundedness. Everything is perfect and peaceful. And there are no doors and no years, nothing but this place and this moment you are in. All is right with the world, and I just rest in that.

Transports as a Threshold

It may be that transports, as exotic and blissful as they are, are merely threshold events that occupy a transitional place between normal reality and even deeper experiences, the way hypnogogia, a distinct state of vivid imagery and fantasy, is the threshold between wakefulness and sleep. Hypnogogia, which is similar to daydreaming, may contain the remnants of the everyday world and thought processes but it also contains fantasy elements, imaginary visions, and illogical connections. Just so, transports may retain elements of a recognizable landscape and sense of self but stray into imaginal realms of otherworldly landscapes and no discernible time. Transports can even venture beyond the present.

Jill, for instance, whose underwater experience appears earlier, had other visions that seemed to come from the past. She once saw herself and her lover in a Renaissance-period Italian city. The vision of this urban setting was incredibly detailed, but oddly enough no one else was present except for the two lovers. Jill began to receive other impressions, words and phrases that came to her, but they belonged to her lover, not to her, and they came from his past:

> Some of the impressions were songs, like the sounds of bells, or I'd hear a word. I'd ask, "What significance does this have for you?" And he'd say, "Oh yeah. That was real important to me at such-and-such a time" or "That was a symbol that was important to me for a while."

Another woman felt as if she were traveling on a train through the countryside in spring. Through the train's window, she watched as a breathtakingly beautiful orchard of cherry or plum trees in full bloom passed into view. Framed by the mass of pink blossoms was a woman sitting in "a kind of Art Deco outfit." The image of the woman seemed rather stylized compared to the realistic naturalism of the rest of the scene. The intense pleasure this image evoked and its beauty made a deep impression.

Transports then can shatter temporal as well as spatial boundaries. They may very well be the threshold to states where time, space, and self all are altered beyond the normal— the sexual states that sweep people into past lives.

The Shattering of the Vessels

Everything was dropping away, no sensory perception, and there is no way to describe it. There was nothing but union in that moment, but I couldn't tell you union with what. And immediately afterward there were the tears, tears of joy, incredible joy that I felt the privilege of having, this incredible gratitude and awe.

—Marta

Time Travel and Revealed Truths: Falling into Past Lives

It's like I was there during the time when the Roman Empire was invading Gaul, and [Dee] was killed during this battle. . . . I was a Celtic priestess, and I have a sense that I died in a Roman prison. Some of the most excruciating pain I've ever experienced was this vision that I had right after we'd made love, that [the Roman soldiers] were burning my sacred trees, my groves. —Ardrigh

[Ardrigh] was a [Celtic] high priestess, and I was a warrior. . . . We met when she was conducting some sort of pagan ritual in the oak grove, and I was hiding, watching her do this . . . I threw her on the ground, and we made love right there. It ended up with my stealing some horses. She said, "And you died, and I was captured." And that was how it went. I died, and she was captured. It was a very tragic ending. That's the story of the oak grove. —Dee

INTENSE LOVEMAKING—even of the ordinary variety—can rob us of our sense of time. Who has never come crashing back into the regular passing of the hours from a passionate interlude— "Oh no, it's Tuesday, and I was supposed to have a meeting at eight!" "Did we eat today?" "When did it get dark out?" Time becomes plastic, usually slipping away too quickly for normal reckoning, at other times spreading out into an infinite pool. Gwen, a busy executive, commenting about how this aspect of ordinary sex can shade into transcendent sex, said, "One time I was so far gone that I bolted up, suddenly scared that I'd missed my train, but only five minutes had passed. Five minutes! I thought it had been about two hours. I even made my lover get out of bed to look at another clock because I was sure the one by the bed had stopped."

For many people, this kind of absorption is only a distant memory from the earliest days of a relationship. Falling in love activates such widespread neurochemical changes in the brain that infatuation can be technically considered a mild (and of course very pleasant) psychosis. As relationships progress and partners become more accustomed to each other, this brain chemistry gradually dissipates, and lovers become more easily distracted. Soon, instead of losing time *during* sex, they start to put time *around* it: "We've got about half an hour. How about a quick one before I go to the office?"

In transcendent sex, however, people can find themselves completely loose from their temporal moorings, a state possible even in long-standing relationships. The clock's hard confines are transcended, either molded by the lovers or sucking them into the past.

Their Time Runs the World

Sometimes couples feel as though they can magically control the flow of time through their lovemaking. Francine and her husband were the founding partners of a housecleaning service company. They regularly supervised different teams of employees on their jobs, but they themselves also functioned as a team, frequently working together cleaning their customers' homes.

Francine was a little embarrassed during our interview, but with some encouragement she finally confessed that she and her husband shared an extremely powerful attraction that allowed them to communicate telepathically with each other, drawing them together at the same instant to fall into each other's arms. She blushed when she admitted that this paranormal attraction frequently overtook them on the job. "We'd be in a customer's house working in separate rooms, and suddenly we'd both come together on the staircase. It was spontaneous, and then we'd do it," she confides shyly. When they were suddenly and silently drawn together in that way, sex became magical.

> When we made love, it was like a band between us. We'd fall into that state like a dance where we just knew what the other wanted. We'd be in a trancelike state so that we could move smooth and graceful, making eye contact, and with every sense that you have, you are paying attention to your partner. You become one being. It was like a dance, like synchronized swimming where one stance would just flow into another. In the exhilarated feeling, the lightness of being, when all my senses were engaged I was not even in my body all the time, but feeling as though the whole world is in me, and I'm the whole world. That's a beautiful feeling.

When these lovers united, they also seemed to become one with time, moving *with* it rather than having it flow over them. Francine continued:

> We created a feeling that, in that mode, time is not a problem. It was the right thing to do in that moment, and *in that moment, our sex ran the world.*

Once we started, we were *completely* safe, completely safe. It was as though, somehow, through our strong desire to make love and our freedom from embarrassment, we were never caught. With this particular man, our love was so confident and sure it seemed that the universe honored the magic in us.

Their sense that their time ran the world flourished because they were never caught, which also affirmed the rightness of their actions "because our commitment in making love was a good thing. . . . We always had experiences that were not rude or cheap, but magical, a way to create a magic that would keep us safe. Those weren't obnoxious things to do in that state. In that state, everything was always okay." In support of this view, Francine cites the countless times they finished before their customers came back.

We were *never* caught, ever. We must have made love in our customers' houses *hundreds and hundreds* of times. We always did it at our own pace, never hurried. It amazed me that it was only just as we were putting ourselves back together that the customers came back. *Never* before.

And this *always* worked for us, whenever we made love like that—even at a New Year's Eve party we were giving, even when we made love in the middle of the day at my parents' house in the living room when they were home. Nobody ever caught us.

I don't know how I could do this. I didn't feel like I could create other people's lives, but I could always create mine at those moments.

They are not alone in their sense of time control. One man in the study told me how he and his girlfriend created a vehicle in time he likened to a fairy bubble: "Remember how in the cartoons, they would show a fairy [appearing] in a bubble? And in *The Wizard of Oz,* the good witch comes in a bubble? Erotic play would generate the bubble." Once it was created, the couple would try to stay in it all day as they went about other activities. As soon as the bubble arose between the two of them, everything seemed to be magical, just as Francine reports. Things and events appeared and disappeared in a way that seemed orchestrated to create the most pleasant conditions. In describing it, he says,

> In this bubble, you could flow anywhere. You know that old joke, you need a parking space, and it's right there. You need this, and it's right there in time. It was like a symphony, like its own work of art that would modulate itself through these different blendings of experience, all of which were equal to each other but which all referenced and played off each other in extraordinarily synchronistic ways.

> In this bubble, the morning was like a year had gone by because every experience during the day would have created a hundred minor but memorable experiences. A day seemed to last forever because there's more experiences per unit of time.

While such claims can't be verified, regardless of how convincing they feel subjectively, they have precedents in venerable traditions from all over the world. Magicians and other spiritually powerful people are able to transcend time. For example, Joshua, in the Old Testament, prays to stop time so that the Israelites can conquer their enemies.

Then spake Joshua to the Lord in the day when the Lord delivered up the Amorites before the children of Israel, . . . "Sun, stand thou still upon Gibeon; and thou, Moon, in the valley of Ajalon."

And the sun stood still, and the moon stayed, until the people had avenged themselves upon their enemies. . . . So the sun stood still in the midst of heaven, and hasted not to go down about a whole day. And there was no day like that before it or after it. . . .[1]

Modern theories of physics and experiments about the plasticity of time also suggest that the flow of time is not as absolute as it was once imagined to be.[2] The subjective sense of time may be closely related to electrochemical activity in the brain.[3] And alterations in brain activity are deliberately cultivated in spiritual practices, such as ingesting sacred psychedelics, engaging in repetitive activities such as dancing, drumming, or chanting, or shutting out sensory input through prayer and meditation. Sex can bring about similar states.

The Brink of Time

Lovers who feel they can control time are rare compared to those who find themselves deposited on the shores of the far-distant past. Several people I talked to mentioned puzzling visions that seemed to be underdeveloped glimpses of the past, as if they were teetering on the brink of time but, for some reason, couldn't quite make it over the edge. One woman found herself rapturously flying above a breathtaking forest. As long as she is in this mode, she has the ecstatic experience typical of transports, discussed in the previous chapter. However, at times, she finds herself "coming to earth" in the scene, which then transforms into the terrifying experience of a past life, in which she is a Jewish fugitive being hunted by Nazi prison guards and dogs through the forest.

Why do some transports fail to develop into full-blown past-life episodes? Perhaps the person isn't yet psychologically ready for the information that will be revealed. For unlike the rapture of transports, past-life episodes are almost invariably disturbing and tragic.

One man was so scared that he stopped making love to his partner to make the transcendent experience go away. They had been making love on the floor of an empty house the woman had just purchased. Warmed by a cheerful fire in her brick fireplace in the gathering gloom of a late winter afternoon, he began to slip away into another world. "I had this distinct impression that, instead of being in her living room in Ohio in nineteen-sixty-whatever, suddenly I was in another place, another time, like in a cottage or a hut. There was a fire in an old stone fireplace with a black kettle over the fire. Suddenly we were a husband and wife making love in another time, ancient England. It was frightening, scary. . . . I pulled out." Despite this man's ability to have altered-state sex frequently, he has never gone back to this place and time.

Past-Life Experiences

Past-life experiences that occur during sex, like those that occur in other settings, can be extremely disturbing. They represent a dislocation of the three dimensions of normal reality: time, place, and person. People are dislocated from the here and now and transported to another period and place. They no longer are themselves but someone else. Their partners are strangers.

Furthermore, past-life episodes strip people bare, revealing truths about their present lives they would rather not know by showing them how ruinous similar behavior was in the past. It is as if past-life stories are backward-looking divinations, fore-telling what must be worked out for a positive future. During these temporal dislocations, one or both parties appear to exist simultaneously in the present and the past. Even individuals who don't believe in reincarnation suddenly find themselves reliving events that seem to come from previous incarnations. Somehow a rather complete knowledge of the previous life presents itself, as if all the significant happenings are crystallized in a single moment that contains a message about the present relationship.

Some past lives seem to involve the person's direct, lineal ancestors. For instance, a Chinese woman in San Francisco may relive a life of hard labor as a male relative building the railroad spanning America in the 1800s. At other times, individuals may find themselves living in a culture they have always been drawn to but that has no discernible link to their origins. For instance, a man of Mediterranean descent who vacations regularly in the Pacific islands experiences a past life as a powerful kahuna. Or the previous existence may be utterly at variance with real life or fantasy: men may see themselves as women, or homosexuals as heterosexuals. Instead of finding themselves in cultures they admire, they may be in ones they never liked, reduced to circumstances that are miserable rather than romantic.

Regardless, the past life is usually a cautionary tale of some unpalatable truth. Significantly, the lovers may not perceive the parallels *at the time the event takes place,* no matter how obvious. Often, the true meaning of the story dawns on them much later—sometimes when it is too late.

There are many theories about the source of past-life "biographies," regardless of how they are generated: during sex, regression therapy, body or breath work, meditation, etc. Some believe that like dreams, they are the subconscious mind's attempts to bypass psychological defenses and the rational mind.[4] Others think they are actual biographical material from historically verifiable past lives.[5] Still others believe that they are ancestral memories from the collective unconsciousness, or that they originate from a spiritual source, such as the Higher Self.[6] No theory has been proven. The value of such experiences, wherever they come from, is in their potential for personal growth.

Lessons from a Tantric Guru

I met Donald when he was a graduate student in his late twenties. With his strong, muscular body, blond good looks, and careless charm, it has always been easy for him to attract women, and he has enjoyed numerous casual liaisons. His family, originally Roman Catholic, had converted to a fundamentalist Protestant denomination. Once he was on his own, he began to study Vedanta, a yogic spiritual practice, which was reflected in the Indian furnishings of his home where I visited him. Although he has never studied Tantra, Donald discovered during a past-life sexual experience that he had once been a Tantric teacher. But he was dismayed to find that, instead of being a compassionate and enlightened spiritual teacher, he was extremely selfish. In fact, he was debauched. The guru was grossly fat from overeating. He sexually exploited his female devotees. This unpleasant image of himself as the guru came as a wake-up call to Donald regarding his behavior in the here and now.

I was looking down at this scene where I was watching myself with a woman in a past life. This was probably the 1300s in

India, and I could see the whole costume getup. I was a Tantric teacher, and she was one of my Tantricas, one of the highly advanced [female] students. I had maybe twenty to thirty students in a building like an ashram. I'd go through a process of initiation [with them] and so forth. . . . I was a *lot* heavier, *really* heavy.

I was watching us make love then, and at the same time we were making love in our physical bodies here and now, and I was aware of both of these experiences at once. My lover and I in this life had this intense sexual connection because of that past life, and I realized that a lot of the experiences I'd been having came from that past life and from what I knew in that past life as a Tantric teacher. . . .

I wasn't using a lot of that knowledge for the highest consciousness, or the highest good, so I'm now dealing with my ego, which I didn't do in that life. I'm learning how to use that Tantric energy without ego and selfish motives. So even though I might have picked up a lot of tools then, I didn't have the ethical foundation to go with it. I was not good at seeing the female's point of view, so I was turning women into objects, and it was happening over and over.

Leaning forward and speaking with intensity, he added that he had had to experience the flip side of his own behavior by becoming a woman in past lives, as well as an oppressor of women. "I've been a woman in past lives, too, and I remember being raped," he adds. "I've also had experiences where I am raping a woman in a past life. I reexperience this during sex as the energy is going through me, being in extreme pain. As this energy releases, the memory of being raped or raping hits my brain, and I remember."

Living both the victim and the persecutor roles produces an almost perfect karmic balance. It is a pattern that appears regularly in ancient as well as contemporary spiritual records, especially those of psychedelic and near-death studies.[7]

Compulsions and Couples

Past lives arising from sex have two qualities that make them unique: they are almost compulsory, and they can entrain both members of a couple in the same events. No matter how ugly the picture revealed, nothing seems to stop it from being shown once it starts. Most of the states described in this book happen more or less involuntarily, but none feels so intrusive and overwhelming as past lives. These stories seem to have a will of their own, pulling lovers into the experience in spite of themselves. Past lives seem to be the only states couples regularly share. In most instances related here, only one partner at a time is having a transcendent episode; on the occasions when both partners were, they tended to have very different subjective experiences. With past lives, however, both frequently slip into the same field of a previously shared existence, seeing the same things, reliving the same events, but from the perspectives of the two separate individuals in the former existence. The next two stories illustrate these qualities.

Light and Dark

Richard and Jude were longtime friends who lived in Minneapolis. They shared the same birthday, and a passion for the African-American culture of New Orleans, especially its jazz and voodoo heritage. Gay white men, both Richard and Jude had always enjoyed the company of black people, especially those from Louisiana, even though such opportunities were comparatively rare in their lives.

Richard's affinity for black people had run counter to his upbringing. Indeed, it had been an early source of conflict, especially with his mother—one that got worse as he grew up. Although the family lived in Minnesota, she was from the South and was, according to Richard, "always real big on skin color, much more than is usual even for a southern white." She constantly remarked on the relative lightness or darkness of the complexions of the African-Americans they encountered. Her obsession centered on very light-skinned people with black ancestry who could "pass" for white. One of Richard's earliest childhood memories was of an incident when his mother had pointed out a light-skinned man they were passing on the street, remarking, "Look at that man. He's so good-looking. Too bad he's not white. He's almost white." Even as a small child, Richard thought that this was peculiar because "I've always liked light-skinned African-Americans myself. I find them very attractive, so I thought, why should he be white? He's fine as he is." The event was impressed on his young memory because it seemed utterly nonsensical.

Years later, Richard and Jude were dining out when they were surprised by an increasingly strong, mutual sexual attraction that engulfed them. In all their years of friendship, they had never felt the least bit interested in each other sexually. They felt compelled to leave the restaurant for a hotel. Their passion had an odd, alien insistence. Richard became aware that it was not he and his friend who wanted to make love, but two other people—a *heterosexual* couple—who wanted to use their bodies: "We were taking off our clothes when this past-life energy intruded, so that before we were actually having intercourse, we were already in that state. It really felt like *they* wanted to have sex, our two counterparts, so *we* did. Boom! It just happened."

The alien feeling of possession continued, as Richard insisted, "But it wasn't my idea. It wasn't his, either. It was this other energy. Although we're friends, we're not really compatible sexually for various reasons."

Jude became a dark-skinned black man, apparently the husband of this married, heterosexual couple. I was unable to interview Jude, but, according to Richard, Jude, who is blond, identified happily with his very dark-skinned counterpart. They seemed to dissolve into a single embodiment. Richard, however, found himself outside "his" body, which now appeared to be that of the Creole wife. He was observing the heterosexual couple from a height of about six feet. Richard said each experienced the couple's story from his own separate vantage point as the husband and wife.

Richard's Creole counterpart was a beautiful, fair-skinned woman of mixed race who had been the kept mistress of a successful Caucasian planter. As was the custom of the time, he maintained her in her own household in the city, visiting her when he came to town from his plantation in the country. Creoles, octoroons, quadroons and mulattos at that time enjoyed progressively higher social standing, depending on how "white" they were, literally and figuratively. The lighter their skin and eyes, and the straighter their hair, the higher their status. Prestige also came from the degree to which their education, manners, and lifestyle emulated those of the Southern gentry. The New Orleans demimonde had its own social code of status and privilege, much like its counterparts in nineteenth-century Europe, and a light-skinned, mixed-race woman whose wealthy lover maintained her in her own establishment with fine clothes and her own servants enjoyed a high rank indeed.

Richard and Jude "knew" that this Creole woman had borne

her white planter-lover three children, all quite light in color. Then the planter was killed in action during the War between the States, leaving her without any means of support. She soon married "a very dark-skinned man, a black man, for financial security" and went on to bear him three children as well. This was the husband whose body Jude occupied. Richard, speaking as his wife, says, "I was really clear that money was why I married him. Although I loved him and he was very devoted to me and we had a very good life, frankly, in my social class, we didn't do that. It was considered a disgrace for a Creole to marry a black, even after the Civil War."

Then switching back to his own voice as an observer of these events, he continues, "Just as I felt somewhat detached watching this from outside my body, I felt she was the one detached also. He really loved her, and she did this for security. She loved him, too, and the sex was good, but she didn't love him the same way she loved the father of her [first three] children. So it was not primarily an emotional love experience for her as much as it was good sex and a bonding."

Speaking once again as the Creole, he adds that her black husband "was a good father to my children [by the planter]. He thought they were spoiled, and he thought they were uppity and all, but he treated them well. I was satisfied."

Richard and Jude didn't become lovers, "even though we had had this interesting experience. . . . It was like an overlay, so that their reality was stronger than ours because they were happily married, but us, we were just friends." But the episode highlighted differences that had been simmering under the surface of the men's friendship. Ultimately, it drove them apart. When they were talking over what had happened, Richard inadvertently hurt Jude's feelings when he said that his Creole alter ego hadn't been as committed to the relationship as Jude's alter ego had been. "I tried to say this to Jude diplomatically after it was over, but I think I really insulted him," he explains. "But it was true. He always loved me more than I loved him in that lifetime."

Over time Jude began to pressure Richard to express himself more sexually, something Richard was reluctant to do privately as well as publicly. He was not "out" in many areas of his life. "Jude made me uncomfortable after a time, asking me to confront my sexuality in a more direct way because I had a long period of celibacy in the 1990s," Richard says regretfully. "He's very open, very up front, and it finally drove us apart. According to our experience, he was a very sexual man in that life, very comfortable with his sexuality, and he's that way in this lifetime, too. I couldn't deal with it at the time." Such was the end of their long friendship, over reasons that might not make any difference to the two men today, as Richard's attitude about his sexuality eventually changed, and he became much more sympathetic to Jude's point of view.

Sometimes Lessons Can't Be Learned

Sometimes people can't apply the warnings of the past to the present, no matter how good their intentions. Martin and Carolyn embodied the good life of northern California. He is an auburn-haired artist who travels all over the world. She had been involved in scientific studies most of her career, and she dismissed any suggestion of the supernatural, although she was intrigued enough to read about it, if only in order to mock. They had been married more than ten years when I met them, talking first to Carolyn, and then interviewing Martin at his studio. Their romance began at a party honoring one of Martin's closest friends. The chance meeting bowled him over.

Carolyn walked in, and she was carrying a basket of blueberries. She'd just come down from an island in Maine. She had an olive drab shirt on. It had such a large neck that it kept slipping down on the left side so that her shoulder was bare. She had a big straw hat on and that wonderful blond hair came out from under that hat.

The idealized woman for me was suddenly there before me. I felt an immediate soul connection, even though I hadn't spoken to her at that point. Much, much deeper than a sexual attraction. Later, I came into the kitchen. She was at the freezer where a bottle of wine in there had frozen and broken. So I helped her clean it up.

While they were working on the mess in the freezer, Carolyn and Martin discovered that they were coincidentally reading the same book, Shirley MacLaine's *Out on a Limb*, about past-life experiences. They crept away to a quiet spot where they could talk without being overheard. Carolyn said, "Somehow we started whispering about this book over in the corner. The people we were associating with at this party, it wasn't the kind of thing you talked about. It was considered far out, *way* out."

Martin's irresistible attraction to Carolyn threw him into a turmoil. Unbeknownst to Carolyn, he was married. Normally he never attended parties when his wife was unable to accompany him, but in this case she was ill. He went alone because the party was honoring his best friend. Nothing like this had ever happened to him before. He was dedicated to his wife, and to his family. In fact, he took great pride in being an ideal family man. Growing up in a large brood himself, Martin had always looked forward to fatherhood, and in part, he had been drawn to the woman who became his wife because she already had two children. They seldom had dated as a couple in the formal sense because he loved taking the whole family on outings, and enjoying not just a courtship, but a feeling of having his own "instant family." After only six months, she told him she had become pregnant, despite taking birth control pills. He seemed destined to claim this family as his own, and they were married. All the kids were now in school. Yet here he was, lying awake night after night in "the perfect family house" he had built with his own hands, his loved ones asleep around him, while he fought his feelings for Carolyn.

It was a losing battle.

Carolyn had also felt a strong attraction to Martin at the party. When she learned he was married, she determined to squelch it. She refused to take his calls, refused to meet him. But his feelings were so powerful that Martin, without any encouragement, formally separated from his wife after months of soul-searching. When he was free, Carolyn agreed to see him.

The second time they went to bed, they found themselves caught up in a distressing past-life story whose painful events and emotions were utterly foreign to the roseate joy they felt as fresh lovers. After climaxing, just as they were disengaging from each other, an unprecedented experience began to intrude on their minds. Carolyn says,

It was sort of like watching a video. It was a very bizarre experience. We started at the same time synchronistically to have this same internal movie start to play. We started talking about it out loud. Like telling a story, only *it* was telling *us*. And we were seeing the same thing, kind of in your mind's eye. We were just lying there, and it didn't arise out of our conversation. It didn't seem to have any reason to be there. A story started to unfold, and I now believe it to be a past-life experience. I'd turn to Martin, and say, "Are you seeing what I'm seeing?" and he'd say, "I'm seeing the same thing."

Carolyn and Martin were almost finishing each other's sentences, as the story unfolded in three scenes. It opened with Carolyn's descending a staircase in a grand mansion during the Victorian period. She was impressed by the formality and richness of her surroundings, especially the numerous paintings on the walls, the long, sweeping staircase, and the magnificent chandelier lighting it. Her hair was pulled up in an elaborate style, and she was wearing a formal ball gown over hoops with lots of petticoats. It came to her that she was in her father's house, and that he was very wealthy and influential. She was a headstrong young woman.

> I was rather scandalous because I was in my late twenties and had refused to marry up to that point. I was very spoiled, strongwilled, and arrogant, and I could get away with it because I had a wealthy father. I had pretty much refused the societal norms at that point and was bordering on the fringes because I had suitors, so there was no reason for me not to have married. My father wanted me to marry, and it was just sheer will on my own part that I chose not to do that. . . .

> I had a red dress on to make a statement. It's funny because I don't really resonate with that kind of personality, and at the time I had this experience, I was doing my damnedest to fit in and always feeling a little outside, kind of the opposite of someone who would wear a red dress. So I remember this bright red dress, bordello red, you might say. Probably not socially acceptable.

> And that's how the story opened, with me coming down this staircase and seeing this large chandelier and all the paintings. I sort of became her, having her feelings, and it was odd because it wasn't a story that appealed to me.

She was late in coming down to her guests. Downstairs, in the ballroom where the party had already begun, Martin was dressed, like all the other gentlemen, in tails. He was eagerly waiting to see her, yet dreading it as well. In contrast to Carolyn's Bohemian personality, he was a very proper man who had met her through being associated with her father in business. Martin's well-to-do family wasn't in the same social class as Carolyn's, but mutual financial interests gave him entrée to higher circles. He handled certain investments, a genteel business that allowed him to rub shoulders with wealthier, more prominent families. In his past life, he was also a good father and husband.

> I was in something like an arranged marriage with a very beautiful, soft-spoken wife who was intelligent, but who kind of waged her will in such a way that she could make things happen in the family without directly confronting me. I managed our family's money. We had three children, all of whom I loved very much.

> But there was a real small part of me that felt trapped within this structure. When I wasn't in touch with that fear, everything was fine. My parents were still alive, my wife's parents were still alive, and all of us would get together. I was a dutiful husband, and I was seemingly empowered in the family, yet my wife would pull most of the strings. We lived in a multilevel town house that was beautiful, but I felt afraid somewhere inside that I was giving up being myself.

> I don't know how I met Carolyn in that life, but I had the same kind of attraction that I had in my real life. I hadn't been looking for anyone. I wasn't unfaithful to my wife. I was somewhat pious, but that little part of myself kept describing my piety as

kind of artificial. It was still covering up something deeper in myself that I needed to retrieve.

Our conversations weren't the kind that I'd ever had, and that little part of me just opened, and it forever shattered the world that I was actually living in. But I was still connected to it with ties that kept pulling me back. I made an excuse to travel, and I would spend whatever time I could with Carolyn in that life. I went back and forth. When I returned home, I would close all that down because it was too terrifying to bring it back home.

The two became lovers, and in a time when birth control methods were so primitive as to be almost nonexistent, Carolyn became pregnant. Martin continues, "That scared me to death. The reality of having a child that Carolyn was going to carry to term meant that suddenly all the taboos of Victorian England were coming down on my head, and this affair I had done so much to keep secret suddenly seemed to be in danger of breaking into my regular life."

The next scene was their parting at a train station. Martin had refused to leave his wife, but he had used his money and connections to obtain a home for Carolyn in the country. In the time-honored tradition of nineteenth-century bourgeois morality, she was being sent away to avoid shaming her family. Martin handed her an envelope filled with currency as she departed, whispering final words of love, believing he would never see her again. "I wasn't buying off the relationship. I just wanted her to be well. I just couldn't take the social humiliation," he said. "Divorce just wasn't there. Divorce was, well, you were crucified instead." Despite their tearful parting, Carolyn was confident that he would indeed leave his wife and join her soon. She never thought that theirs was anything but a temporary separation—and one of short duration, at that. Carolyn's more avant-garde spirit wasn't bowed down by the events, even though she was making what she considered to be a short-term concession to convention. She was proud of their love, confident that Martin would come to her in the country home he had arranged with such care and that they would live happily ever after. Her conviction never wavered that his devotion would lead him to flout convention, just as she had.

In the final scene, Martin did leave his wife for Carolyn. Martin recalls, "She lives in the country, and I've been in remorse. She's never left me [in my thoughts], never for a moment. I was in a place I'd call purgatory. I was considering leaving my family. I'd tried to live with it for so long, and I finally got to the point where I almost had no choice but that I *needed* to find her."

It was too late.

Carolyn had lost the baby, but that was not the source of her coldness. He had waited too long to join her. How could he not have come to her sooner, not have been with her through her ordeal? How could he have lacked the courage she had when their love and humiliation were equal? In Carolyn's words, "The baby was gone, and I wanted nothing to do with him because it was too late. It wasn't about not loving each other. It was about timing for me, unmet agreements and expectations, and the pain around that. The disappointment that he had not come to me before was so great that I couldn't rejoin with him when he was ready to be there."

This final discordant scene rendered Martin bereft of everything. "I was in purgatory in that I couldn't go back. All that time I'd held the hope she would take me back, and this visit was in the despairing hope that she would, but I was too fearful to really face what that would mean if she wouldn't," he explains before continuing in a dull voice. "I just returned to my old life, but it all closed down. I didn't have any other place to go. There wasn't another woman to seek out. She was the *one*, the spiritual absolute I'd been able to find that once in my life. My former indecision and inability to break loose had resulted in her not being able to hold on."

For Carolyn and Martin in real life, newly in love, the story was extremely upsetting at several levels. Carolyn, whose scientific orientation did not include such happenings, happy or sad, doubted her sanity. Reading Shirley MacLaine was one thing; actually having a past-life episode was something else.

> We were caught off guard by it. The story was dictating to us, like watching a movie, and you don't get to change it if you don't like what's going on. It was playing out, and we were being shown something. My reaction was, that wasn't going to happen to *us*. That was my relationship to it.

> I didn't see any similarity in it with us at that time, though it did say something about why we felt so compelled to be together even though we didn't know each other that well, why we felt so familiar, like we'd always been together.

> It was overriding my logical mind, which was a big override for me. The rational part of me dismissed it. I'd say to myself, "Oh, you were just daydreaming."

As much as she tried to dismiss it, though, Carolyn found she could not escape the story. Several weeks later when she was traveling, she happened to go into an art gallery where she was dumbfounded to recognize a painting as one she had seen hanging in her father's mansion in her past life. Putting her skepticism to work, she decided to research the painting's ownership history to satisfy herself about the reality of her experience. The artist was obscure, but she managed to find a book about him and his works. Before she could finish the task of tracing the previous owners of the painting, though, she became frightened, and thrust the entire project away as too uncanny.

> I'd never seen or heard of the artist before. I really felt strange about seeing the picture. I bought the book because it bothered me enough that I wanted to know more. But then it gave me such creeps at this point in my life that I threw the book away. It was just too strange for me. It wasn't a pleasant story in the first place, and the whole thing was just too weird and spooky for me. It was a secret that we couldn't tell anybody.

These events were almost a decade in the past when I met Carolyn and Martin. Carolyn never resumed her research into her past life. She and Martin had married and lived happily together, though their life was beset with difficulties, including three miscarriages. They never were able to have children, a tragedy for them both. After drawing a glowing picture of their relationship, Carolyn surprised me by saying abruptly that she was seeking a separation. Martin was still hoping she would change her mind when I talked with him. She had come to regard their past life as a karmic lesson, foretelling what they needed to learn in order not to make the same mistakes with each other again. She believes they failed:

> When Martin today gets pushed into a situation where what other people think is important, he has a tendency to surrender to that. There is this timing thing where I feel betrayed, that our relationship should be more important than whatever else it is that is keeping him from making a choice, and that usually has to do with outside appearances. So now there's that sense that it's too late again, that it's not about love, but about his making

choices too late for me, and my need to move on. I have this
urgency that I can't wait.

I believe we were given an opportunity to be with each other in
a different context, but we haven't been able to do it. We made
the wrong choices again in this lifetime.

It's too painful to continue.

The Gift That Keeps on Giving

Many of the spiritual systems that incorporate reincarnation,[8]
of course, are founded on the belief that earthly attachments
create the conditions that keep human beings entrained in the
cycle of birth and death in the material order. Spiritual
advancement depends on learning the lessons of past experience to reduce, and eventually eliminate, a self-created karmic
legacy. The goal is liberation from choiceless reincarnation.
Today regression therapy is based on the idea that past-life
material can help resolve problems by revealing destructive
patterns that keep repeating. It's clear that Donald, Richard
and Carolyn all retrospectively interpret their past lives as providing them a second chance to do better this time around.
None of them benefited from the lessons in ways that preserved
their relationships. But they did gain something else.

Donald learned to take direct action to redress the wrongs
he believes he perpetrated on women, including redressing the
wrongs of others. He actually found a way to do this through
sex. He discovered a talent for picking up impressions of abuse
from his partners, not from previous lifetimes, but from the
more immediate past. The first time this happened, when he
was still flitting from woman to woman in transient affairs, he

was frightened away. Near orgasm with a woman he had picked up in a strange town, he suddenly had a vision of her crucified, writhing in pain on a cross. "So deep was her pain that it scared me. I was scared getting this insight into her experience," he admits. "I felt she had been abused an incredible amount. Images flashed through me, like telepathically receiving images of incest and stuff, pictures of her in darkness. And it scared me so much that I didn't call her again because I knew I couldn't relate to her. It was beyond my ability to empathize at the time. It felt to me like she was in a hell realm, and she was just stuck there, wanting me to save her."

Although he avoided that woman, Donald couldn't avoid receiving similar impressions from other partners about previous trauma. Gradually, he learned to open himself to their pain, and to help them using some of the techniques he had picked up from the Tantric guru he had once been.

I began to have insight, a specific sort of insight into women who had been sexually abused, and about various things that go on in the body energetically and how they're like doorways into the memory system of the women and to events that happened when they were younger. I learned to work with those energies to help heal them.

It became a common occurrence to be making love with a woman, and at some point I could feel images arising to my third eye. A lot of times I sensed their energy would change. They would suddenly close down.

The energy would be moving as we became more and more engaged, and all of a sudden there would be *bam!* a shutdown. I'd feel it in me, and when I felt it in me, I would intend to see what it was about. What lies here in me or the woman that is shutting down? And images would come, or questions would come. I'd ask, "Has such-and-such ever happened to you?" I would always have a general idea, and it would usually be accurate. At one point, I even knew at what age the woman had had this trauma.

My body seemed to sort of know how to move the energy. A lot of times, I would see where the energy was stuck, and I could move my hands in a certain way, and send energy through my hands or through my second chakra, my penis, or my heart, and I would allow it to flow and flow into the wound in a way to try to move it. A lot of times there would be a breakthrough. . . . It was incredible empathy.

In time, his helping others also eliminated the traces of exploitation from Donald's present way of life. His conscious intention now is not to engage in sex, as he did before, "mostly for pleasure, to have huge orgasms, to get high, to get off." Instead, he says, "I began to make a commitment to healing if I was going to partake in sexuality with a woman—that it would be for healing as the primary reason rather than pleasure."

Richard's past life helped another troubled relationship. It provided a special insight into his mother's irrational and embarrassing preoccupation with skin color. Instead of faulting her for having a racist attitude, he now assumes responsibility for the way she behaves. His voice breaking with emotion, he said, speaking as the Creole wife, "I had six children in that life. Three of them passed for white because their father was a planter, a white planter. One of them, one of the children who passed for white, is now my mother in this lifetime. She was my son in that lifetime."

With the greatest tenderness, he explains that the light-skinned son she had borne in New Orleans escaped the devastation of the postwar South and his mixed-race heritage, moving north to Minneapolis where that son successfully passed for white. Crossing racial lines was an anxious business in those times. This man lived in constant fear of betraying himself by some little slip or running into former acquaintances who knew of his parentage. Richard traced the parallel between his son's life and that of his real-life mother, who, he said, had also been born in New Orleans and had eventually settled in Minneapolis. So far as he knows, his mother actually has no African American blood, but Richard shoulders responsibility for her fixation. He sees her obsession with skin color as the karmic residue of the self-loathing he, in another lifetime, had instilled as her Creole mother who despised and blamed her dark-skinned husband and the children she had by him for compromising her social status. This realization has enabled him to have compassion for his mother, and for himself, as he accepts their interconnectedness in both oppressor and victim roles.

Carolyn, too, found a gift, even though she and Martin may not be able to save their marriage. She credits this past-life experience with being her spiritual awakening from hard-bitten scientism, an opening that has steadily blossomed to the point where she now possesses special talents for a healing vocation.

It was an invitation, and it even felt like that at the time. That's a funny thing to say, but it felt like an invitation. It's always stayed with me somehow, no matter how much I wanted to push it back into the closet. Something would come up in my life, and it would be there again.

This was my first experience in a personal way that God spoke to me, and it came at a time when I was trying to be oh-so-rational in my scientific program. I almost didn't like it because it felt like the back of the wardrobe opening, and I didn't want to go in there.

Carolyn likens this episode to discovering she had a religious calling that would transform her life, and take her away from scientific pursuits. "I now operate from a completely different worldview," she says, "that continued to open into the spiritual to this profound relationship that I have with God or Spirit or Whomever that's completely changed my evolution. I now have a knowing, a voice inside me that tells me what *is*. Now I run prayer groups, teach laying on of hands, give readings to people from that voice about their well-being. . . . It's a completely different life, but it's one I had to step into."

CHAPTER 8

Being in Nothingness:
Sex and Nirvana

Maybe it started with that dissolving quality, but then the two of us were not two anymore, but we weren't just a melding of two. We were in a larger oneness. And then there was a dissolution of that. We were dissolved into this larger thing that was included in everything, and the boundaries to that dissipated or disappeared so there was a sense that it was the whole. We were the whole. —Ann

I can't remember who said it, but they were talking about how people get a sense that the point of meditation is that I'm like a drop in the ocean, and I'll connect to the other drops and become one with the ocean. But it's not at all like that. Rather it was more like when you open yourself, suddenly the whole ocean flows into that one drop. It wasn't that I have now connected to all there is, which is fabulous enough, but like all there is has come into me. So I was all there was, much expanded, greater, glorified. —Lynn

KABBALAH, OR MYSTICAL JUDAISM, envisions the ten essential energies underlying the cosmos as vessels. When the Light of Creation was poured into them, the seven lowest vessels were too weak to contain this exalted power, and they broke in an event called *shevirah*, the Shattering of the Vessels.[1] Something very like this happens when people come close to Spirit: the Absolute cannot be contained by the limited vessels of normal consciousness. Direct perception of Spirit bursts the containers of space, time, and self. Reality as we know it implodes. It is like nothing we know, nothing we can imagine.

Full realization of Spirit is the highest goal of Eastern and Western religions, though it takes a different form in each. In Eastern spirituality this state is one of no definition or emptiness, popularly called enlightenment. But it has many other names, some better known than others: nirvana (Buddhism), *satori* or *kensho* (Zen), *wu wei* (Taoism), and *moksha* and *samadhi* (yoga).[2]

The goal of Eastern paths is the banishment of illusion, which produces complete liberation through correct and pure awareness of What Is. In other words, enlightenment is an awakened mind, conscious of the true nature of things. Thus Eastern forms of enlightenment focus on the cultivation of the right perception of reality rather than on becoming one with God, which is the goal of Western religions.[3]

People believe, with good reason, that both states—enlightenment and union with God—can only be attained through years of arduous spiritual discipline, especially a rigorous meditation practice. But virtually all religions also maintain that a person can suddenly become awakened. Ramana Maharshi is one well-known twentieth-century figure who attained enlightenment in a flash, as it were, as a result of investigating the fear of death. Whether moments of enlightenment occur through an intentional practice or spontaneously, they are most often just that: momentary events. It typically takes considerable practice to sustain pure awareness so that it becomes a constant state of mind.

Some respondents in this study reported timeless moments of awakening during sex that appear to be identical to those described in the sacred literature of East and West. These brief glimpses are sufficient to change their understanding of reality and their place within it. This chapter concerns sexually produced experiences of the Void of nirvana. The next covers unification with God.

Looking into the Jewel

Before delving into these stories, it's important to point out that these experiences are both more rare and more uniform across participants in the study, just as they are in mystical traditions. One way to understand this is to liken the body of altered-state experiences to a huge, imaginary diamond. People looking at its crown or table would see all the reflections of its various facets. Each person would have a unique vision of dazzling scintillations, depending on his or her line of sight, like the diverse stories reported in earlier chapters. But fewer viewers could simultaneously crowd around to examine the narrow bottom point of the diamond from different vantage points, and what they would see would tend to be the same: the refractions and colors would be fewer, and the image more nearly uniform, regardless of their angle of vision. So it is with the experiences of enlightenment, though they are no less remarkable for being similar.

And a word of warning is in order: the concepts presented in this chapter challenge our normal levels of understanding. When the ways in which we know things are shattered, our experience is impossible to express in words. Ineffability is actually one of the hallmarks of mystical events. That's good news, in the sense that the difficulty is a mark of authenticity, but bad news because it renders the core of these experiences hard to grasp. They are beyond the rational, linear, word-based way of thought because language always creates categories, and enlightenment is, by definition, the absence of categories. As the Upanishads, one of the oldest texts on mysticism, declares:

> There the eye goes not,
> Speech goes not, nor the mind.
> We know not, we understand not
> How one would teach it.[4]

The classic tag for this impossibility is the English paraphrasing of the *Tao Te Ching*: "The Tao that can be spoken is not the Tao."[5] Or, as another Taoist source more humorously puts it, "If it could be talked about, everybody would have told their brother."[6] This is one reason that some of the most useful representations for enlightenment are pictorial, like the yin-yang symbol of the Tao or the Zen series of ox-herding pictures. It is also a reason some practices employ methods to shatter the confines of rational thought, such as the mind-bending Zen riddles called *koan* (what is the sound of one hand clapping? what was your face before you were born?).

When words are used, the sacred writings usually revert to dizzying paradoxes to convey the sense of nonduality: polar opposites and categories do not exist, but neither is everything one monolithic absolute. The Buddhists use the phrase "not-same, not-different" to convey the idea expressed in these three different sacred texts:

> I am the ritual and the sacrifice; I am true medicine and the mantrum. I am the offering and the fire which consumes it, and he to whom it is offered.[7]

[I am] control and the uncontrollable.
I am the union and the dissolution.
I am the abiding and I am the dissolution.
I am the one below,
And they come up to me.[8]

Jesus said . . . , "When you make the two one, and when you make the inside like the outside and the outside like the inside, and the above like the below, and when you make the male and the female one and the same, so that the male be not male nor the female female . . . then you will enter [the kingdom]."[9]

It is not only difficult to communicate what has happened to others, the subtleties of such experiences make them extremely difficult even to recollect in their entirety once they have happened, one reason mystical writing is so abstruse—or that little has been committed to writing at all but remains a living tradition passed along experientially from master to aspirant. Contemplative Rabbi Nachman of Bratislava observes: "You may have a vision, but even with yourself you cannot share it. Today you may be inspired and see a new light. But tomorrow, you will no longer be able to communicate it, even to yourself."[10] Expect to struggle with this material, unless, you, too, have had an experience of enlightenment.

Norberto, originally from South America, was a Roman Catholic priest for fifteen years before leaving the Jesuit community and eventually marrying. He is still a devout Catholic, though now mystically oriented. He describes the difficulties of talking about the enlightenment experience he had with his wife with reference to Taoist terms:

The sensation of time and space disappears, too. It's unique, something that is difficult to express, but someone who has had the same experience would say, "Yes, yes, yes, yes. I know what you're talking about." You know how when they say the Tao you can speak is not the Tao. You can't say what this is.

Cutting Vegetables

Ann is in her forties. She was reared in an agnostic family with little knowledge of any religion, certainly not Eastern ones. Her first experience of transcendent sex occurred, against all odds, under rather unpleasant conditions. Ann's marriage was troubled, and sex with her husband had "never been good." Despite her dismal experience, Ann persisted in believing that sex could be spiritual, a conviction she says she must have been born with, because, she says, grimacing, "No church I'd ever been in—and certainly not my parents—had any words for that, or even a need for that. Even if my parents had been thinking in a normal Christian mode, that wouldn't have been part of their picture of how things are."

One night, while enduring sex with her spouse, Ann tried to derive a modicum of enjoyment out of it by shutting him out of her mind completely. To block him out, she concentrated instead on what she was feeling in her body.

Moments later, her whole world changed.

She dropped into the Void of all realization, and it transformed her life. As a result of this experience, she went on a spiritual quest that culminated in her becoming a Zen Buddhist. It led her to divorce her husband, and to go to graduate school to incorporate spirituality in her career. Consequently, her story contains some Buddhist metaphors she acquired later, but they were not part of her understanding at the time the events took place. Here's what happened.

I am aware of how it arose, though it's a very intimate thing to talk about. I was just concentrating on my own body. I blocked [awareness of my husband] out of it. That's how it happened. I was really going into the sensation.

I would compare it to a Zen practice of cutting vegetables, where all you do is cut the vegetables. Cut, cut, cut, and that's all you're doing. And then suddenly there's only cutting. I was in the moment of that stimulation, and then there was only that. There was *nothing* except that.

There was nothing there. The boundaries of the body *went,* and yet there was an awareness of doing, but the sense of the body was *not*. There was this dissolvingness, and this losing of boundaries.

And then there was this incredible nothingness and every-thingness. Out of this feeling of nothingness and no-self, there was yet all possibility and all potentiality.

It was probably for only an instant, but in that instant there was no time and no space. Yet there was an awareness of what was happening, an awareness of something and nothing all at the same time.

There was no difference between my husband and me, so there was no feeling *for* him or me, but at the same time a total com-passion, and then even that was instantaneously gone some-how.

It was just some kind of depth of insight, but insight sounds dualistic somehow. There was just a more complete sense of really pure awareness, just no sense of self. The completeness of the nothingness was enormous.

Ann was overwhelmed by the vastness of the event. Her first emotion was amazement, which rapidly turned into "hugeness and awe because awe has a bit of terror in it" that occurred just "before everything was gone." Everything collapsed, and, then the indescribable effervescence and hilarity of the experience crashed into Ann like a wave. Although she doesn't recall how the moment of enlightenment resolved itself, she remembers clearly the rush of emotion in its aftermath:

> Then when I began again, when there was this coming into myself again, there was this joy. I can't describe it. The joy was part of the expansiveness in that awareness of all possibilities.

> I was laughing and then crying and then laughing at the absurdity of it all, the freedom of it, a large joyousness that wasn't a normal oh-boy-isn't-this-nice kind of thing. It was *Whoa!*

> It left me with a wonderful, deep-seated peacefulness, somehow, a gratitude, a thankfulness. Not at [my husband], like thank-you-because-you-brought-me-to-this kind of thing, but to the universe. A cosmic gratefulness.

Ann felt "that I needed to put a lid on it," as she didn't want her husband to think she was nuts. These events are so earth-shattering they are virtually impossible to hide when they occur. People's reactions are invariably like Ann's: amazement, awe, laughter, tears, and a thunderstruck hilarity at finally understanding everything, an appreciation of the absurdity of how hard we humans make the quest for happiness that can barely be contained.

When she was finally able to get outside her experience to realize how it appeared to her husband, she was overcome with other emotions. "That brought up a huge amount of sadness with it and some anxiety. Who knows what he would have done if he'd thought I'd gone off the deep end or something? I was almost hysterical-sounding, laughing and crying. I can see him thinking, 'My wife doesn't usually do this when I make love to her.'" She continues, "I remember him coming at me and asking, 'What happened? What's the matter?' And I said, 'Don't ask me,' and I remember pushing him away and saying, 'It's all right, I'm okay.'"

Like others who have had this experience, Ann had a life-changing realization: "There was nothing I could have said to him, nothing I wanted to say. I didn't even want to share it because there wouldn't have been a resonance, a receptivity for it."

What began as something of a sexual ordeal turned into a conversion experience. She says, "It galvanized me into looking for a practice, that's for sure! I began looking around. The first time it was an affirmation for me of who I was growing up. I always felt this sense of oneness but never said anything to anybody, so it wasn't totally strange to have an experience like that."

Ann began searching the literature in an effort to find something—anything—that remotely resembled what had happened to her. It took a couple of years, but she finally found it in the Zen descriptions of *kensho*.

"I'd always had the sense of how close sex and spirituality were, I don't know from where, don't ask me. The sadness was that I had this experience during a sexual encounter, but it didn't have to do with sex per se, and I knew that. It showed me that the experience can happen. I didn't know then that there were people out there meditating to have it happen." She adds, "I wished my husband had been in on it, but he wasn't. . . . I found out if you can have it once, you could maybe have it together somehow. I got the sense that I was okay, not so far off.

This can happen, maybe not in this relationship, but in other relationships. It had a huge influence on my life. It taught me something about myself as a woman in a physical body, that there is no difference really between my spirituality and my sexuality."

The Path to Enlightenment

Ann's story contains all the components necessary for an enlightenment experience: achieving a single focus, narrowing awareness to what is occurring in the immediate moment (sexual stimulation in her case); transcending the boundaries between the perceiver and the perceptions (her analogy of going beyond cutting vegetables to nothing but cutting); then dissolving perception so totally that self, time, and space explode into nothingness; and the arising of bliss.

The first step is fairly easy to understand, but hard to do. Ann successfully confined her attention to her sensations, just as meditators strive to banish all distractions from their minds. Contemplatives cultivate one-pointed attention by focusing on the breath, on a word or phrase used as a mantrum (*om mani padme om*, for example, or the names of God or the Jesus prayer), on a physical object like an icon, or on their own stream of perception, such as their arising emotions, mental activity or bodily sensations. A meditator might attempt, for example, to be fully and only aware of eating a banana. It's easy to understand how sex could provide a concentrated focus, even when a person is not trying to screen out distractions, as Ann was.

Ming, a second-generation Chinese American woman who does not practice meditation, says, "I just let it happen, and it doesn't happen all the time. I have to try to force everything out of my head, and that's hard if I'm feeling stressed out or any-thing. It's almost like meditation, I guess. I try not to think of anything else except what I'm actually physically feeling."

A woman named Blythe doesn't have to practice because her lover's touch focuses her attention easily:

I am so responsive to his hands on my skin that the rest of the world seems suspended. . . . If I could draw a picture of it, every-thing but that one tiny point would be dim or out of focus, just a blur.

I can't sense anything else. I can't track visually. I can't attend to sound. Wherever he touches me is the focus of my world and all my being. Everything else drops away into oblivion.

A somewhat discomfiting aspect of this experience is that the partner actually vanishes at some point! Ming, laughing abashedly, says, "It's weird because I lose track of who I'm with. I suppose this would be bad news for the people I sleep with, but when it happens, it doesn't really matter who it is. I'm just in the sensation."

Ann, who now has attained *kensho* experiences in medita-tion but still sometimes has them during sex, has attained the same experiences with her new partner, subsequent to her divorce. This beloved man disappears without her intent:

I totally forgot both of us, not really forgetting, but I just went *beyond* us. And I thought, "Isn't that incredible that you can have such intense feelings about somebody, and at the moment of this great oneness, [he's] not even there?" It had nothing to do with love. It just made no difference for him to be there somehow, any more than it made a difference for me to be there either.

Shattering Self and Form

Even when the focus of perception has narrowed to a single point—the vegetable cutting Ann mentions or Blythe's sexual touch—it is still composed of separate elements: the perceiver, the act of perceiving, and the thing that is perceived. True realization comes when these subtle constructions vanish altogether, according to the Upanishads:

> You cannot see the seer of sight,
> You cannot hear the hearer of hearing,
> Nor perceive the perceiver of perception,
> Nor know the knower of knowledge.[11]

The observing self is transcended, so nothing remains to perceive or be perceived. The person can no longer be divided from All That Is, so there is no separate self. Individual consciousness *is the same as* Cosmic Mind. The soul dissolves into the World Soul, or Atman.

> The shining Self dwells hidden in the heart.
> Everything in the cosmos, great and small,
> Lives in the Self. He is the source of life,
> Truth beyond the transience of this world.[12]

Enlightenment is a state of pure self-reference without content—not the blank mind of nothingness, but no-*thing*ness. In Eastern traditions, the first enlightenment experience may feature intense light, stunning ecstasy, and an immediate grasp of reality that dwarfs all previous comprehension. These feelings are typically accompanied by an absolute conviction of the import and truth of the realization. It is aptly called an awakening. Philip Kapleau, one of the first Americans to become a noted Zen master, describes his first split-second experience of enlightenment, which occurred just *after* a meditation session:

> All at once the roshi [his Zen teacher], the room . . . disappeared in a dazzling stream of illumination and I felt myself bathed in a delicious unspeakable delight. . . . For a fleeting eternity I was alone—I alone was. . . . Then the roshi swam into view. Our eyes met and we burst out laughing.
>
> I exclaimed . . . , "I have it! I know! There is nothing, absolutely nothing. I am everything and everything is nothing."[13]

Compare this to the following description from a woman in the study who knows about Buddhist meditation—and uses its language—but does not practice it:

> Everything in the room was suddenly lost in a bright, white light. Then suddenly everything appeared again as though the floodwaters of the light were receding only with form. I can't even say things appeared because that implies a separate vantage point. But there was really no separation between the things: the bed, the dresser, the window, my lover, me. I was not separate from everything, though objects had the usual edges. The "spaces" in-between were as alive and full as the "objects." We were all not-same, not-different. There was only being. It was all part of me, and I was all of it, just the is-ness.

These statements point to the "fullness of the Void" in the sense that three-dimensional objects are not different from "nothing." A Zen master expresses it this way:

> Form does not differ from Voidness, and Voidness does not differ from Form. . . . Voidness and existence are complementary

to each other . . . not in opposition. [An] enlightened being sees both aspects at the same time. . . . *Voidness is simply a term denoting the nonsubstantial and nonself nature of beings. . . .*[14]

Bengt, the director of a continuing education department, offers another perspective. Of Northern European extraction and Protestant upbringing, he has made a study of yoga, Zen Buddhism, Taoism, and Sufism. He has now converted to Islam. Here he describes the Void he encounters during sex:

> I see that I'm there, and my partner's there, and we're connected, and everything's connected. Everything in the room is connected. There's no space between us, and yet I can actually see from one standpoint the outline of her body as a separate thing. But that's just an outline within the fullness of being. The exterior surfaces of our bodies are actually very permeable, and in and through this is *being*.
>
> That just happens in a snap. I'm aware of the passing of time, in the sense that there is a sequence of events, but there's also nothing but that moment.
>
> It is an awareness of the manifest world in which there are names and forms. I experience this person named Bengt, my lover, and the objects in the room. But although I can see form, I can also see that, as the Buddhists say, the forms are inherently empty.
>
> On the one hand, everything is being. On the other hand, being is not full of a whole bunch of forms, but the *appearance* of a whole bunch of forms. It's very real from one standpoint, but at the same time you can see straight through it.

Just as things appear to change radically in some altered states and then vanish at the moment of dissolution into the Void, the boundaries reappear again, but people's understanding of what they are is forever altered.

Shattering the Tyranny of Time

Perhaps the most stable category of experience is that of time, no matter how flexibly it stretches in other transcendent experiences. We are always thinking in contrast to the future and the past: what we will do next or what we have done. The present, for most of us, is merely a viewing platform from which we are constantly peering forward or backward, unaware of what is supporting us. But Ann described one timeless instant whose duration was impossible to gauge, when time ceased to "pass" at all. This is the Eternal Now of enlightenment, and it is the core of realization. Says the Christian mystic Meister Eckhart:

> Time is what keeps the light [enlightenment] from reaching us. There is no greater obstacle to [realization] than time. And not only time but temporalities; not only temporal things but temporal affections; not only temporal affections but the very taint and smell of time.[15]

The Eternal Now of enlightenment doesn't come from anywhere (past), and it's not going anywhere (future). It is not an eternity stretching out forever from the distant past to an unimaginable future. As Ken Wilber, one of the most articulate advocates of meditation today, says, "Eternity is not an awareness of *everlasting time*, but an awareness which is itself *totally without time*. The eternal moment is a timeless moment."[16]

There is no beginning or ending to *this now*, to *this very moment.* Now can only be *now.* Pure consciousness lives in now-ness, and nowness is eternal because it neither arises nor fades away but exists absolutely. It is neither permanent nor impermanent, yet, paradoxically, it is also experienced as one with the passage of time. According to Zen master Dogen, "For time to fly away there would have to be a separation [between it and things]. Because you imagine that time only passes, you do not learn the truth of being-time."[17] Of this kind of time, Blythe says:

> Experience drops away into nothingness, without the flow of time, without even desire because in that moment everything is there.

> There can be no desire because that suggests something to desire, something separate, and everything is there; there is nothing that isn't there in that moment. Desire suggests a future, wanting something *out there* in time. But there's no time, so there's no *out there* there. Time just doesn't exist somehow.

Another experiencer, Norberto, agrees, "I feel there is eternity in one moment. But you don't care if it's one second, two seconds, one hour, three hours. That moment is eternal."

The Arising of Bliss

Eastern traditions don't dwell on emotions, which can produce undesirable attachments as people seek pleasure and try to avoid pain. Enlightened masters are characterized by a sublime tranquillity, since they are free from the suffering caused by desire. Effortless serenity and compassion are hallmarks of spiritual attainment. But Elaine, a librarian who has practiced Buddhist meditation for over twenty years, wrote a letter to me about the emotions her sexual experiences created. She finds them more compelling than her formal practice. In describing the gifts of her sexual episodes in the Void, she said:

> I entered an area of No Time. I was suspended without the ego, yet somehow with an awareness because I could remember it afterward. It was as though I was inside a Vortex where there was no sense of you/me/other. At the same time there was an almost overwhelming feeling of love *toward* the other person involved.
>
> While in the Vortex or the Still-Point, I was aware of a silent question being asked; that is, I had an understanding— although I have no idea what the question was—but I also knew of no other answer, except *yes!*
>
> I suppose when I describe it, it will sound like a form of psychosis: the boundaries are completely dissolved, and there is no longer any "you" or "I" but simply *this*. Then the "this" becomes love/compassion not only for the other person, but for something (or some*one* if you're a theistic person) comes up from the depths so that there is only one word to describe it: *yes!* But this "yes" that comes from the deepest depths is a "yes" to the entire universe, to a point where there is no longer a god out *there*, but rather one is dissolved into the God/Numinous/Universe.

Such joy is the natural heritage of humankind, not truly an extraordinary state, as Zen master Huang Po adjures, "It's right in front of you!"[18] Elaine echoes this sentiment, with an emphasis on embodiment of the enlightened state.

> I have often thought about this later and have come to a conclusion that our very cell structure *must* already have the Ulti-

mate/Bliss/Awareness programmed in. . . . We "individuals" are simply a part of the giant hologram of Existence and that we can return to the state of bliss through a sexual experience like the one I have described. Whenever I hear the phrase "God is already within you" or "The Buddha Within," I think of this cellular structure we can tap into.

The Fruits of Enlightenment Through Sex

The "high" of enlightenment, of course, is not the goal of spirituality. The goal is the fruits of realization: an end of suffering, right perception of reality, and effortless compassion. Contemplative religions urge meditators to practice diligently until they can remain in a state of realization at all times. However, most traditions hold that even a split second of nirvana will have transformative effects.[19]

Nobody in this study made any claims to enlightenment—or even to sagacity or compassion. But everyone who had a momentary experience of the Void said they had changed in some way. Norberto and Bengt felt they were healed in ways that had not previously been possible given their respective sexual histories.

"When I was a priest, it was a value to make a sublimation of sex or a repression," Norberto reflects, with particular reference to "bad" sex, such as pornography. But now his attitude is different and much more in accord with sacred writings about the nonduality of opposites:

There is not something that is bad or good, not something dirty or clean. There is only how we approach reality, and that was a very, very important realization for me. It all depends on your eyes. Once you have had that experience, it is difficult—not impossible, but much more difficult—to go back to seeing things in the ordinary way. Another thing I was discovering in this sexuality was my feminine side. For someone with my Latin American background, this is probably the hardest thing for a man to contemplate. . . . I'm enjoying it, to have a whole piece of my life like that.

For his part, Bengt was physically and sexually abused as a child. He is unique in this study for having used the skills he developed in meditation to help him have sex. He explains how hard it was for someone with his background to remain present during sex:

One of the frequent experiences of almost any survivor [of childhood sexual and physical abuse] is [that] of dissociation as a response to trauma. So as an adult, many survivors experience disassociation during sex . . . whether it's fantasy or just going through the motions physically but with the mind somewhere else. Or the person is just numb or not there. . . .

I've gone away in fantasy. Normally when I'm in a high state of arousal, I'm *out* of here, *long* gone, far away. I'm very split off and very dissociated. So being fully present [during sex] doesn't come out of my history.

It's taken a long time of spiritual practice, mindfulness meditation, Zen meditation, learning how to be in my body to sense all of it. . . . I can be present, looking into my lover's eyes . . . , and feeling her, and moving together. And the second thing is being able to dissolve to my essence, becoming transparent to my lover, and seeing into her essence . . . in a most intimate way.

And then in these nondual experiences . . . I can be right *here,* right *now*. That's a miracle for someone with my history, a miracle.

But healing is not the only fruit of enlightenment through sex. Elaine stresses how knowing she is part of everything has made her entire life different when she returns from those moments:

> You are changed but in a good way; your other relationships are enhanced by the experience, also because you have changed. Somehow a string of that love experience is woven throughout your other relationships, career, etc. [You gain] tolerance for others who are not so knowing . . . and great compassion.

> The impact of such an experience is immense: the world's colors, sounds, smells are very intense, especially afterward, and I've gotten to a point that I can "become" a tree, a cloud, a lovely smell, in the same way in which I experience lovemaking; they are no longer separate in my daily routine.

> Matter is viewed in a different way; it "feels" almost as though the world becomes (for a while at least) a prism and that you've seen the light piercing through, creating the rainbow colors. The light is sometimes named God (if you're from a theistic faith) and the rainbow colors represent matter. Knowing on a *deep level* that . . . everything is dependent upon everything else, that there is nothing that exists *independent* of something else.

Life isn't bliss for those who have these insights during sex, but it can provide access to deep knowledge and peace. Blythe, a woman who has been troubled with depression all her life, who doesn't meditate and who has had only the openings to the Void that come during sex, feels she has a different attitude toward life now. She acknowledges that for all its ups and downs, life has become paradoxically infinitely precious and yet something to be held lightly, not taken very seriously anymore. Perhaps she sums up the wisdom of Eastern saints and sages in an ordinary, contemporary voice when she says,

> When you know, *really know,* that you're not separate from anything, that everything is You, life can be nothing but beautiful and good. Sure, I still have trouble with the day to day, and sometimes passing events get me down.

> But at a deep level, when I remember, I know what they mean now when they say, "How marvelous! I chop wood, I carry water!"

> Because it *is.* There is this still point that you never lose sight of where you know beyond any doubt that everything is okay, that you are okay, that life is good no matter what is happening. This kind of experience during love shows you that. You only need eyes that see, a heart that remembers.

CHAPTER 9

Divine Union: One with God

You're just shot into the white light. It's not actually a portal, but a medium. The white light is God. You know you're not dead, so somehow you maintain your congruency or coherence in the process, but you're just bathing in it. It's so pure and it feels so good, and you're just connected. You know that every-thing separate is an illusion because you're not separate from God. The white light is communion. It's God, Goddess, asex-ual, and yet it's also homey. It's home, that deep sense of con-nection with a purity, a sort of taken-for-grantedness where we don't acknowledge how special it is because we're just there. You only know when you come back. You know then that there's more. —Maureen

At that moment the universe was revealing itself, and all the secrets are there. They're not intellectually revealed but just known. Because we were expanding through everything. And in all of that is contained all experience, and all knowledge about experience. So we're all-knowing. We're all experience. We're the universe, and there is this incredible peaceful qual-ity, this peaceful quality. And it's all here all the time. God is surrounding us and in us. We really are All That Is. We are. We are All That Is. All That Is. —Laura

IN THIS CHAPTER, lovers tell of losing all touch with everyday reality to become One with an unfathomable, ineffable Mystery so great and so free of content that it can only be realized once the person "returns." All ontological categories are shattered, but unlike going into the Void, people fall into *unio mystica,* mystical union with Spirit:[1] *devekut,*[2] which means cleaving, in Judaism; the Kingdom of God or the Kingdom of Heaven in Christianity; and *fana-f'illah,* which translates roughly as annihilation or "passing away in God" in Islam.[3]

Unio mystica chiefly differs from Eastern enlightenment states in the way it produces ecstasy and a feeling of relationship with Spirit, a uniting to become the One of existence, rather than falling into nothingness, the Zero of annihilation in the Void.[4] Judaism, Christianity, and Islam emphasize the love of God, and their contemplative forms often enjoin devotees to approach God as a suitor. In fact, sexual metaphor is a prominent feature in their sacred and inspired writings.[5] But none of the participants in the study, most of whom were reared in a Judeo-Christian culture, knew much, if anything, about these contemplative paths, nor did their religion predict whether they would have an Eastern or Western experience. Instead, the determining factors seem to be more related to the process they were drawn into during sex. People who had Void realizations seemed to get there through focused attention and the deconstruction of perception, while those who had unitive experiences seemed to go through a process involving progressive changes in their relationship to the environment.

Unio mystica can occur in different ways during sex. Occasionally a person suddenly breaks the boundaries into unity, but it can also happen when the self-boundaries widen to include increasingly greater horizons until they dissolve utterly. For instance, a person may arrive at this state after an experience of the Third, as Laura, in an earlier chapter, indicated when she said, "Yeah, the two becomes three becomes One."

Dissolving into God

One of the most complete descriptions of progressive dissolution into Spirit, though it is idiosyncratic to a particular relationship, comes from Blake, who is ethnically Jewish, but was reared without religion. He frankly admits that his greatest spiritual openings (before sex) came from taking psychedelics and from working with certain marginalized populations. Blake attributes his unitive sexual episodes to a special connection with his partner.

> When I'm with her, it goes beyond a sense of merging. . . . It's no different from a religious person who goes to church and is so inspired by a sermon or a hymn or some beautiful artwork that they're immediately taken away and drawn into God. It's the same thing. It just happens when I'm making love with this particular woman.

> Making love in this way is not just like praying to God, but like a bottomless surrender to the Infinite. It's the most perfect feeling I can imagine. It isn't just a kind of awareness, but an ecstasy, a feeling state suffused with joy, rapture.

> All I have to do is offer myself and somehow through her I get to God. I don't know why she's the channel. I really don't, except maybe because of the feeling she draws out in me. It's odd in sex where there are often no words, but I feel like I'm often most in communication with her that way, coming both *to* her and

through her: to her in terms of union, and through her to something beyond. She's that opening to me.

According to Blake, he proceeds from awareness of his lover and the feelings induced by lovemaking to a place of infinite surrender and rapture, in which no categories exist, including, paradoxically, the normal category of his lover as a separate being.

> My awareness of her [becomes] intermittent. . . . It's as though I'm moving through her to something beyond her, beyond me. That's the religious part. She's a conduit, but then in that state, bodies become irrelevant, and in a way, she does, too, I'm embarrassed to say.

> I'm actually opening myself to God and surrendering to God and feeling God entering into me. The energies are so strong. . . . It's something which is only articulated for me in the language of feeling. . . . This takes me beyond the edges of language. It's a combination of yearning, giving way to surrender, a tremendous joy, and it explodes into God in a way that doesn't even have any content. Feeling God's rays streaming into you, being lit up by that.

> But not as though I'm an object, not like feeling the rays of the sun on me. There's no sense of me and other in this experience. I can't even say it's a union because that implies that I am separate from it. You are aware of more of what you are, and you open yourself to it, and you *are* it at the same time.

This new way of experiencing reality, though, cannot be grasped when it is happening because it is a nondual state in which the observer is one with the observed. Apprehension of what is transpiring is only available after the fact. "When I go in it, it's not a blank, but I only feel the immensity of it after I come back," Blake explains. "I'm not comparing it with nirvana—you know how they say you only recognize nirvana after you come back from it—but it's a little like that."

For Blake, the salient feature of his unitive experiences is their transcendent rapture. From his reading, he associates this ecstasy with mystical Judaism, Christianity, and Islam and their view of God as having the quality of absolute love, in contrast to Eastern traditions that are about the deconstruction of illusion.

There's no sense of union because that implies one thing merging with another. But there's a predominance of transcendental feeling, not like the sometimes rather bloodless descriptions one finds in Buddhism, but more as in the ecstatic traditions like Sufism and Christian Gnosticism. Saying no-mind or nirvana—those don't capture the feeling.

It isn't just a kind of awareness, or if it is, it's a kind of awareness suffused with feeling, joy, rapture. It's an ecstasy, a feeling state. It's a feeling of opening to the Divine, feeling its Being.

Is there a sense of union? No, but there's not a sense of duality either. There's no sense of me and other in this kind of experience.

I break apart, where I fall into the Light . . . merged into the fires of God like a planet plunging into the furnace of the sun. It's every possible good feeling, and it lasts just a second, but there's no sense of time. There is joy flooding everywhere, light everywhere.

The World Well Lost

Blake's narrative can serve as a road map for unitive experiences. One of the first things lovers report is an opening of the usual self-boundaries. This can be a deliberate practice, as, in Western mysticism, teachers like Sufi Ansari of Herat, say: "Know that when you learn to lose yourself, you will reach the Beloved. There is no other secret to be learned. . . ."[6]

But self-dissolution during sex can take people by surprise. Armand, whose encounter with Spirit was prefigured by a visitation from his dead sister, just "disappeared." We were sitting in my cramped office when he began to tell me his story:

> I just let go into [what my partner was doing] . . . and I felt myself disappear. It was like nothingness, in the sense that I wasn't as I am now. I couldn't feel that normal sense of myself. My sense of my body was gone, completely absent. There's a point at which I *wasn't*.

> I would describe it by saying that it was like an abandonment. I felt more and more like I was letting go of boundaries as the experience progressed, and just abandoning myself to this, abandoning defense structures, abandoning my body sense of self. Like I don't need to hang on to this anymore.

The self is not the only category that breaks down. Christian saints Augustine, Monica, and Gregory of Nyssa, to name a few, stress the transcendence of thought, space, and time in *unio mystica*, just as Eastern mystics do.[7] Speech and rational ways of processing events no longer exist in such moments. According to John of the Cross, "All that the imagination can imagine and the reason can conceive and understand in this life is not, and cannot be, a proximate means of union with God."[8] When those things collapse, all that remains is light.

"The room was pitch black, totally dark, but my partner wasn't there in the normal way that I knew him, and the bed wasn't there, and the room wasn't there in the usual sense," Armand says, gesturing broadly. "I didn't seem solid anymore, and as my body dissolved, there was light everywhere. . . . No bed, no partner, no me, nothing but light and also at some point maybe a sense of my little sister. But mainly it was this light, not like anything that I've seen normally, this incredibly pure light."

The light is then revealed as the Light of Spirit.

Esther, a soft-spoken teacher from a mid-Atlantic state, had a similar experience: "The boundaries definitely disappear. It's a very boundaryless time, and then comes the Light."

This Light is different from the lights of kundalini experiences because nothing but the Light exists at all. Western religions consider such pure illumination the hallmark of the Presence of God.[9] Uniting with the Light destroys the ability to observe it, as the last boundaries that create observer and observed vanish, but it is extremely difficult to sustain this timeless moment. Esther describes how this occurs: "I'm content in the Light because I'm also there observing it. I love it when this happens, but there is that moment when it begins, and I step in it without that awareness. It is maybe nondual for a few seconds, and then I'm there observing it, so it's not there."

Esther's report parallels a stage recognized in Sufism known as *ma'rifa*, which precedes the unitive experience *fana*.[10] In *ma'rifa*, the person retains a vantage point of the experience, as Esther does, but when *fana* occurs, the vantage point collapses along with the person's identity as a witness, just as the perceiver and the perceived vanish in Eastern traditions. The

Christian mystic Meister Eckhart, sounding very much like the Upanishads, said, "The knower and the known are one. Simple people imagine that they should see God, as if He stood there and they here. This is not so. God and I, we are one in knowledge."[11] Thus, when uniting with God, the concept of God breaks down, as noted in the Gnostic gospels:

> Names given to the worldly are very deceptive, for they divert our thoughts from what is correct to what is incorrect. Thus one who hears the word "God" does not perceive what is correct, but perceives what is incorrect. So also with "the father" and "the son" and "the holy ghost" . . . and all the rest.[12]

Or in the more familiar canonical gospels, Jesus says, "I and the Father are One."[13] He also says, of aspirants to this state, "That they all may be One; as Thou, Father, art in me, and I in thee, that they also may be One in us."[14] Similar ideas of God's omnipresence are conveyed in the *Ra'aya Mehimna* and the *Tikkunim* of the Kabbalic *Zohar*.

Finally, the experiencer Laura discusses how time breaks into the Eternal Now, a concept well documented in Christianity where it is called the *nunc stans,* as opposed to passing or streaming time, the *nunc fluens*. First, to distinguish the two in her own experience, Laura, in speaking of the Third, says, disarmingly, "There are times I feel [God] is right behind me when we're making love, if I could just turn around fast enough and look." Then she goes on to say:

> But the only time I really get to see It is when I can stop time. It's there, I know It's there, but my brain is proceeding in time, and my experience is in time. But It's right here and now. During this kind of sex, my brain can stop time.

When I go to that, I also start to lose content. I've learned that as soon as I start to observe It with my little self, I can't stay out there.

The notion that any sense of passing time keeps people from directly experiencing Spirit is as central to Western mysticism as it is to Eastern thought. Sufi adepts, for instance, are known as "the sons of the present moment." Christian contemplative Jean-Pierre de Caussade observes, as Blythe did in the previous chapter, "There is never one moment in which I cannot show you how to find whatever you desire. The present moment is always overflowing with immeasurable riches, far more than you are able to hold."[15]

The Face of God

What is the core of the *unio mystica?* If all the saints and spiritual masters—and the lovers from this study—are correct, it is finally achieving the soul's desire to see God. But when people are taken into God, they find that Spirit has no face at all—or no face other than all of What Is, *no other face than their own.* Our own.

The mystical experience of God transcends the symbolic descriptions of the canonical Bible and rabbinical literature.[16] Mystical Judaism, Christianity and Islam all describe something very different from any personified being—and very different from anything that can easily be conceived. For instance, Sufi mystic Abu Yazid Bistami, who began by courting God as a lover, tells of his gradual abandonment of any notions of an anthropomorphic God as his contemplation deepened:

I gazed upon [Allah] with the eye of truth and said to Him: "Who is this?" He said, "This is neither I nor other than I.

There is no God but I." Then He changed me out of my identity into His Selfhood. . . . Then I communicated with him . . . saying, "How fares it with me with Thee?" He said, "I am through Thee; there is no god but Thou."[17]

Sufi mystic al-Hallaj was martyred when he proclaimed his own experience of God in the words, *"Ana'l Haqq,"* which can be translated as "I am the Truth" or "I am the Absolute."[18] Or as the Christian saint Catherine of Genoa said, "My Me is God, nor do I recognize any other Me except my god Himself."[19] In the King James New Testament, Saint Paul's words are similar: "I live, yet not I, but Christ in me,"[20] which can be more contemporaneously translated as, "But I am living, not as I, for it is Christ who *lives me*."[21]

The same staggering realization reverberates throughout the reports of lovers during transcendent sex. According to one man, the moment of recognition is the purest ecstasy and awakening.

It's *real!* I can embody all my spirit, and it is divine. At the same time I felt it coming from the outside, it was also coming from the inside. It was evident that it was also in me. I participate in divinity in a direct, inclusive way. There's no separation at all. . . .

It wasn't a call, it wasn't a sign. All the things I had interpreted as it weren't true. Was there a face to God? No. Or a presence? *The presence was us.* We were just there. It just *was*.

Or, as Laura said at the beginning of this chapter, "We really *are* All That Is. *We* are. We are All That Is. *All That Is*."

Coming Back to the World

The glorious revelation of *unio mystica* is so unexpected and blindingly all-encompassing that it is only after some reflection that people are able to grasp the totality of their experience. According to St. Teresa of Avila,

> For during the time of this union [the soul] neither sees, nor hears, nor understands, because the union is always short. . . . God so places Himself in . . . that soul that when it returns to itself it can in no way doubt that it was in God and God was in it . . . even though years go by without God's granting that favor again. . . .[22]

For Armand, whose *unio mystica* during sex remains a one-time happening, his comprehension of what occurred came in an awestruck and emotional dénouement to the experience itself.

> I remember that after I came back to myself, it was totally dark, and I was in this room, and I had to recall all that had happened. But what especially brought me back to my senses at some point was that [my partner] noticed that something was wrong with me, that I wasn't reacting anymore . . . , and he started asking, "Are you okay?"

> And he repeated that until I finally said, "I'm here."

> He asked me what had happened, and I said something like, "I was just with God," something about God.

> Then I realized that I remembered my little sister, and I started having this reaction. I remember sobbing, actually sobbing, after I came back, one of those instances where sobbing felt like

joy and sadness both at the same time, and I couldn't tell which was which. I was laughing hilariously and really crying at the same time.

Lovers are bemused with rapture like the Sufi master who was "inwardly drunk [with God] and outwardly sober."[23] The *unio mystica* that arises during sex can be as completely life-changing as the *unio mystica* experiences that occur among people of religious vocations.

The Story of Artemis

A woman who asked to be called Artemis was a musician from the Deep South, where she was reared in a fundamentalist Southern Baptist faith. When I met her, she had been happily married for eight years.

Her story began with a friendship she had made in college with a woman several years her senior. Their relationship, which stretched over the years Artemis was in school, had always seemed special. At the end of her undergraduate college course, Artemis married her fiancé, the man to whom she is still wed. Within the year, her friend also married. The two couples lived at some distance from each other, but they visited from time to time. On one such occasion about six months after Artemis's wedding, the husbands were working on computers together and the women were exchanging confidences in another room in their customary way. The atmosphere in the room felt charged, and it dawned on Artemis that the distinctive quality that had always set this friendship apart from others was actually a sexual attraction. Before Artemis fully realized what was going on, her friend leaned over and kissed her. "It was the first time anything like that had ever happened to me,"

Artemis observes, "and I instantly became aware that I wanted that."

The sudden awareness of this sexual attraction made sense to Artemis, but it posed an enormous moral dilemma for her. Her religious and cultural upbringing not only forbade homosexuality, but also any form of sex outside of marriage: "I didn't hang on to many of the rights and wrongs from my childhood, but monogamy in marriage was one of the things I'd held on to," she states frankly.

Despite her beliefs, Artemis had a strong intuition that an exploration of this attraction would be all right, and she decided to proceed.

> It was paradoxical because [along with the moral problems of homosexuality and adultery] there was a feeling that there was *nothing wrong* with this. I went to where my husband was with her husband, and said, "This is what has happened, and this is what I want to happen. How are you with this?"
>
> And he said, "I can't explain it, but it's okay."
>
> I asked, "Are you *sure?* Because if it's a problem tomorrow, I won't appreciate that."
>
> And he said, "No, no, it's okay."

What happened next is a complete mystery. To this day, Artemis has no recollection of what transpired. She believes that she and her friend began to make love, but in her words, "I don't know what happened. The only memory I have—the *only* tangible, concrete, worldly image I have—is lying down." She was lost in a unitive experience.

And then there was just this engulfing white Light. It could have lasted a minute, it could have lasted twelve hours. I don't know.

There was nothing to focus on because that was all there was. There were no thoughts. I didn't have any cognitive processing while the white Light was present.

There was just this engulfing white Light. That was all I was aware of, and this incredible sense of compassion and love. It was just that Light, and this overwhelming feeling of love and compassion and coming into myself and going beyond myself at the same time.

[That feeling of love] was different because there wasn't the fear of losing it. I never thought about that before, but in your normal everyday relationships, like the love I feel for my husband, I'm always aware that things could change. Because of the attachment I have in my everyday relationships, there's a fear that I could lose it, lose the love. This time, that wasn't there. It was just so encompassing. I can't even say that the thought of abandonment from that or losing that sense of that experience was there because thought wasn't there.

There was an experience of the actual radiation of the Light, the energy of that going out and flowing out, and I was very aware of being that sensation. I can't say I was *having* a sensation. The sensation was just what was.

She only came to interpret what had happened to her after it was over and she had returned to normal reality. "Once thoughts came back—once I got out of the experience to a point where there were thoughts again," Artemis remarks, "that was definitely the first idea that hit me cognitively: this was an experience of God."

Of course, the idea that a forbidden relationship could be the ground for a spiritual awakening directly contradicted the teachings of her religion. But like others who have had their religious convictions overturned by a direct experience of God (such as Saul of Tarsus who persecuted Christians and whose experience led him to become Saint Paul, the great Christian evangelist), Artemis is as certain of the Spirit inherent in this as St. Teresa, who, speaking of her own dissolution into union, declared,

> Now, you will ask me, how did the soul see this truth or understand if it didn't see or understand anything? I don't say that it then saw the truth but that afterward it sees the truth clearly, not because of a vision but because of a certitude remaining in the soul that only God can place there.[24]

Artemis has the same assurance about the sanctity of the event, despite its apparent conflict with her Baptist beliefs concerning adultery and homosexuality.

> It's really funny because this totally taboo thing gave a lot of the religious stuff I'd heard more meaning and made it more real than any hellfire and damnation preachers ever did. It was so paradoxical to be doing all these things that were definitely wrong, and to have it be *the* spiritual experience of my life. And the sacredness of it, I *never* doubted. This was the first experience where I never doubted it.

> Compared to other religious experiences I've had, this was by far the most powerful one. Not that prayer doesn't have its place, but this was the most sacred experience of God.

One other time I had a dream, and in that dream Christ came to me. Now that may depend on what theory you buy, whether or not it was really Christ. But I'm actually leaning toward the fact that I saw an actual divine Presence in the dream. It was very powerful, very moving, very humbling, and it was something that was out of my control. But even that wasn't on the same level as this. This is the only time and the only place where I *know* I had an experience of the Divine.

This turn of events, controversial and shocking as it may be, is exactly what happens in mystical experiences: they smash preconceptions, burst through conventions, and contravene social norms to reveal the Ultimate, which has nothing to do with sacred cows. Spirit is never what we think, as the martyrdom of so many who have later been recognized as saints and avatars attests. Direct spiritual experience often is a social affront, a shattering of everything previously known, believed, and even valued.

Transformation

Artemis's story has an unusual ending in several ways. She fully expected that most people in her conservative southern, fundamentalist culture would condemn the sexuality of her experience as forbidden, immoral, and, therefore, unspiritual. She was less prepared for the attitude of her close friends who, far from objecting to the sexuality, had trouble with the *spirituality* of what had happened. In her cohort of Generation Xers, homoerotic experimentation is considered commonplace among women (if not *en règle*). They dismissed the significance of her experience, but for the opposite reason: it was too banal. "Most people in my life who know about that experience automatically say, 'It's just [a sexual] orientation thing. What's the big deal? You figured out that you're a lesbian. No wonder you had a good time.'" Artemis makes a face. "But it's so totally *not* about sexual orientation. It was about something else entirely."

On the surface, life returned to normal. Artemis and her husband said their good-byes to the other couple the next day as though nothing unusual had happened, and went back to their routine in the town where they lived. Artemis, however, quite predictably attributed aspects of her experience to her partner, especially the sensations of overpowering love. She wanted nothing so much as to connect with her friend after this incredible experience.

Her feelings were not reciprocated. Though her friend had initiated the sexual contact, she would have nothing to do with Artemis. Thus began a long, excruciating period of rejection. "I reacted by really wanting to pull her closer. I realized I'd been in love with her. Her reaction was the opposite," Artemis says, "She dropped off the face of the world for two years. She wouldn't respond to me. It was very hard. I got depressed."

Finally after two years, her friend got in touch with Artemis. They had a long conversation, in which the friend said that she had not been frightened away by her feelings for Artemis because she had toyed with same-sex love before. In fact, she was, generally speaking, much more sexually liberated than Artemis. Rather, it was the intensity of the experience and, Artemis believes, its spirituality that had made her friend draw back. "It wasn't about making love with a woman," Artemis says. "The answer to that is that she sensed something bigger was going on."

Other things about Artemis's life changed. Subsequent to that weekend, she and her husband of only six months were now "in a marriage that neither one of us ever felt that we would find ourselves in." But their love for each other was deep, genuine, and abiding, as their eight-year commitment in the wake of these events attests.

> It changed a lot about our marriage. Here we became aware of several things: a) that we really loved each other; b) that we really wanted to be married; and c) that there was really a deep part of me that needed an intimate relationship with a woman. So we started really looking at what that would mean. We've negotiated it through the years, and we continue to negotiate it.

At a personal level, Artemis was restored as parts of her psyche damaged in early childhood were made whole. The immediate change was so obvious people remarked on it as soon as they saw her after that fateful encounter, but it produced long-reaching effects, as well.

> When my adviser saw me in class on Monday, he said, "What the hell happened to you this weekend? The way you look has completely changed." He's pretty intuitive and knows a lot about the transpersonal realm and things, and he kind of figured out I'd had a spiritual experience.

> Other people said, "You look like this incredible load has been lifted off you."

> And I felt *alive*. There was a lightness to me.

> It changed not only how I viewed myself in terms of my sexuality, but many things made a lot more sense to me about myself. My life changed on every level. There was a whole part of me that was awoken that had been dead for a very long time.

The feminine part [of me] came to life. This sounds analytical, but it's true. I had a real scary and out-of-control mother, and at a really young age, I rejected the feminine and became a tomboy. I grew up being one of the guys, and because I grew up with a bunch of guys [brothers] anyway, it was an easy place for me to be in.

But after that experience, being female was no longer something that was evil and horrible. It was the first and only really positive, powerful experience of the feminine I'd ever had. Being a woman mattered, and I began to integrate that part into my life. It mattered to me to be a woman.

And there was more than that. A real presence there, and a realness, just a sense of some sort of inner peace.

In addition to all of these changes, there was her spiritual rebirth. Artemis ultimately left her musical profession to take up several years of rigorous training in preparation for a spiritual vocation.

It changed my whole spiritual and religious focus because at that point in time, I went from trying to *understand* God in a cognitive way—does God really exist?—to just wanting the *experience* of God . . . and feeling so overwhelmingly grateful. That's why I'm seeking this career now.

I don't know why it happened at that particular time and in that particular way, although I can give you guesses. It could only have happened with a woman, I'm convinced, because of the power behind that for me [given my family history]. But ultimately, it was just an act of God. Ultimately, it was grace.

It's not an experience I could *have*—I didn't do a damned thing for that to happen, and it may never happen again. But just that one time, no matter what happens in life, it's worth it.

Finally, in language reminiscent of the born-again tradition from which she comes, she adds,

There are other changes that didn't happen immediately after the event but that I'm convinced would not have happened had that event not taken place. They're still unfolding.

It's like having lived two lives in my thirty years. There was my life before that, and there's another life now, after that, that's totally different.

In conclusion, it is not the specifics surrounding *unio mystica* events that give them their power, but the insight into God that changes lives—especially how it illuminates the veracity of spiritual teachings and creeds whose meanings have been obscured by overfamiliarity. The truly thrilling (and frightening!) residual of such encounters with Spirit is suddenly knowing, beyond a shadow of a doubt, that those things that have been articles of faith are real and true and absolute, a knowledge that demands a different way of being in the world.

Using the Knowledge
of Transcendent Sex

Spiritual sexuality is a very precious thing. . . . That doesn't mean that it's going to make life easy; it will make it rich.
—*Sabu*

CHAPTER 10

Why Didn't Anyone Tell Us About This Before? The Dark Side of Transcendent Sex

I wouldn't encourage people to go out and do this because it may have a negative impact on people's lives if . . . they don't have a place to put their experience somehow or a way to bring it into themselves. I certainly don't go out and encourage people to take LSD. If they're going to take drugs, go to somebody who knows how to use them and has good stuff so you don't do something to yourself. Maybe it's the same for these kinds of experiences. There's no one guiding it, no signposts, no preparation along the way, and there's no integrative support at the end. —Ann

During sex, you can activate a lot of thoughtforms when you're in a heightened energetic state—injurious, horrible, lovely, supportive, destructive, inflammatory, calming—and part of our system grabs on to these. If you don't have a balanced, grounded reference point, you can adopt some of these forms so completely that you lose your ability to return to the center, never mind your sanity, in the moment. —Muntu

TRANSCENDENT SEX IS NOT all sweetness and light. It has a shadow side that can be frightening, seductive, and dysfunctional. Altered states per se are not indicative of any higher or more evolved way of being—spiritual or otherwise—so being in an altered state during sex does not necessarily mean something hallowed is going on, no matter *how* it feels. "Altered states" refers to any state different from normal adult waking consciousness, not merely the sublimity of meditation but also schizophrenia, drunkenness, vertigo, hallucinations, and the like. There is nothing particularly sacred about the plasticity of time, place, or self; these characteristics of altered states have been associated with both spirituality and madness depending upon the context and on their effects—whether such states lead to life-enhancing or life-diminishing transformations.

Experiencing an altered state of any kind can be destabilizing, creating breaks with "normal reality" from which some individuals may not recover. The allure of nonchemically induced altered states can be as psychologically addictive as those that create a physiological dependency. Mystical traditions routinely warn against becoming attached to the pleasures and powers associated with altered states. All spiritual traditions using altered states—whether attained through trance, prayer, fasting, contemplation, or sacred medicine— have stringent requirements and exclusive rules for initiation into their mysteries.

In short, the spiritual path is full of danger.

So is sex, even the ordinary kind. The combination of high emotion and physical arousal is a cliché for violence, the "crimes of passion" in which people, frequently considered to be temporarily insane, stalk and kill lovers, themselves, and sometimes the children of their unions. When sex and altered states intersect, strange powers and pleasures amplify the dynamics between partners at a time when personal boundaries are in flux.

This is one reason Taoist and Tantric sexual training are best done within their original spiritual frameworks, which include ethical standards to safeguard the integrity of the practice and protect initiates from exploitation and inappropriate fixations. Some Western teachers and schools of sexual training maintain these ethics, but, unfortunately, many do not. Marketing sexual techniques is sufficiently lucrative to attract unscrupulous "teachers."

Risk also exists for those who, like the respondents in this study, find themselves catapulted into transcendent sex by accident, totally unprepared. In a culture where sex is not recognized as triggering nonordinary states and large segments of the population lack experience with waking altered states, few people are likely to have the resources to integrate a transcendent sexual event constructively. (Many participants said they wished a book like this had been available when they had their first experiences to help them understand what had occurred.)

Few people reported negative experiences during the course of this study.[1] Those who did have initially destabilizing events ultimately yielded positive outcomes. Many of these involved the revelation of disappointing material, such as the failed relationships portrayed in past-life experiences. However, some were severely disturbing. Even for respondents who came to view their histories in a positive light, the anguish they endured, often for considerable periods, warrants caution. In some cases years of therapy were needed to achieve integration.

Regardless of the way they were interpreted or their final resolution, real dangers exist. Perils fall roughly into two major categories, dangerous liaisons and overwhelming intimacy. In dangerous liaisons, the primary issues concern the dynamics of the relationship, which, in transcendent sex, can be boiled down to an unhealthy, transpersonal bonding with the partner. Someone might remain in an otherwise unfulfilling—even damaging—relationship in order to maintain the "high" of altered-state sex possible with that partner, for example. Overwhelming intimacy occurs when the person's sense of self (ego) is in danger of being overrun by other powers. Dangerous liaisons and overwhelming intimacy often overlap.

Dangerous Liaisons

One type of dangerous liaison comes about through the rapture generated by transcendent sex, much like the desire to reexperience an ecstatic high from drugs. But in this kind of sex, the high is a by-product of an event involving another person. Sometimes individuals crave the pleasure so much that they begin to exploit others to achieve it. According to Laura, "You can't jump into this kind of sex without having your feet planted firmly on the ground. . . . The first problem is addiction. It produces an incredible amount of endorphins [brain chemistry associated with pleasurable sensations], I'm sure, and so you can become very promiscuous. I've seen people go from one partner to the next, with unprotected sex because this becomes very spiritual, the spiritual quest."[2]

A related problem stems from attributing these experiences to a particular partner, especially when a long-term relationship with that person may be neither possible nor desirable. It's extremely difficult not to become infatuated with a fantastic lover even if the sex is only great in the ordinary way, never mind extraordinary. Just as terrific ordinary sex is not enough to sustain a relationship, neither is transcendent sex. Several people in this study, after separating from the only partners with whom they had had transcendent sex, despaired of ever again achieving such heights—and feared remaining solitary for the rest of their lives, as a result. Betty, a hardheaded businesswoman, had the fortitude to tear herself away from her first transcendent sex partner because she had been forewarned that altered-state rapture was not necessarily the basis for a good relationship. She was ambushed, as it were, by an electrifying connection with someone she met at a conference, but she kept herself from becoming overly attached because she realized how easily she could mistake ecstasy for love:

> I loved it in terms of the color I painted it afterward. It was just *pow!* knock-your-socks-off wonderful. I remember immediately after feeling like, if this isn't going to turn into a relationship, then somebody's going to have to put the brakes on because this is the kind of experience that people infer magical things to. People including me.

> I remember a friend saying about a [nonsexual] altered state, "Be careful. You're going to have the urge to merge," and that was really good advice since this [lover] was not someone I knew well.

> So a warning went off in my head about "urge to merge," and the feeling was that this wasn't about *dating* somebody. Oh, no. My feelings were about *getting on a horse and riding off into the sunset!* I knew that if I let that part of myself that will misinterpret this as happy-ever-afterness go, then that part of me would say this is supposed to be a long-term thing.

As Betty suggests, the powerful feelings created during transcendent lovemaking can easily be attributed to the lover as the creator and sustaining partner for such experiences. Her advice is excellent: the feelings that occur during these altered states are not necessarily indicative of an exalted, fated-by-the-stars relationship, so all the usual cautions and caveats should apply—*or be given even greater credence.*

If falling in love too easily is a problem for one person in the relationship, other problems attend those who seem to trigger transcendent sex. Individuals whose sexual fields are so strong that they invite transcendent experiences in their partners may have difficulty maintaining the integrity of their relationships. For a woman who asked to be called Sabu, transcendent sex has been a way of life. She realized that she was being sought for the experiences she produced in others. "It's like nectar, you know. You just drip with nectar, and people want to suckle. Doesn't matter if they're men or women, they want to. Whether you'll allow that is up to you," she says. At first, Sabu enjoyed the sense that she could provide something people seemed to need so badly, but eventually she found that road too hard, leading to unsatisfactory, one-sided encounters. If her lovers were unable to go with her into transcendent realms or to handle the intensity, she held back in order not to endanger them. The result was that she herself began to suffer. When she held her own energy back, she began to have nightmares of herself "with no arms and no mouth, all wrapped up like a cocoon or a mummy in a coffin." This type of personally repressed sex deadened her until she just couldn't take it anymore.

Sabu began to screen her partners more carefully and to tone down her persona to avoid difficult entanglements. She didn't want to have relationships based on the altered states she could provide for her partners; she wanted to be in mutually fulfilling relationships based on reciprocal desire rather than an inequity of neediness.

Sex Between Unequals

Not everyone is so scrupulous. One man interviewed for this research who studies spiritual disciplines is a smart, good-looking, aggressive go-getter. He revels in his strong sexual presence, using his gifts to attract, seduce, and have sex with as many beautiful women as he can. He speaks proudly of employing the paranormal powers he has cultivated through his practices, such as telepathy and other, less subtle techniques, to make women respond to him. He is not interested in their feelings, or even in reciprocity, so much as he is motivated by his own pleasure and conquest.

His actions point to the most publicized nexus of sexuality and spirituality—the exploitative relationships dysfunctional gurus often have with members of their communities. Tales of sexual abuse and spiritual betrayal abound, ranging from the crimes attributed to cult leaders like Charles Manson, to the charges of adultery and pederasty leveled at TV evangelists and Roman Catholic priests, to the scandals surrounding internationally known figures, such as Swami Muktananda, the Bhagwan Shree Rajneesh, Sai Baba, Yogi Amrit Desai, Sogyal Rinpoche, Da Free John, Chögyam Trungpa, and countless others. While it is impossible to say whether sex with any of these leaders involved altered states, it is nevertheless reasonable to conclude that their power in the spiritual sphere somehow influenced the sexual relationships they developed with their followers. And this brings up the vulnerability of any individual in a sexual encounter between unequal partners. The same dynamics occur when devotees engage in sex with spiritual leaders or when a person believes a particular partner provides their altered-state sex. A partner may come to be associated with altered-state "highs" and ecstatic feelings, creating the potential for an unequal pairing with extremely strong power and different needs.

People bond intensely to partners who embody the most potent dynamics of their relationships with their parents or primary caretakers during early childhood.[3] Transcendent sex may even be more likely to occur when the partner embodies the "ideal" parent, or when the partner embodies the "shadow" parent, often two sides of the same coin. Add to this the fact that both psychology and religion recognize the relationship between spiritual figures and parents (employing titles such as Heavenly Father, Father Sky, Father O'Malley, the Great Mother, Mother of God, Mother Superior, etc.), and combine those powers, and it's easy to see how the conflation of primal sexuality and spirituality can become institutionalized.

Whether a sexual liaison with a spiritual leader is coerced or consensual, such a connection might indeed feel like the ideal relationship, thrilling and numinous beyond words. Hard as it may be to resist becoming the chosen partner of a charismatic figure, relationships based on the inherent inequity between devotee and teacher have the potential for devastation, whether the liaison involves altered states or not. From all the press coverage of such debacles—and the tedious frequency with which new scandals break—it would appear that no warning is sufficient for some believers.

Still, it is worth repeating since devotees or members of religious communities are not the only ones at risk. Anyone who attends sex workshops should be alert to the dangers of teachers, facilitators, or gurus who focus sexual meditations and techniques on themselves (even if they never actually touch a practitioner). In the first place, the leader can create a mindset in the unwary that can guide a subsequent altered state. Rituals and suggestions, even very subtle ones, may substantially influence the kind of state a person enters, determining, for instance, what kinds of imagery emerge and how that imagery is interpreted. Thus, the ideology presented, instructions given, ritual gestures or invocations used, social expectations created—any number of things—can shape an altered-state experience, and thus may be reified afterward. It is wise to be alert to, and highly critical of, all of these elements before going into the increased vulnerability of an altered state. Responsible teachers do *not* function as surrogate partners or as objects for sexual contemplation. Instead, they have participants work with their own personal imagery and bodies or with a partner of their choosing. Responsible spiritual masters have transparent egos, always pointing beyond themselves to the greater reality and actually making it difficult for aspirants to "grasp" enough of their personality to form a personal attachment, even when certain types of devotion are encouraged.

In fact, Muntu, a professional body worker, likened the desire to connect with a powerful sexual partner in transcendent sex to the love of a disciple for a guru. His advice is excellent for those enjoying transcendent sex with a partner, as well as for devotees:

> In the initial state, people frequently identify very completely with the person who allows them to have that experience, but that should be just an initial thing. Some people think that's falling in love because there's this fascination and wonderful excitement that happens in sex, especially in this over-the-top kind of sex. But the real teacher or serious student knows that that's only temporary, one of the ways people use to find their way beyond to the next level.

Bonding with a Bad Partner

Certainly the vast majority of current relationships reported here suggest that the altered states enjoyed by the participants represent bonding with an ideal partner. But someone who appears to be ideal at first—perhaps like some rascal gurus—may turn out to be a very dysfunctional partner in the end. A transcendent experience can tap into unhealthy complexes and then magnify them, as one participant named Gwen learned. She regressed to a state of complete psychological dependency in a liaison that began well but soon replayed the worst of her relationship with an abandoning and emotionally unavailable father. After nonordinary sex, she gradually became incapable of separating herself from a man with sociopathic tendencies.

Gwen had the world by the tail. She was a successful, put-together executive on the fast track. She had married a well-respected executive several years her senior, and the two enjoyed a jet-setting lifestyle that combined business with pleasure. Soon, however, her husband's career faltered. He began drinking heavily, missing work, staying out all night, and generally behaving irresponsibly. He denied that anything was wrong, and flatly refused all attempts by his friends, family, and Gwen to get help for his situation. Within a short time, her life became a series of stressful events: the miscarriage of her first pregnancy, her husband's self-destructive and often dangerous behavior culminating in an incident of physical and sexual abuse, the threat of legal action against her husband for malfeasance at work, his irrational demands during the divorce procedure, and great financial uncertainty as the company Gwen worked for was put into play during a merger.

In the wake of these events, she met a man who swept her off her feet. Where her husband had become neglectful and cruel, Scott was warm, kind and attentive. Where her husband had sexually humiliated her, Scott was the most exciting lover she had ever had, a situation that shortly triggered Gwen's first transpersonal experience.

We really hit it off in bed. I've seldom had so instinctively "right" a lover as Scott, and it was during one of these occasions that my ego boundaries collapsed. It's easy for me to call it that now. I had no idea what happened at the time, except that it was something very strange and in some weird way, it seemed to seal our togetherness in a way I had never been with anyone before. We just merged.

I can remember exactly when it happened. My thoughts, usually completely abstract during sex, began to form his name and project his face behind my closed eyelids, so that soon I was mentally chanting his name in time with our movements. I wasn't trying to do this. It just happened. At some point, it was as if his image got bigger and bigger, filling the screen of my mind until *Scott, Scott, Scott* became *me, me, me*.

The fusion didn't dissipate . . . during sex or after. I felt dazed and disoriented afterward . . . , but it felt okay. I had no true reflection except an awareness of how odd I felt, how different. I couldn't have said that it was bad or good, but I somehow felt more complete. Only there wasn't exactly an "I" there.

I was one with Scott, not in love with him, but some kind of unquestioning, almost flat acceptance of this fusion. I was so totally *with* and *in* him that feeling *about* him wasn't really happening. It wasn't like love or joy. It just was.

Gwen and Scott began to spend more time together, even though at first she had doubted that their relationship would have a future because they were from very different backgrounds. In hindsight, Gwen could chart how her fusion during that one embrace (the feeling of merging was never repeated) began to spread like a creeping disease in other venues of her life, as her normal intentions shriveled and were replaced by his.

I hate to sound like a snob, but Scott just wasn't in my social class. He was a redneck, and he liked to do things like hang out in cowboy bars and go to tractor pulls. I'd not only never done anything like that, I would have laughed if you'd told me I ever would. His whole world was alien and unattractive to me, but soon I went wherever he wanted to go. I was content to do whatever he suggested. It was as if my mind had just checked out.

I was no longer depressed about my divorce or the miscarriage or the problems at work, but I wasn't happy either. I sort of had a mindless type of mild contentment. After work, I'd go home and putter around or watch TV, previously a rather boring activity for me, waiting for him to call. I used to read five or six books a week. Now I did all this mindless stuff. I didn't read at all.

When we were together I became more animated, but I didn't sense my *self* more than when I was alone. I thought about him constantly, just pleasant daydreams with his name and image, like some kind of unfocused, half-formed obsession, like a junior high school crush.

Gwen felt a distant sense of wonder at the change in her life and interests. She was perfectly content to spend all her time doing household chores, the kind she used to hurry through before in order to read or go out with friends. An upper middle-class college graduate, she found herself envying a woman she would have pitied, a poor, pregnant teenager who lived next to Scott's mobile home in the trailer park.

The monotony and lack of initiative I felt was strangely comforting. It was enough just to be around Scott and involved in concrete tasks—making the bed, making coffee, getting dressed, watching TV.

I began to envy people who had concrete lives, like the woman in the next trailer. She was your basic barefoot and pregnant type, probably seventeen years old. Her whole life was nothing but housework, women's magazines . . . and daytime TV and having dinner on the table at five o'clock when her menial-labor husband came home. She'd have her babies and the years would pass, but every day would be the same mindless round.

That kind of life seemed simple, uncomplicated, and good. I wanted that routine for myself, not all my responsibilities.

The relationship quickly became addictive. Gwen needed Scott. She gave up more and more of her self-determination to stay with him. He became increasingly demanding, insisting that she not go out with friends but sit home waiting for him. Gwen did whatever he asked, dreading his anger when she transgressed his desires. Their connection through sex soon became the only time she could "have enough" of him. No price seemed too high to pay.

I know now that this is how an abusive relationship starts, where the man makes more and more demands and the woman isolates herself more and more. It sounds crazy to me now, but at the time I was apologizing when I had to go out of town on business and I was canceling important business dinners just to sit home and wait for the phone to ring.

But his calls were fewer, and he kept making excuses about working late. He was actually a pretty good liar, and it took me a while to figure out what was happening.

I began to realize he lied about everything, even the unimportant stuff. He just lied all the time. And I also found out he had a violent streak. . . . He picked fights with people in bars, really liked beating people up . . . [including] some of his previous girlfriends. I was dismayed but never even considered breaking up with him. Is that sick, or what?

He would treat me in humiliating ways, and I didn't care. I suspected he was cheating on me. Although I despised myself, I wasn't truly introspective.

I know this sounds sick. It *was* sick. I'm ashamed to even be telling you this. It was the lowest point in my entire life. . . . I know now how easy it would be to become an abused wife, to put up with things just because the only time and place you feel whole is when he's inside you.

The erosion of Gwen's sense of herself as a capable and attractive woman prior to meeting Scott had certainly undermined her psychologically, perhaps making her easy prey. So did Gwen's history. Her father, who spoiled her when he was at home, had been absent for most of her childhood, predisposing her to select partners who appeared to be available to her but who, in fact, were emotionally withdrawn. Scott was the most extreme version of that kind of a partner for Gwen.

She did eventually break from Scott after finding incontrovertible proof of his infidelity, but getting back to normal was a difficult process. In spite of everything, she found it almost impossible to stay away from him, even after she had begun psychotherapy. It was months before she could resist his phone calls. Years afterward she was still terrified that "somehow, someday, I'll find myself back in that horrible place where my whole self is lost in someone else."

At the time I interviewed Gwen, her relationship with Scott was more than fifteen years in the past. She is now in a joyful relationship involving transcendent sex, which brought her into my study. But the scars from her first boundary-breaking encounter remain tender, and she is still haunted by fear.

> When I first was drawn to [my present partner], I was scared to death. I started having these strange experiences, and they felt terrific, wonderful, just great. And I had no reason to be afraid of him, he was so loving. But I had to wonder.
>
> I realized that the more special these experiences were, the more they bound me to him, and the more I would suffer if we ever broke up. I didn't feel lost in him, but it was scary to feel that I might be dependent again, like I was with Scott, that I might be in love so much that I couldn't survive without him.
>
> I went into therapy right away and stayed in for three years, and I guess I've worked most of it through. But I always feel like I'll be vulnerable there, like I'll always have a little danger of losing too much of myself and that maybe I won't be able to recover from it.

Highly charged altered-state sex in which ego-boundaries dissolve to include the partner can seriously jeopardize psychological integrity. Getting professional help, as Gwen did, is the most efficacious solution because the primal patterns activated during such dangerous liaisons may be as hard to mitigate as they are debilitating.

Overwhelming Intimacy

Overwhelming intimacy refers to times when the content of the altered state threatens the ego as alien material seems to impose itself on a person's mind in an invasive manner. Since people in this study weren't seeking to have an altered state during sex and may never have experienced an involuntary, waking altered state before, they were taken by surprise the first time extraordinary events began to unfold. Sometimes they were unable to avoid hallucinations, such as the changing of a partner's face in *trespasso,* or to control the content of their own minds, such as when they felt possessed by another being. Naturally, any suspension of "ordinary reality" can be frightening. Sometimes the person can stop the experience, like the man who managed to stop the past-life experience by disengaging from his partner or the woman who tried to shake off the illusions of *trespasso* by changing focus, closing her eyes, looking elsewhere and concentrating. But not everyone has the presence of mind or capacity to banish alien thought processes.

Keiko, a charming African American advertising executive, told a story about his never-fulfilled attraction for a man he only met in passing. The stranger lived in the first neighborhood Keiko moved into in New York. They passed each other on the street, and Keiko always noticed him. Keiko moved twice, and the stranger appeared in those neighborhoods, too. They never had a meaningful conversation, only greeting each other in passing. Keiko always sensed some subtle connection, though. After mentioning his mild but persistent interest to a fortune-teller who said the two men had been sisters in a past life, Keiko was satisfied to let the matter rest.

Then one afternoon when Keiko was making love with

someone else, the stranger suddenly appeared in a frighten-ing vision—frightening because in the first place, Keiko was unaccustomed to having fantasy images of another person during sex. He says, "I wanted to think it was in my mind, but I know for a fact he was nowhere in my thoughts at that time. I'm not one who imagines a person when I masturbate or have sex with someone, even if it's a person I have seen or know."

Second, the apparition seemed like a disruption of normal reality for Keiko, which he found extremely unnerving. "It was definitely a very scary experience at the moment of its happen-ing. It freaked me out," he avers. "It *totally* had to stop, and I totally, completely lost it for a few minutes. I couldn't talk; I was speechless. It threw me for a loop. . . . I just let a whole reality slip out of my hands." To make things worse, the stranger's mes-sage was menacing.

I could see his face clearly and could hear his voice extremely clear. . . . It was really scary, because he said, "You want to hang with the big boys? Can you handle that?"

And it was really him showing me how big *he* was, and in that one moment, he was really in my face. I tried to remove myself, to shake myself a little bit, but he was just there, *he was just there.*

But then he was just gone, and I was losing my erection and everything. It took me twenty minutes to recompose myself, and I never really talked about it.

The uncanny appearance of the stranger and his threatening question haunted Keiko for the next two or three years: "It wasn't so much a spiritual experience as a rude awakening, the way it felt. He was asking me what I wanted and then asking, 'Are you ready to play with the big boys?' He basically told me that the reason we hadn't connected was that I wasn't ready. I mean, this is really *crazy*."

During the interval when Keiko was attempting to come to terms with the apparition, he learned that the stranger had been killed in an accident. This enabled him to reengage the process. He came to interpret the message as a spiritual challenge to himself.

Since he's no longer around, and I finally figured it out, over the last year I decided to take it a step further. Basically I asked his spirit to help me understand.

The message I got was that I was never strong enough in myself, and I never believed enough in myself to approach him to communicate directly, face-to-face, eye to eye. It was all about . . . how I felt about myself, not feeling worthy.

He was a big player, he was large, and if you really wanted to play, you had to come forward, strong. Not like you're a big player to win, not in that sense, but at least self-secure enough that you can approach the issues.

Since then, it has changed my whole thinking. Now I'm more aggressive about things, if I want to know this thing or this person or have this experience. I definitely go for it more immediately. . . . I can always relate back to that. . . . I've used it as a form of healing myself.

If it was true that we were in past lives, then I have closure now. We never said more than "hi" or "good-bye." I may have thought that we looked at each other in a way of "I know you," but it could have all been in my head. Nothing had ever been said. We were like two strangers in this realm. But I kind of thank him all the time, you know? I really do.

Bad Endings

For Betty, the intensity of the connection with another partner put her in a severe psychological crisis when repeated altered-state experiences threatened too much of her understanding of reality. She was in a long-term marriage when she began having an affair with a colleague who lived across the country. Despite their infrequent meetings, the charge of their relationship rapidly escalated into transcendent sex. "There was definitely a transcendent quality of being in intense contact with somebody. I can still wake him up in New York by thinking of him in the middle of the night. If we're 3,000 miles apart, this is not possible in my world," she remarks, referring to just one eerie aspect of their connection,

> What set it up for us was when we were physically together, we could move [with] the mundane to the transcendent . . . being able to descend into that place of vulnerability, of total release, a total letting go of yourself. It had all that, and this spiritual, transcendent part and also the underlying thread of how things were between us. We knew from the beginning we were connected in a place that was a rare thing, and that it was a bonus that we could go to these other places.

But these new abilities exacted a price from Betty, who saw her reality deteriorate as a result: "When this started happening to me, [I was close to] a psychotic break . . . because it so thoroughly disrupted my reality to admit that things like this exist, these other realities. It was not possible to go on with my life . . . [the way] it was before."

Within a year, Betty's life dissolved into chaos. She divorced her husband, brought her lover into her family to the extent their opposite-coast commitments permitted, and then suddenly kicked him out of her life without a word. She was also involved in "all sorts of life changes" because she couldn't sustain her normal understanding of reality anymore. She finally came full circle, but she says, "It took time and long-term therapy to realize that, oh yeah, this stuff *does* happen, and it can happen in the context of an intimate relationship. It was, 'Honey, you ain't in Kansas anymore!'"

Confusion, questioning the meaning of life and reality, and making significant life changes usually follow in the wake of spiritually transformative events, from being called to become a shaman to having a near-death experience. Betty's experience is not unusual in that sense, and she now celebrates the changes in herself, such as an increase in compassion that informs all her relationships. But her former husband, children, and lover were not so fortunate in the way their lives were painfully affected by Betty's erratic reactions to transcendent sex.

In a different example, Laura had a short-lived marriage with a former Catholic priest. Because she had had a splendid prior relationship characterized by mutual transcendent sex, she and the former priest attempted to induce transcendent experiences during lovemaking using meditation. In hindsight, she believes these experiences helped destroy him. They had married after a only a two-month courtship, and she was not aware of his psychological fragility. She now believes he was suffering from an undiagnosed mental illness as well as alcoholism, and that their sexual experiences pushed him over the edge.

I saw him disintegrate, I saw him go downhill. I know he had the priesthood and all that [guilt], but the kind of sex we were having probably speeded up the disintegration of his ego.

This kind of sex is very, very, very, very powerful. I've seen it burn through ego, just backfire. It's hard to lose your ego during these experiences and then have to come back and get in your body and get on with life. It's dangerous for people who haven't worked on themselves psychologically.

This kind of sex will burst you. It will burn through blocks in your energy field, blocks in your memories, blocks in your psychological well-being. I put myself back in therapy.

Altered states are nothing to play with. They can exacerbate preexisting problems, even in apparently stable individuals. Professional counseling with someone knowledgeable about transcendent experiences, such as a therapist trained in transpersonal psychology, is warranted.

Invaders and the Invaded

Intrusive intimacy can be damaging when the integrity of the separate self erodes and as aspects of the partner invade personal boundaries. For instance, lovers who are sensitive to the body's energetic fields may have difficulty separating themselves from impressions that arise in their lovers. Muntu, for example, who has experienced several transcendent sexual episodes, has had to learn how to protect himself since he can be affected by his partner's physical states.

It's important to me to remain me . . . at different levels of surrender . . . at the same time that we get closer and closer. . . .
When I engage in sex, I can feel my [body's energetic] fields
going all the way around a person and getting totally intermin-
gled. . . .

It's an indication of how intimate this is, in that if a person is an
alcoholic or has had a fair amount to drink, I will pick up that
alcholness [sic] and become drunk. So therefore, I don't make
love or get involved with people who are drunk. Same thing
with other drugs or chemically altered states.

Unwanted intimacy can work in both directions. Take Mike,
who had a profound peak experience when he was in Vietnam,
that led him to pursue a spiritual path on his return to the
States. He married a woman who was also a spiritual seeker, but
they always had sexual difficulties, and in fact, their eighteen-
year marriage was unworkable at many levels. Mike tried past-
life regression therapy to work out their marital problems. The
therapy enabled them to enjoy sex for the first time, and stabi-
lized the marriage for a while, but ultimately it collapsed.

Mike had a second spiritual opening that lasted about six
months. While he was in this exalted state, he could "see the
mystic picture of the world from everybody's perspective I
knew," including those of his lovers. This enabled him to have
transcendent sex. This openness to others remained, long after
opening, and it has become, in a way, the bane of his existence.

His capacity to see the world from others' perspectives was
overwhelming in the fast-paced hurly-burly of the business
world. Worse, he couldn't keep others from sensing his access to
their minds. Some responded positively, but others were completely repelled. He gave up his successful career for the more
restricted life of academia and began living reclusively.

Many people find me too intense now, especially in business. . . .
I don't like the fact that I'm a professor now, but I tried to go
back into business several years ago, and found it was just too
painful.

You see, I'll get the positive, that I've touched people's lives very
deeply. I see the beauty in them, the Buddha in them. But on
the other hand, some people said I was making them too aware
of what they saw as their inadequacies, although that wasn't
what I was seeing about them at all.

Over half the women I would go out with—and some who were
very attractive to me—cannot stand to be around me. One said
it very well. She said it was that she couldn't be herself. She felt
so overwhelmed that she was throwing up.

"My sensitivity is very difficult to live with. Many people are
just not aware of the level of pain that they have. They don't
even know they're suffering," Mike says, reflecting a fairly common problem reported by people who are considered "spiritual
sensitives." This group comprises individuals who have had difficulty most of their lives in screening out awareness of others'
psyches,[4] and those whose sensitivity is adventitious, such as
the result of near-death experiences. Regardless of how such
porosity of emotion occurs, most people find it both a blessing
and a curse. According to Mike,

I would prefer to be more alive and to feel the pain than to be
more comfortable and out of touch, and I'm having to deal with
that question right now because of what I've been feeling. The
more I am sensitive to it, the more pain I feel. And it's not my
pain anymore. When I go out and interact with people, I feel
very dense energy. . . .

I can't tell you how much it hurts and yet feels good to be alive. Right now I'd have to say the pain is excruciating and also sweet and elegant—so joyful and so excruciating at the same time.

If Mike is unable to screen out the world at large, he has at least found ways to protect others from being aware of his powers. However, the permeability still remains in lovemaking. There he can attain depths of intimacy beyond his wildest dreams, which over the years has led to transpersonal exchanges and kundalini-type energetic events. But Mike's sex life is an admixture of intense pleasure and pain. He has difficulty maintaining the integrity of his boundaries. He derives so much ecstasy from the fusion of lovemaking that he craves it, even when the encounter has damaging side effects. He would be affected by his partner's bodily states and experience and would also gain such high levels of energy and sensitivity that he had trouble living a normal life.

I was sleeping two hours a night, writing a book, teaching during the day. The only way I could stabilize myself was to practice, to learn how to do TM [transcendental meditation], which grounded me so I wouldn't get stuck in all that energy. Since meditation, I've increased my sleep to five or six hours. . . . I would like to sleep more soundly, not wake up a lot in the night.

Fusion with a partner also made it difficult for Mike to hold on to his own thinking initially: "I can feel the other person, not just myself in this incredible bond and intimacy. It was very destabilizing for my mind. My mind had a hard time keeping up, even though I could understand what was going on."

Sexual commingling gives him depths of intimacy so

exciting that he was willing to endure painful aftereffects. Mike's language suggests addiction to a spiritual-sexual "high."

I was with a woman who was having a problem being open in general. She wasn't having orgasms. She just wanted to be close to me, and she's not very open at all, very tied to her parents, especially her mother. She's half Japanese, and she was brought up with a lot of restriction.

Making love [with her] felt so good I didn't want to live anymore. It actually felt so good I wanted to die . . . but then as I became more bonded to her over time—to give you how bizarre this is—I wound up not being able to have sex with her more than once a week, then less, then not at all.

What I experienced making love to her was a very exciting, wonderful bond, but afterward I'd revert to a terrible state of fear and upset. It was peculiar. I just could *feel* the problems in her that she was going through. She's performing to her mother's perceptions and expectations. I had some very severe reactions—stomach tensions, throwing my food up, back problems—and I just couldn't think and be myself in that relationship anymore.

But my obsessive desire for that kind of union was so great that I would not pass up the opportunity to be with her, even though there was an aftermath of working hard to be myself. And I actually had to work *very* hard, writing papers and disciplining my mind to being a professor.

Now this woman was working in a large customer service organization and . . . thirty percent had lost their jobs. They were just called into an office, one by one, and told they were fired in about ten minutes. She was in a pretty tough environment, and then add that to all [the problems in] her relationship with her parents.

I couldn't keep her environment out. If we went to parties together or something like that, the same thing happened, but it was no big deal because you can come home and sleep it off. But if I had sex with her, this would *last*. It would take weeks. And it began to take longer and longer [to get over it], and the pain was so intense.

But the joy of it was also so intense that I couldn't stop myself. As soon as I'd get well enough to do it again, I would.

When I interviewed Mike, he had decided to abstain from sex because it was just too fraught with difficulties, yet his years of living alone were painful. He had just been on a trip where he had stayed with friends; in their peaceful household, he slept better than he had in months, and his intimacy with them was pleasant and trouble-free for all. His yearning for a harmonious balance between his delight in intimacy and a love relationship is poignant:

I'm actually choosing to abstain from sex right now because it's like I've had enough perspectives, and I'm really tired of it. It's very confusing.

I can live without sex easily. I look at myself as a monk in that way. But I cannot live without intimacy. They're not mutually exclusive. Sex in the right situation with a person is not just about sex, not about that moment, but about what's going on in their lives.

I really want to bond with a woman and just have a home and stability, but there's a certain amount of unease, not knowing what that might be. The difficulty in this perspective is that I'm afraid I'd find myself getting sucked into something. Can I be sexually intimate and be okay and not lose my capacity to feel and then to be with people in general?

I cannot live without intimacy, and I'd rather err on the side of intimacy and less on the side of sex.

Precautions

In conclusion, transcendent sex is no guarantee of ultimate happiness, spiritual attainment, or the true union of soulmates. Like any powerful event, its value isn't intrinsic but depends upon the way the experience is understood and used. Sexual altered states can happen to anyone at any time—ready or not—so it's important to find ways to promote their healthful integration. The following recommendations can help you recognize and mitigate situations that may be potentially hazardous, whether you are deliberately seeking altered-state sex or have experienced its accidental occurrence.

1. *Check into any practice carefully.* If you are seeking training in altered-state sex, investigate the teachers and organization carefully. What credentials and training do the facilitators have? If their training comes from a religious institution, ask what tradition they follow and about the lineage of their teachers. Are they affiliated with a formal organization or recognized as having formal credentials in their tradition

that permit them to teach these techniques? Do they and their organization enjoy good standing in the larger community? Major traditions are supported by a wealth of published material, and you would do well to dip into their major texts to determine whether their approach and affiliation accord with the spiritual heritage of that tradition. If the teachers' credentials include some form of counseling or body work, are these individuals duly licensed by a recognized accrediting body? Do they furnish referrals to independent, third-party specialists, such as therapists, if you find yourself in trouble? If not, do you have backup support resources of your own? Even if you just decide to read Tantric or Taoist or other manuals at home for experimentation, it's wise to investigate precautions and have a backup support system of knowledgeable experts lined up in case you experience uncomfortable dynamics.

2. *Proceed with caution.* If the organization and its teachers have a clean bill of health, remain alert to the ideology, injunctions, and rituals surrounding participation. Any of these elements can profoundly shape an altered state, and the way that state is interpreted. When such matters are overtly addressed by teachers or facilitators, they are "setting the intention," a phrase that recognizes the ability of mental predispositions to foster certain outcomes in altered states. Remember that ideological suggestions, the wording of instructions, and various aspects of ritual are frequently subtle or covert—and may well coexist with their stated intentions. Pay heed to any suggestions or expectations that might shape your experience.

3. *Learn how to stop an altered state.* Whether accidentally or deliberately, if you find yourself starting to slip into a nonordinary mode of awareness that is uncomfortable for whatever reason, cease immediately any activities that might be

supporting that state, especially repetitive motions, touching, and vocalization. Alter your visual field by opening your eyes and focusing clearly on a succession of near and far objects (which will help change your brain's electromagnetic waves to the beta signature of normal, waking consciousness), by blinking rapidly, or by closing your eyes if they have been open. Change your physical stance, preferably to a more upright position unless you are dizzy. You may wish to disengage completely from your partner, turn off any music, increase the lighting, lower the room temperature, walk around, or even quit the area entirely for a while.

4. *You're not crazy.* If this is the first time you have ever experienced a waking altered state, you need not fear a loss of sanity. Altered states are more common than most people believe, and they can happen at any time. The states associated with sexual activity are not very different from those associated with many other types of experience that normal people have under other circumstances. They represent subjective realities, it's true, but except for individual details, explorers and researchers have mapped most of these realities for thousands of years. These things *do* happen, and they can happen to anyone.

5. *Nothing is necessarily sacred.* The presence or absence of altered states is not indicative of the goodness of your relationship or of your partner. Transcendent sex can happen in good relationships and bad. It can occur once in a lifetime, more with one partner than another, or it can be the way some individuals just always have sex, regardless of their partners. As yet, too little is known about what triggers transcendent sex, although altered-state experiences may occur more often when something in the dynamics of the relationship reactivates one of the partner's primal parental connections. Since the dynamics of early childhood can replay the

ideal good or bad aspects of the parental relationship, the altered state can be hazardous. Having transcendent sex with an individual does *not* mean that you were meant for each other or that the relationship is somehow blessed. And the presence of transcendent sex is no reason to stay with a particular partner. If you have had it once, you may have it again with someone else.

6. *It's not about your holiness.* The presence or absence of these states is not indicative of your own goodness. Some people are more prone to altered states than others, but this does not mean they are more spiritual or more highly evolved. In fact, research shows that individuals with certain developmental disorders and those who have suffered severe early childhood trauma are more likely to have altered states.[5]

7. *Slow down.* If you are aware of an unusual connection with a partner that either has led to transcendent sex or seems likely to, use good judgment, and if possible, slow down the level of physical involvement until you are reasonably sure that the relationship will be mutually beneficial and that the potential partner is not likely to engage in power games.

8. *Monitor yourself.* Critically examine your reactions, and your own level of self-control. If you are disturbed—for whatever reason—by *anything* associated with your partner, relationship, your own reactions to what is happening, or your nonordinary experiences, seek professional counseling from someone competent to give guidance in this area. Conventional psychotherapists and sex therapists may not have the training needed to deal with altered states and their aftermath effectively. They may also be inclined to bury your experience by medicating you with prescription drugs. You need a counselor who will treat your experience

as subjectively valid and who will not dismiss it as a product of your imagination. Therapists who specialize in spirituality, spiritual emergencies, and transpersonal psychology usually are knowledgeable about altered states; some of them employ altered states in therapy. It is worth locating competent guidance rather than relying on the low-cost, short-term, mainstream services offered through most managed-care plans.

9. *Consider unusually attractive people potential hazards.* Beware of people using charismatic techniques to arouse your sexual interest, including potential partners, retreat facilitators, sex therapists and teachers, and spiritual guides. Research suggests that intentions can influence the behavior of living beings and inanimate objects, while centuries of tradition suggest that spiritual masters have unusual mental abilities and powers. Without encouraging paranoia, it is wise to honor your intuition: if you feel you are being manipulated in some subtle, unnamable way (a hunch, a creepy feeling), better to err on the side of caution.

10. *Remember the greater good.* Always ask whether you are motivated by what is helpful, kind, and true. It's especially important to ask yourself whether your partner seems motivated by what is helpful, kind, and true. Do your actions reflect those motivations? Do your partner's? Does your relationship reflect that? Even when spirituality cuts like a sword or shakes us out of our mindless habits, it is always life-affirming, life-enhancing.

There is no foolproof way to avoid potential trouble or confusion, but caution, careful self-monitoring, good judgment, self-control, and professional guidance can make the path safer. Sabu's experience provides these kernels of wisdom:

A low form of sex makes for a low form of spirituality, and a low form of spirituality may make for a low form of sex. The quality of the sexual experience relates to the capacity of the individual to hold it in a spiritual place. Spiritual sexuality is a very precious thing. . . . That doesn't mean that it's going to make life easy; it will make it rich.

CHAPTER 11

Grace and Practice:
Facilitating Transcendent Sex

Some . . . native peoples call it the Great Mysterious, and I like that better. Moving into that greater Force. By our coming together and touching and caressing and loving, maybe there's something that we're doing that is the kindling in the midst of that fire, but . . . that fire comes from somewhere else, not just from the two of us. . . . Making love . . . is a way to go to church, talk to God, connect with God, however you might understand that. —Roland

It makes me so happy to know that just by living our regular lives, we can connect with something so beautiful. We don't have to do anything . . . but just be open to it. —Rhonda

WARNINGS ABOUT TRANSCENDENT SEX are fine, but after hearing the heart-stoppingly beautiful accounts of ecstatic sex, people always want to know how they can invite such experiences into their lives. There's an easy answer to this question, and a more complex one. Both are valid.

On the one hand, how-to books about sex abound, including books on spiritually based approaches from Taoist and Tantric models or eclectic Westernized versions of these ancient traditions. The vast majority present techniques for opening the body and becoming more consciously aware of its capacity for sensual pleasure, especially learning to sense and manipulate the energetic fields represented by the meridians and vortices of the chakras. Methods emphasize overcoming old patterns of shame attached to sexual activity and promoting mutual trust between partners. These are worthy goals, and all of them are conducive to transcendent sex.

But none of them can account for the experiences participants in this study cited, for several reasons:

- Few were sophisticated lovers, knowledgeable about their bodies, subtle energy systems or esoteric techniques.
- Some people were carrying lifelong habits of shame.
- Many were not in relationships of high trust.
- The kinds of activities they engaged in varied considerably so that it would be impossible to suggest that any particular practice produced a certain state.

However, certain patterns did emerge, and these were congruent with the advice provided by standard texts on esoteric sexual practices. Most of these patterns represent a collective wisdom, and they're offered at the end of this chapter.

The question of how to facilitate transcendent sex also has a more complicated answer, one that lies at the nexus of grace and practice.

Re-creating Transcendent Sex

There's no doubt that transcendent sex experiences are compelling, even when they aren't ecstatic. One of the most affecting stories I gathered came from Katherine, a vivacious Hispanic executive in a high-profile, high-tech company. Her one transcendent sexual episode concerned her roots in a past life. During sex, she says, she became aware that "another part of Katherine had tapped me on the shoulder and was trying to get my focused attention" away from the part of her in bed with her lover. This other part was making love in a place that seemed to be her ancestral home in Spain surrounded by vineyards. Her impressions were from the 1860s, she said, and she had the haunting feeling that she was about to learn where she came from, what she was doing in the world, where and how she *belonged*. But the spell was broken too soon. Her normal analytical mind took over, stranding her in the present, bereft and shortchanged. "I remember a lot of sadness afterward that brought tears. . . . There were so many leftover questions. . . . *Wait a minute!* I want to go back and see the end of this. . . . I just wasn't ready to come back here."

Katherine desperately attempted to repeat the episode. "I tried to do everything I could when I was with this man to recreate it, remembering what I was eating, what I was drinking. It took almost three months for me to just let it go. I was very stubborn about it and getting frustrated," she says. It began to affect the quality of her relationship.

> I didn't want that to have any effect on the current relationship. It was like, every time, I'm not living in the moment, but trying to recapture that. I was very analytical about what should have been a very loving and emotional place. That was the goal, and maybe it will come around, and I'll get Part Two, the continuation of the saga.
>
> But I finally had to let it go.

Katherine's yearning was by far the most pronounced of any respondent's, and in some ways, it is a lone voice. Although a number of people, like her, had had only a single instance of transcendent sex in a lifetime, few expressed more than a wistful nostalgia. Actually, the ones who expressed the most need to have such experiences again were those who had enjoyed transcendent sex fairly regularly with a particular partner. They attributed their experiences to something inherent in that special relationship, and, if the relationship had been terminated—or was on the verge of ending—they expressed sadness and fear that their access to transcendent episodes would end. Their concerns, however, focused more on the need to re-create an unusually intimate connection than on a need to identify techniques that would reproduce a particular experience. And significantly, none was so desperate that he or she was willing to remain in an unsatisfactory relationship in order to keep having those experiences.

In fact, only a handful of participants said they attempted to cultivate practices they thought would increase their ability to have transcendent sex, and these practices were quite personal—ones that seemed to be natural outgrowths of their own idiosyncratic activities. *None* had undertaken a course of study in sexual technique subsequent to transcendent sex. If ecstatic sex is so wonderful, why aren't these people doing all they can to re-create the experiences they reported?

Grace or Practice?

The answer seems to be a preference for spontaneity rather than practice in the sexual arena. Even participants who doggedly adhere to spiritual disciplines favor adventure and grace over practice when it comes to making love. They are content to invite, but not engineer. Since some of them know about Tantra, their reluctance to study and use such techniques, or even to attempt to re-create (and perhaps ritualize and thus institutionalize) their own techniques, suggests a willingness to trust the process and keep it free from manipulation and performance expectations. According to Donna, "I've read about chakra control, and I've had some experiences in yoga that I wouldn't want to drop. But when it comes to sex, I haven't done that. Maybe at some point I could try them, and I imagine it would deepen and ground my experience. But I don't want sex to be work."

In the first place, most people said that although it's possible to create a certain readiness and openness for such experiences, ultimately they can't be forced or controlled at will, any more than meditators or worshipers can guarantee what kind of experience they will have in contemplation or prayer. Second, sex with a partner isn't as easy to "control" as solitary prayer or meditation: partners have their own ways of doing things, may be unskilled or may resist participation in a deliberate practice (which isn't a requirement for transcendent sex, anyway). Third, sex is already greatly regulated by the same forces that influence public behavior—social, religious, and legal norms of what is acceptable. In this most private arena, many people choose to express themselves with as much freedom as possible. They have little interest in practices that encroach on their spontaneity and creativity. And last, for many, the idea of trying to "force" a spiritual episode is just plain absurd. If it *could* be done, it would violate the sanctity of the experience altogether, or as one participant, Kirill, a physicist who studies such things, put it, "Transcendental experiences are to some extent causeless."

Pascal, another participant, is a married Episcopalian who faithfully observes the prayer and meditation discipline of the Benedictine order in his spiritual life He describes his sex life this way:

When you're hungry, your body tells you in a physical language that it has something going on, that it needs something. It doesn't use words, but you can translate that into an intellectual, mental language to tell someone you're hungry.

That's true in a spiritual experience where at a mystical level you use spiritual language, and to try to mix the two is like the equivalent of your stomach explaining logarithms. It doesn't have access to the language and it can only react viscerally and dump chemicals, like your mind, which can only spew words and dump ideas but not get at what is really happening. I'm convinced there are connections of the spirit, and I've learned to trust those to take care of themselves at a level beyond my conscious intention.

The lack of a conscious spiritual need or desire for a transformative experience is present in virtually all those whose experiences are recorded in this book, even for people who had profound episodes. For instance, Suzette, Armand, Zebediah, and Artemis were just going about their "normal" sexual business, looking forward to a pleasant but ordinary interlude in the sack when they were ambushed by Spirit. Artemis even says that she believes it was impossible for her to "have" the experience because it was a lightning bolt from Spirit, an undeserved and unsought act of grace, nothing for which she had the remotest desire or ability to produce.

And this is the very point many lovers make: looking for something, trying too hard, is a sure way to prevent such an event from *ever* occurring. Steven, a high-powered lawyer whose faith combines Congregational and Quaker prayer and meditation, puts it this way:

I know men who say, "I want to have sex with that woman." I say, "That's not right. Perhaps you want that woman to want to have sex with *you*, but any further than that and you're in deep trouble. Do *not* want to have sex with that woman." The point is, *no objectives*. Just be there. My sense of this sexuality is that it's a spiritual practice of transcendent knowledge, but the only way to enter it is not to have an objective.

Thus even people who are highly disciplined contemplatives and who have transcendent sex prefer not to bring the same kind of intentionality to lovemaking they bring to meditation. Roland, a participant who is a professor and recognized expert at altered-state sex and meditation, offers this view of keeping the unpredictable and humble human touch in the picture:

> I'm not sure I want to have somebody regulate what I'm doing in bed with my partner. If spontaneity doesn't help with the science, so what? Are you going to be preprogrammed, like okay, we're going to have cosmic sex now?

> People can with Tantra, certain breathing and positions, some prescribed manner. For me, that misses it, though.

> I like the mystery, the not knowing. The underground path to ecstasy has a lot to recommend it. I've spent a lot of time on the [meditation] cushion, but I don't have that sense of control in sex, and that's part of the excitement. . . . It's an exploration. . . . Wow, we're doing this together and where are we going to go? The profundity is how the relationship with my partner is shifted, changed, solidified, expanded, and it's also about the relationship with God and the human-to-human connection.[1]

How Can We Find Out What Works?

The lovers in this study didn't "practice" transcendent sex in the same way that Tantric or other practitioners might. That's one reason their experiences vary so widely: they were following their own idiosyncratic paths rather than institutionalized disciplines. This poses a dilemma for discussing what can be done to facilitate transcendent sex based on this study for several reasons:

- A number of participants had only one episode in a lifetime, and they had no clear idea how or why it occurred on that occasion, nor any thought of how to re-create it deliberately.
- People had diverse preferences concerning partners, values, and practices, so their activities and approaches vary considerably.
- What worked for some, such as the need for the trust and security of a long-term, committed relationship, was not true for others, who had transcendent sex in a first-time encounter in a casual relationship or one-night stand.

Thus, the tips that follow aren't a unified, foolproof blueprint that will guarantee results. The methods are as idiosyncratic as the people, and the results less predictable than those of prescribed contemplative practices. Some suggestions directly contradict others. They are offered as a range of possibilities for selection, and, if you choose, as a starting point to be pursued only in view of the caveats mentioned in the previous chapter. Most, if not all, have direct parallels in the annals of esoteric sex, including self-discovered ways of manipulating breath and energy. Moreover, other parallels lovers discovered partake of the deceptively simple injunctions for contemplation: they sound easy on the surface, but are challenging to grasp in their subtlety.

If transcendent sex is a serious goal drawing you to a more structured practice, by all means investigate experienced teachers and methods, such as Taoism and Tantra, and use the guidelines in the previous chapter to help you select a safe approach. But consider the following list first. Some items may match your values, some may not, and some may seem more possible than others. If certain suggestions are appealing, try practicing these approaches to see how comfortable they are for you. If you respond positively, that may be sufficient, but you may still decide to take up a structured practice under the tutelage of a guide or using manuals to direct your efforts once you know what is possible.

The Underground Path to Ecstasy

The following suggestions are known to facilitate transcendent sex, even though none, alone or in combination, can guarantee a particular result. Don't expect immediate results. It may take several weeks of practice before openings present themselves.

The Partner

1. *Be alert for connections that may prefigure altered-state sex.* Electric connections where sparks seem to fly between two people who may not have exchanged a word ("love at first sight") represent a strong potential for transcendent sex. Respondents frequently mentioned magnetic attractions that drew them to strangers for transcendent encounters, even if the liaisons were extremely short-lived. People variously described them as "incredible chemistry," "magical," "karmic," and "lightning-bolt" connections. They mentioned such uncanny events as ecstatic visions of a stranger prior to

their meeting, preternatural recognition, being transported into another realm upon sight of the other, and actually "seeing" or feeling the sizzling thunderbolt connecting them to the partner. The nature of such attractions is mysterious, but there is no denying they happen—and when they do, they indicate a high probability for altered-state sex. In fact, for some couples, coitus is not even necessary: they can go into transcendent states through the touch of a hand or a kiss. These attractions are *in no way* predictive of a healthy relationship, so consider the risk before taking action.

2. *Choose a partner you can trust.* For some people, transcendent sex was possible only with a partner in a long-term, committed relationship "without duplicity," someone with whom they felt totally comfortable and with whom it was safe to be vulnerable, even out of control. Most sex workshops and manuals encourage activities to build trust between lovers, and the respondents in this sample emphasized the same issues, especially the importance of feeling unafraid to reveal and enjoy their bodies and to express and explore their sexual needs, no matter what they are.

3. *Select a partner who can revel in intensity.* Partners who are uncomfortable with emotional, psychological, or spiritual dynamics are unlikely to support some experiences related to transcendent sex (assuming they are sensitive enough to notice what's going on in the first place). Although it's possible to have a transcendent episode with virtually any partner, respondents were uniformly disappointed and isolated when their partners were unresponsive to, uninterested in, or mocking of intensely emotional or spiritual happenings. Some partners may be frightened away. As Cougar notes, "Having these experiences has spoiled me, and it's difficult to find somebody who is willing to be intimate on that level." Elaine has now been celibate for a number of years because

she is unable to find partners who can tolerate the intensity of such experiences, and she is unwilling to settle for less.

4. *Clear your relationship.* Everyone knows how unsatisfying one-sided lovemaking can be when both partners are willing but one or both is not fully present. Distractions can range from nagging worries, to smoldering resentments, to the proverbial but often quite real headache or other body misery. Or a partner may just not be in the mood for sex. Honor that. Even the most devoted couples had trouble reaching an ecstatic place when they felt out of sorts with each other, even at a subtle level. One man says, "If we've had a period of intense closeness already or if there's already a kind of opening, it's easier for me to get to that particular place than if we're tired, or we've quarreled, or there's stuff to get through. It's better if we find ourselves in that state of communion even before we start making love."

5. *Cultivate an attitude of gratitude and devotion to your partner.* For some, adopting an attitude of adoration toward the partner is the key, whether it arises on its own or is more deliberate. Some spend time honoring the other, whispering words of love and adoration before and during lovemaking, creating an exciting, accepting sacred space. The more certain individuals were of achieving a worshipful state toward their partners, the deeper they could go into a transcendent experience. (Again, be cautious that the partner will be a safe place to repose adoration.) According to Donna, "I get in a place where my experience is more meditative . . . and out of that arises a devotional quality where my lover becomes the most beautiful, precious, divine thing there is. That's what opens me, and a quality of gratefulness that I can have this experience of devotion." Others create a ritual or consciously seek to see the divine in their partners, a practice central to Tantra, but in these instances, done in very per-

sonal, private ways. Ardrigh says, "I have this sense that I'm making love with the Goddess. I try to project that on [my partner] a little bit, and make it really sacramental. We have some ceremony that is extremely sacred to us, but then everything Dee and I do is sacred, in a way."

Preparation

1. *Be grounded and centered in your life.* Although this is always an extremely tall order, it's true that for many people transcendent sex happens when their lives seem to be in good order. As one man says, "It tends to happen more often if I have been tending to my daily prayer and meditation, and the family and kids are doing well, and the job isn't just hideous. It primes the field when I have time to relax about things."

2. *Be alert to the potential afforded by exhaustion and hypersensitivity.* When people are tired—not just physically but also mentally and emotionally—they often are more able to enter an altered state. This is not a reason to force sex when you're fatigued, but it is food for thought. Several individuals had their only, or most moving, altered-state sex just after a physical or emotional crisis.[2] Some made love after extremely long hikes, when lying down felt good, though their bodies were otherwise exhausted from temperature extremes and exercise. Others had extraordinary episodes in the wake of great personal loss, such as the death of a loved one, when they were emotionally exhausted, raw, and open.

3. *Have sex in a special place.* Not surprisingly, transcendent sex is more likely to occur when people are out of their everyday environments. This means making love in places free from distractions and reminders associated with the responsibili-

ties of housework, errands, repairs, work, and family. It was much easier for respondents to let go when they made love out of town at conferences, on vacation, in the partner's home, out of doors, etc. The change of scene is liberating, enabling people to let go and relax. Sex experts suggest creating a sacred space using candles, incense, draped fabrics, and the like to emphasize the sensual and reduce the "noise" of everyday demands. A couple of respondents had gone to great lengths to create such environments, elaborately decorating a "love pad" apartment they leased in the city exclusively for sex.

4. *Give yourself plenty of time.* New lovers spend hours upon hours in bed, one reason the early stages of relationships may produce more transcendent sex. In record after record, people cited making love for several hours or setting aside two- or three-day weekends in places supplied with everything they might need so they wouldn't have to get dressed or go out for food or drink. According to Gloria, "It's not going to happen if we have someplace we have to be. It happens when we have all the time in the world, and we're both relaxed so we can engage in prolonged lovemaking when our energies aren't fragmented and our minds are just with each other."

5. *Invite the experience, but then release the intention.* Holding an openness to transcendent experience can increase the likelihood of having one. For instance, just knowing that they are possible and "setting the intention" through private reflection, a moment of prayer or meditation, or a ritual invitation may prepare the ground. It is as important to form the intention as it is to let it go. One man says, "I'm just grateful to know about it and invite it. I never think what it's going to be like or wonder if I'm going to get there. Even though it doesn't always happen, there's enough just to know it hap-

pens that I can touch aspects of it even if I don't have the full experience."

What to Do

1. *Enjoy and protract sensual play.* Many lovers found it easier to let go and to heighten their sensitivity through ritual and erotic activities. Some read poetry to the other; brought special perfumes, lotions, and oils for massage; selected special music for dancing and lovemaking; dressed in exotic clothing; offered favorite foods; surrounded themselves with candles and flowers; or touched each other with items of varying textures, such as feathers or furs. Sensual play can heighten sensitivity, desire, and the connection between partners to electric levels even before "actual foreplay" begins. One woman said, "Forcing myself to concentrate on the sensuality, the gazing into each other's eyes, the minute feelings through touch, taste, etc., caused a softening inside me so that I could let go of my resistance and tiredness. This concentration seemed to be the setting-off point. . . . It was a losing of oneself and then regaining oneself and then losing oneself again into the sensual experience."

2. *Enhance your connection through foreplay.* Respondents often began to "fall into" their lovers after just kissing them or caressing them. Protracted, deep kissing, or repetitive stroking shuts out other input and focuses a relaxed kind of attention on the partner or the "flow" of the experience. Letting go of discursive thought and sinking into the wordlessness of immediate sensation facilitates the open alertness that can lead to transcendence.

3. *Be the passive partner.* For a majority, transcendent experiences occur when they are "on the receiving end," whatever that may mean in the course of their activities. It is easier to

let go into the sensation of what is going forward when they are unconcerned about what will happen next, when there is no intentional motion, and when they are not responsible for balance or rhythm.

4. *Narrow attention in a relaxed way to a single point.* Becoming absorbed in any activity can produce a flow state of relaxed but focused concentration that shuts out awareness of the environment so that people are often "lost in their own world," oblivious to noise or other distractions, as well as the passage of time. The ability to become absorbed in the experience is critical to transcendent sex.[3] Certain people can become absorbed into touch, but others may lose themselves in sounds, music, or perhaps their own or their lover's vocalizations. Still others may become lost in imagery, whether it is the play of flickering candlelight against the darkness, their lover's eyes or face, or visions that arise within their minds. The focus doesn't matter; becoming absorbed is the portal.

5. *Go with whatever arises.* There is an extremely subtle difference between distractions, self-produced fantasies, and the "stray" thoughts or images that may herald the beginning of a transcendent experience. These stray thoughts may be triggered by something in your mind or environment, but they seem, somehow, to slip into awareness without intrusion or intent. Rather than banishing them (unless they are frightening), "follow" such thoughtforms where they lead. For instance, what appears at one moment to be the blank wall or ceiling beyond your partner may become a portal to another reality, or the "daydream" that starts to form may become a transcendent vision.

6. *Give up any outcome.* Forget about orgasm—yours and your partner's. This kind of sex is *not* about orgasm. There are no objectives, including, ultimately, having a transcendent

experience. It's about getting lost in the process of making love and forgetting about any possible goal. Just as the practice of meditation is a path that is spoiled by grasping for a goal, so is transcendent sex. The only way to get there is to be unconcerned with getting there. As one woman said, "In my tradition, you had to work hard to get into heaven, but maybe the Bible's right and heaven's here on earth. It helps me to remember that so I can let go of the notion that I'm going to miss something."

7. *Prolong erotic contact, including genital stimulation and penetration.* High levels of arousal and repetitive stimuli during sex bring about altered states just as they do in spiritual practices such as trance dancing. Protracted, monotonous stimulation helps focus attention, relax or exhaust defensive systems, and raise bodily energy levels. According to Kim, "You have to be pretty excited, in a high-passion connection. It's not casual, like one of those let's-have-sex-before-we-go-to-sleep kinds of thing. You have to be physically excited and mentally engaged."

8. *Do what comes naturally.* Participants mentioned time after time falling into a wordless place where they instinctively, without deliberate thought, engaged with their partners. Their movements went from the deliberate to the dance, and from the dance to an effortlessly entrained oneness. Lynn says, "I just know intuitively what to do, but it just feels completely natural to surrender to it. I just don't think about it, just surrender and then it somehow feels familiar and natural and loving so there's no sense of separateness but we're this one being."

Afterward

1. *It isn't necessarily over when it's over.* Many people found that their transcendent states, especially out-of-body and past-

life experiences, actually began when they were relaxed but exhausted after orgasm. They collapsed with their lovers in comfortable positions post coitus without engaging immediately in any distracting activities, such as reaching for a drink, adjusting the lighting, removing any clothing, contraceptives or sex aids, or going to the lavatory. They remained awake and attuned to each other, albeit in a diffuse, even dreamy manner. Give yourself time to enjoy this state until it fades into its natural conclusion, whether that is sleep or wakefulness as other needs manifest. This interval, rather than lovemaking, may actually produce a transcendent experience.

2. *Be accepting of whatever happens, or doesn't happen.* Making judgments about an experience—a "big" one, a "little" one, a "good" one, or "nothing" isn't helpful. In fact, it's likely to create the very performance expectations that can kill a nascent ability to slip into an altered state, as well as project barriers that will inhibit future efforts. Value the sacredness of everything concerning the gift of sex—or of not feeling sexual. Sacred sex, marvelous as it is, isn't the be-all and end-all of spirituality, and its presence and desirability in your life should be held very, very lightly.

This last point can't be made too strongly. No matter how much you may want to experience sacred sex, it is truly no different than seeking "true love," happiness, or enlightenment. The way life is lived is actually more important than the goal ever will be. It's therefore wise to remember the evanescence of any objectives over the course of life. One participant sagaciously observes,

I used to be a drama junkie, and I really thought it was great to have dramatic experiences, but I may not have them anymore, and I don't care. It's like don't drink that second glass of wine because you'll feel it tomorrow, and you don't need it today to enhance your enjoyment of the first one.

So I don't worry about it anymore, and you know, it's really okay. I think it's having an appreciation for the overall lucidity and value of life with or without these experiences, what I call the Giotto effect, the way he could paint blues with that diaphanous kind of quality where they're blue but they're also so clear they're almost not even there. That's the way I sense and hold all these experiences and everything else now.

CHAPTER 12

Fruits of Transcendent Sex: Lovemaking and the Spiritual Path

It has provided a sense of connectedness as a human to something larger than myself in a very real and powerful way. . . . I am part of a fabric of a timeless, formless, yet reverential reality that's also very human and very natural. It's a transcendental, spiritual, loving place. I don't worry about scratching for a living anymore or much of anything, though I still do the responsible thing. I've learned to accept that the Universe will unfold and provide, and [this sexual event] was the beginning of all that for me. —Eagle

Do not give up on the possibility of always something greater, whatever that is. Do not give up this ineffable longing. I now know I wasn't crazy to want something of that magnitude. Number one: Yes, it's possible; the thing I wanted was real. Number two: It's not out there, it's in me. Number three: I'd rather have had even one experience of that order and never have it again than to have missed out on it because it woke me up to my own spiritual nature and what is possible. —Marta

IN ANCIENT TIMES, the mysteries and pleasures of the primal urge were revered as a blessing, as a way of worshiping, and as a

253

way of participating in the life force sustaining the cosmos. The earliest evidence comes from the prehistoric "Venus" figures of women's bodies with their exaggerated breasts, buttocks, bellies, and pubic mounds followed by fragments from oral traditions of gods, goddesses, and divine hermaphrodites copulating to bring forth the universe. Sex was a ceremonial act of great magic in which priests and priestesses dedicated themselves to hallowed rituals making love with initiates, worshipers, or surrogates of the holy ones. We will never know with any certainty what heights, transcendent or merely erotic, Mesopotamian priestesses, Mithraic priests, or initiates in the mysteries of Isis and Pan attained, but from the stories presented here, we can begin to appreciate the potential of lovemaking for direct spiritual experience.

My study suggests that this capacity exists in everyone. It is part of our human legacy. Transcendent sex isn't dependent upon spiritual expertise: atheists and agnostics are as apt to be swept away as devout believers or accomplished contemplatives. It certainly isn't dependent upon sexual prowess, since Spirit envelops even awkward lovers in the bedroom, as well as those immobilized by abuse. And it clearly isn't something conferred on a lucky few by superior, knowing partners or as a result of attaining the heights of "true love." Transcendent sex may be cultivated through practice, but it's also a sweet, wild, and perhaps random zephyr dancing through the universe, ready to catch and transform us at any time.

Perhaps its very availability and unpredictability is what made religions want to forbid and contain sex over the centuries of civilization. After all, what if everyone or anyone could participate directly in Spirit—without help, without rules, without striving to be "good," "religious," or even deserving, however any of these terms may be defined? What would it mean to know—not merely believe—that Spirit is always here, already and always available to every one of us, no matter what?

Personal, compelling glimpses of the greater reality tend to challenge the religious establishment. Except in tribal cultures where individual spiritual revelation is honored, religious authorities usually condemn experiences that bypass their rituals and ideologies. The idea that Spirit is everywhere and always with us endangers established religions of all kinds. It's the reason Western mystics have been ruthlessly stamped out, the reason Eastern paths narrow spiritual legitimacy to certain lineages of transmission, and the reason near-death experiences have been challenged by authorities guarding the bastions of religion and materialist science alike. The idea that we are already with and in Spirit, already loved, already perfected is a dangerous one. And perhaps it's even more threatening to think it can be realized from something as universal as sex.

Is It a Spiritual Path?

When I began this research, a number of my colleagues immediately said that transcendent sex couldn't be a legitimate spiritual path. If by that they meant a deliberate method for cultivating realization of the true nature of the greater reality, of knowing the Absolute, of becoming one with God, then no, it isn't. Not because it won't produce those outcomes: transcendent sex clearly can and does. But it isn't a deliberate practice. It's not quite so adventitious as near-death experiences— which, incidentally, produce very much the same results. Yet, as ravishing as it is and as much as people would love to think it could happen again and again, it didn't inspire such a craving that the people in this study, at least, began to dedicate themselves to a practice for cultivating transcendent sex. Of course, the intentional sexual paths, such as Taoism and Tantra, do indeed exist and have for centuries. In that respect, yes, transcendent sex is, or at least can be, a spiritual path for those who are looking for a discipline. It just so happens that with sex, Spirit can suddenly pull you into the dance before you are even aware that the music is playing.

If, on the other hand, the greater question is whether sex can be a path to realization—and whether its fruits compare favorably to other paths—the answer must be a resounding yes. And it does so in ways that exceed more unilateral approaches that center on emotion (ecstatic practices, including the charismatic and devotional), that center on the body (postural or movement methods, like yoga or sacred dance), or that center on the mind (prayer and meditation). Transcendent sex unifies *all* the dimensions of human experience. According to Paul, a rock musician who has meditated for many years, it's "way more intense than anything like meditation or making music. . . . Like the arc lights are turned on, much brighter, more clear, much more happening. . . . It's engaging the body . . . this really physical thing happening at the same time as a spiritual experience." Or Ranier, an accomplished meditator in many different traditions, who says, "Sex felt like six different meditation practices all . . . happening at the same time . . . this multifaceted thing [where] . . . all aspects of my being, emotionally, physically, sexually, intellectually, spiritually, were engaged, and it's the first time every aspect of me could feel completely engaged in an integral, transformative practice."

These experiences sanctify not only sex, but also embodiment, relationship, and participation in the material universe in a way many more ethereal practices don't. Time and time again, people emphasized the humble quality of transcendent sex, that somehow spirituality was *not* different from the human or material condition, *not* some evanescent state beyond bodies or beyond the real world, no matter how resplendent. Or, as Pascal says, it eases the need to work so hard for spiritual attainment even though he is still assiduous in his prayer and meditation practice:

> It becomes a marvelous reassurance for your other spiritual practices, like [assuring you] that there's a reason to continue. It's not just empty gesturing, and it points to the futility of grasping, which makes it easier not to worry about trying desperately to experience this. . . . It's easy to say now, "Well, if I don't ever get there through meditation, that's just fine. . . ." You understand that there's this enormous sea of loving Spirit you're bobbing in anyway, even when you're not trying to swim. It's holding you up all the time.

Perfection is here, now, in the world we know. We are already perfect, already in heaven, if we can but realize it. We are already at home in the universe.

Attainment

Ultimately the efficacy of any spiritual path, even of a one-time spiritual experience, is judged not by the Olympian feats required of practitioners, but by whether it transforms the person in ways that also serve the greater good. In this respect, the fruits of transcendent sex can surely be stacked against those of sanctioned spiritual avenues. They are also almost an exact parallel for the transformative effects of near-death experiences.[1]

The most skeptical materialists in my study said their understanding had changed as a result of these experiences; they could now appreciate that reality was far more mysterious and beautiful than they had previously comprehended. Many said their new knowledge had transformed their lives in terms of accelerating their personal growth.

Some left what they now regarded as limiting relationships. Others felt more empowered and confident. Some realized they had greater gifts of mental clarity or presence. Others acquired paranormal abilities to sense subtle energies, perform healing interventions, or access extrasensory forms of knowledge. Still others shed self-limiting beliefs or ceased dysfunctional habits. People made these changes often in the face of great resistance because their new values and behaviors disrupted culturally supported lifestyles or long-standing relationships that no longer served them well.

Experiencers now felt filled with a greater capacity for love, sometimes directed to a partner, but often including humanity at large as they began to be less critical, more accepting of the flaws and foibles of others. They became more self-accepting and full of compassion for humankind as a whole. At the same time, this opening to love tended to make people revere sex all the more and tended to reduce promiscuity. As one man said, "Sex is a way to have a dialogue with a woman, a full person, a way to talk in the fullness of who they are and who I am . . . a way to see the largeness of our being."

The sacralization of sex itself healed those who were taught to hate or feel ashamed of their bodies and desires. Norberto, whose Roman Catholic upbringing and Jesuit priesthood taught him that sex was a low, bestial urge to be despised, conquered, and transcended, now says:

> This is a way to go from repression to liberation. It really is a way to nurture my holiness, and . . . to honor my body, to recognize that, really, life is a continuum and that nothing is a lower-level

type of thing or higher-level type of thing. There is a connection between Spirit and the body.

There is a poem or song in Venezuela that was very inspiring for me about a farmer talking with a priest, and saying, "Well, Father, forgive me, but I think the skies are in the eyes of [my lover] and every night after I pray my Hail Mary, I find God in [her] womb."

I found this to be true. God is not only to be found in the solitude of your prayers or in doing social justice among poor people, but can be found in the womb of my partner. That song and that experience is my hidden music that I can always remember, like an overture of God's love for me.

And, finally, transcendent sex can pack so much transformational power that it becomes a "conversion" experience that reorients everything in a person's life. It convinces atheists and agnostics that Spirit is real, and it makes individuals change from one religious orientation to another. A number of participants were moved to undertake sacred vocations, including becoming transpersonal psychologists specializing in spiritual integration; becoming spiritual guides who help seekers on the quest; becoming healers using spiritual techniques; and entering the priesthood. Ardrigh, for instance, changed her entire life. After rejecting the repressive Christianity of her childhood and taking up a religious path that encouraged promiscuity, she met a partner with whom she fell deeply in love and began having transcendent sex. The immediate result was that she embraced monogamy, gave up her career, moved across the country to take graduate courses in transpersonal psychology, and then entered a Christian seminary. Her partner, Dee, who grew up in an agnostic household and doesn't identify with any particular faith to this day, says:

I'd been searching. I still am searching for something to believe in, and it made me feel connected with the universe, and in some way with whatever you want to call God. It's strange, because I always thought you'd have to get there through fasting and going to the mountaintop, but not through sex.

Of course, an experience like this has residuals. I'm a completely different person, I do feel good, and it wasn't like a finger that came down and hit me on the head and said, "You're changed." A lot of things have happened in the wake of this experience.

But what is different is that instead of conversing about God or reading about God, I can see God the way I can see blue. I can feel it in my body, that it really is true, and I'm a part of it, a part of it all.

There's no question Spirit can visit us with more force and power through sex than perhaps through any other venue. Opening the veil to apprehend the greater reality through sex changes people. Lovers, like other aspirants and near-death experiencers, understand the world in a different way and are transformed by that understanding, without the help, approval, or interference of priests, gurus, ideologies, or disciplines. Isn't it enough to honor what the experiencers themselves are saying? What authority do we need to interpret the value or validity of the miraculous things that have happened to them? These lovers' experiences speak for themselves.

Are we really offered a choice for spiritual realization in life: years of practice, dying, or sex? That may sound like a flippant question, but it warrants consideration. How would we live if we believed our bodies and the life-celebrating and potentially life-creating act of sex were the way? If we believed embodiment was no different from Spirit?

That is the message from these lovers. Transcendent sex is just that: going beyond the bodies that encapsulate our separate selves, our senses, our egos, our climaxes, and our suffering, but without leaving those bodies behind. They become the vehicle for a grace that transfigures all of the human condition. The nexus of Spirit and flesh illuminates and sanctifies all creation. It allows us to see everything, even our naked bodies and our physical desires, in the incandescence of perfect beauty, holiness, and love. As Blake said,

> Transcendent sex gives you a glimpse of the Divine always present in all of us. It . . . shows you: *This is what you are. This is where you are going. This is where you have always been.* It gives you a glimpse of what your true nature is. You open yourself to God, and you find that you are divine at the same time.

This is the gift that is ours. Not a command or a target for striving, but a potential, the heritage of our embodiment. There's no "other side" to get to, no part of ourselves we must deny. We're already at home in the universe if we can be at home in our bodies and in our hearts. How perfect that sex is the way that Spirit becomes life.

APPENDIX

The Research Study

THE OBJECTIVE OF THE RESEARCH was to identify the kind, quality, and range of altered states induced during sex using a heuristic, phenomenological inquiry. The plan was to recruit a sufficient number of articulate participants who could describe extremely subtle, subjective events. Since the range of experiences was unknown, however, there was no preconception of how many individuals would be adequate for this kind of survey. Males and females of any sexual preference, marital status, and ethnicity over the age of twenty-one were eligible, provided they were not taking psychotropic drugs or engaging in Tantra, Taoist sexual techniques, or similar erotic arts designed to bring about altered states or create expectations that might shape either the state or its interpretation.

Owing to the sensitive nature of the subject matter, recruiting was limited to personal and professional contacts and word of mouth. While this might introduce bias, it seemed infinitely preferable to advertising through print and electronic media for two reasons: 1) in the initial stages of the research, it might be difficult to spot hoaxes or fantasies; 2) to screen out responses from people whose sexual interests would be at variance with the intent of the study. Recruiting took the form of email solicitations through professional and personal networks, mentions of the study at lectures given in various institutions of higher learning, and referrals from these sources. Solicitations invited anyone who had had a "nonordinary, altered-state, mystical, or transcendent experience during sex with a partner." All self-selected volunteers were initially accepted, subject to the screening qualifications concerning drugs and altered-state practices.

Recruiting qualified people was not particularly difficult, despite the minimal wording. People who said they had never had nonordinary sex, whatever they imagined it might be, were absolutely certain. The momentary loss of self, time, and space during orgasm is so familiar that people identify this sensation as "ordinary." Only one volunteer's experience did not meet the criteria of alterations in consensus views of time, space, and agency that constitute standard clinical criteria for mental health and the baselines commonly used in consciousness research.

Volunteers were given informed consent forms outlining the protocols. In-person, semistructured interviews were the method of choice, and these were conducted in mutually agreed upon locations, typically the person's home or my home or office. In some cases, telephone interviews were the only feasible means of communication. Interviews lasted from thirty minutes to two and a half hours. They consisted of standard open-ended questions, followed by probes to develop promising lines of inquiry and to clarify. All interviews were audio recorded and transcribed. A few participants preferred to write their responses rather than be interviewed. Correspondence, including clarifying exchanges, occurred through hard copy and electronic media. Names and certain identifying details were altered to protect confidentiality.

The majority of the reports come from only one party rather than both persons in the relationship, since ordinarily only the one individual believed he or she had had transcendent experiences. But owing to the fact that most volunteers said they had never confided their experiences to their lovers for fear their partners would "make fun of," "not be interested in," or "not be receptive to" "spiritual stuff," it was impossible to determine whether their partners might also have been candidates. In other cases, only one person in the partnership was willing to be interviewed. Where both partners had transcendent experiences, these usually differed from one another.

All records were coded and thematically analyzed concerning the content, meaning, and structure of the experience. Themes were aggregated for clusters of meaning, and the results of the analysis were integrated into exhaustive descriptions that were then synthesized into fundamental structures, content, and meaning areas. Once the data became clearer, they were compared to phenomenological descriptions in the altered-state literature.

The Sample

The sample was purposive rather than representative for the reasons stated. Statistical validity was not a goal of this project. Furthermore, no attempt was made to include representatives of the full range of spiritual practices and beliefs, nor of the full range of sexual proclivities. The sample consisted of 91 heterosexual, homosexual, and bisexual men and women ranging in age from 26–70. An unusually large number for a qualitative study, especially a phenomenological one, this number was necessary once the full range of experiences began to emerge. Because it is so large, it permits limited quantitative analysis, though this was not an original aim of the study.

The sample comprised 53 (58%) females and 38 (42%) males (all percentages are rounded to the nearest one percent).

Seventy in the sample (77%) are heterosexual in their preference for partners (37 [41%] females; 33 [36%] males), followed by 14 (15%) homosexual (10 [11%] females, 4 [4%] males), and 7 (7%) bisexual (6 [6%] females,1 [1%] male). Marital status was not a useful category for various reasons: 1) individuals were sometimes speaking of past events unrelated to their present marital status; 2) if married, they were sometimes speaking of extramarital events; 3) those with long, rich histories had had experiences while single, married, divorced, or outside of marriage; 4) for same-sex connections, marital status was not necessarily a relevant descriptor.

The sample is predominantly Caucasian (80 [88%]; 49 [54%] females, 31 [34%] males). Other groups represent 12% of the total: 4 (4%) African American or with African American a primary racial identity (3 [3%] males,1 [1%] female); 5 (5%) Latino (3 [3%] males, 2 [2%] female); and 1 (1%) each Asian (female) and Native American (male). The sample was mainly from the United States with the largest proportion from California (44 [48%]); followed by New York (6 [7%]); with 4 (4%) each from Washington and Ohio; 3 (3%) each from Connecticut and Illinois; 2 (2%) each from Pennsylvania, Texas, and Virginia; and 1 (1%) each from Arizona, Colorado, the District of Columbia, Florida, Georgia, Louisiana, Maryland, Minnesota, North Carolina, New Hampshire, New Jersey, Oregon, Rhode Island, South Carolina, and West Virginia. In addition there were 2 (2%) respondents from Canada, 1 each from Ontario and Quebec; 2 (2%) from Europe, 1 each from Germany and Spain; and 2 (2%) from South America, 1 each from Venezuela and Brazil.

The sample is skewed by age and sex, with a disproportionately large number of women in their forties and men over 60. The average age of women is 41, and the average age of men is 46. The sample was divided into decade cohorts as a more useful way of identifying age differences for some of the later analyses. The cohort from age 20–29 comprised 10 females (11% of the sample) and 6 males (7%) for a total of 16 (18% of the sample). Nineteen people (21%) were aged 30–39 (12 women [13%] and 7 men [8%]). The largest cohort was people in their forties, representing 32 individuals for over a third of the total (35%). This group comprised almost twice as many women (22 [24% of the sample]) as men (10 [11%]). Seventeen people in their fifties comprised 19% of the sample (8 women [9%] and 9 men [10%]). The last cohort, representing people from age 60 through age 70, was predominantly male, consisting of 7 people (8%), of whom 6 (7%) were men.

The necessity of recruiting articulate participants who could verbalize the subtle dynamics of altered-state experiences combined with solicitation venues associated with institutions of higher learning greatly skewed the sample regarding education. Twenty-four (26%) had doctoral degrees (Ph.D., M.D., J.D.); 36 (40%) had master's degrees; 5 (5%) had some graduate education; 21 (23%) had bachelor's degrees; 2 (3%) had associate degrees; and 3 (3%) had high school diplomas. These individuals represent a wide range of occupations. Thirteen (14%) each were employed as counselors, ranging from psychiatrists to social workers, and as educators, including trainers, elementary school teachers, and graduate school professors. Eight (9%) were graduate students. Seven (8%) held management positions in manufacturing, service, and retail businesses, followed by 6 (7%) each who worked as consultants to business, as writers, and as scientists or health-care professionals. Media professionals, researchers, and body workers each comprised 4% of the sample. Three persons (3%) each were artists, entrepreneurs, finance professionals, and professionals in high-tech industry. Two (2%) were lawyers, and 2 (2%) worked in the nonprofit arena. One (1%) each was a hairdresser, a sales person, a retiree, and unemployed.

People were asked about the traditions in which they had been reared and their present religious orientations to ascertain whether they had spiritual beliefs that might have had a bearing on their interpretation of nonordinary states. The vast majority had mainstream Judeo-Christian backgrounds. Forty-two (46%) had been brought up in Protestant households. Of these 10 (11%) were not affiliated with any particular denomination, but the remainder were 7 (8%) each Baptist and Episcopalian, 6 (7%) Methodist, 4 (4%) Presbyterian, 3 (3%) Lutheran, 2 (2%) Unitarian, and 1 (1%) each Christian Science, Congregational, and Church of Latter-Day Saints (Mormon). Twenty-two individuals (24%) had been reared Roman Catholic, followed by 18 (20%) who had been reared in agnostic or atheist households. Seven people (8%) were Jewish. One person each (1%) had a background that was Buddhist and "eclectic."

As adults, most had shifted their spiritual orientation—some as a direct result of their sexual experiences—to follow less traditional paths, a finding that may follow sociological trends for these cohorts but is also consistent with research on persons who have experienced similar adventitious altered states, discussed below. Forty-three (47%) now consider themselves to be spiritual but to have an "eclectic" orientation. Only 16 (18%) are Christian (5 [5%] each "generally Christian" and Roman Catholic, 3 [3%] Episcopalian, and 1 [1%] each Congregational, Presbyterian, and Unitarian). Thirteen (14%) consider themselves atheist or agnostic, though 6 of these used theistic references throughout their narratives in describing their experiences, and another 3 talked of spiritual meanings or causes for their episodes. Eight (9%) are Buddhist; 4 (5%) Hindu/Yogic; 3 (3%) Pagan/Nature mysticism; and 1 (1%) each follow Islamic, "New Age," "Jewish mysticism," and Transcendental Meditation paths.

Finally, the frequency with which people experience transcendent sex was assessed. On a continuum from least to most frequent, 17 (19%; 12 men, 5 women) had had a single experience in a lifetime of sex, closely followed by 16 (18%; 6 men,10 women) who had had altered-state sex on a few occasions. The largest proportion, 29 people (32%; 5 men, 24 women) typically experienced transcendent sex within the context of a single relationship, followed by 15 people (16%; 9 men, 6 women) who were able to invite the experience successfully, regardless of partners, with some degree of frequency. Seven (8%; 3 men, 4 women) enjoyed transcendent sex with some regularity in multiple relationships, seemingly independent of a particular partner or set of conditions. A fortunate 7 (8%; 3 men, 4 women) said they seldom have ordinary sex; their habitual way of lovemaking features transcendent experiences. (In fact, they wondered why anyone would "bother" with ordinary sex.)

How adequate is this sample? For all the reasons noted, the selection was purposive, as well as unintentionally skewed by access, availability and time constraints. Thus, the findings, while suggestive, are not likely to cover the entire range of possible altered-state sexual experiences, but the degree of overlap among 91 cases suggests that this is an adequate first attempt to chart new territory. How trustworthy is the information? People may exaggerate or fantasize about their sex lives or avoid telling the entire story. A further difficulty exists when the events in question involve an altered state, which may be difficult to capture and convey in an ordinary state. This is complicated by the difficulty inherent in communicating phenomenological information verbally. Furthermore, the accounts represent self-reported subjective experience uncorroborated by anyone else. In the few cases where both partners were interviewed, one partner's experience frequently differed significantly from the other's.

Although 91 people were interviewed, their stories represent more than 91 events since a significant number of participants had more than one type of experience. It would be difficult to make any claims for the data if any single experience had to stand on its own. But when person after person describes the same type of event, the same feelings, and the same insights, patterns begin to emerge. Furthermore, these states have independent corroboration in the altered-state literature from diverse traditions.

Defining a Transcendent Sexual Experience

No simple definition of transcendent sex is possible. However, two factors consistently emerge from the narratives as characteristic of transcendent sex. The first, not surprisingly, is participation in an altered state that could not be ascribed to the use of chemicals or deliberate techniques. In altered states, the ordinary sense of time, space, and/or agency (in Cartesian-Newtonian or Formal Operations terms, or what is commonly thought of as consensus reality) is disrupted and transformed. Furthermore, the altered state includes an awareness of the lover, if only as a conduit, and is rooted in the union of the two whether or not actual intercourse between two human beings occurred. There must have been a sufficient sense of a living presence that the participant did not construe the event as a solitary, autoerotic experience.

These altered states are more or less independent of orgasm, which is considered a discrete state of its own. That was invariably true for the men: they entered an altered state that had no relationship to the timing or duration of their climax. It was true for the majority of the women, as well. For a few, however, being non- or mono-orgasmic during sex is either infrequent or impossible. These women were having a chain of orgasms that could last indefinitely, usually until their lovers withdrew the contact, although the events they described as transcendent had little or no (subjectively) discernible relationship to orgasm. (For most men and women in this sample, orgasm was either a nonevent or a problem relative to the transcendent sexual state. Some could not recall whether they had climaxed, they were so much more drawn into other events; some said orgasm became "irrelevant"; others found it an irritating distraction; and for a few, orgasm shattered or ended the state.)

The second factor that differentiates transcendent sex is the felt experience of a cosmic force engaging one or both lovers in the context of their lovemaking. This cosmic force is most often described in the terms reserved for Spirit: God, the Divine, the Oversoul, the Void, etc. Some described it spatially, as a place they could enter, a world of cosmic power, intelligence, and love. For some, the force is implied: it is the invisible source of their journeys into other realms, makes the other realms possible, or causes nonordinary events in consensus reality. The tendency to associate such experiences with the supernatural was marked.

Text from the narratives is presented verbatim. Direct quotations were modified in only two ways: to eliminate repetition of habitual but meaningless phrases ("you know," "know what I mean," etc.) and to create a meaningful chronology. Over the course of the interview, speakers often digressed or began talking about more than one transcendent experience in such a way that the narrative thread was broken. Probes also interrupted the flow. Where I have regrouped a significant number of sentences to keep related material together, I have secured the participant's permission to ensure the intended meaning was not misrepresented.

The Varieties of Transcendent Sexual Experience

Classification of complex human experiences is fraught with difficulties as any taxonomy is somewhat arbitrary and can never reflect the dynamics or richness of an individual's experience per se. I have previously classified these experiences using Grof's phenomenological altered-state cartography.[1] However, a classification by the other criteria structuring noetic experiences (time, space, and agency) reveals somewhat different relationships. For purposes of this study, the classification schemes, with the definitions provided below, are used to parse the experiences of this sample. They are presented in order of frequency of occurrence, not according to the breakdown of time, space, and agency. (In all of these experiences, normal left-hemisphere temporal awareness was disrupted, a finding so universal it is not reported, though other forms of temporal displacement or distortion are noted.)

Each type of experience is accompanied by a brief discussion of the data from the sample. Two sets of chi-square analysis were carried out on the only demographic factors that might have represented significant correlations. The first assessed the relationship between biological sex, the participants' experiences, and their reported outcomes. The second looked more closely at sexual preference within the female sample (the male nonheterosexual sample was too sparse). In neither case was there a significant relationship between the population characteristics and the experiences or results reported. This suggests that the quality of transcendent sex and its results are independent of biological sex and sexual preference.

Merging with the partner. The most frequently reported phenomenon was a sense of merging with the partner, noted by 43 people (47%; 24 women [45% of women], 19 men [50% of men]). Merging is defined as a dissolution of spatial boundaries, particularly the familiar somatic sense that the self is contained within the skin, accompanied by some sense of self-dissolution (loss of ego boundaries) to include the lover but not other objects in the environment. Merging includes a blending of agency into a state of unity and oneness, so that individuals are unable to say which person is causative. Frequently the here and now shrinks so that environmental cues vanish and the blended lovers become the focus of experience.

Kundalini. Kundalini experiences were defined as nonordinary percepts of energy fields in the absence of any discernible stimulus, especially sensations of heat, subtle force fields, light, and liquefaction, congruent with descriptions in various mystical traditions. These experiences occur in the here and now without significant alteration in the usual sense of self. Thirtyone people (34%; 20 females [38% of females], 11 males [29% of males]) reported kundalini-type experiences. These included not only sensations of heat, light, energy, and liquefaction, but forces that caused involuntary movements (*mudras* and *kriyas*), copious female ejaculate (*amrita*), and glossolalia—all well documented in various spiritual traditions.

The Third Presence. An experience of the Third is defined on the basis of a phenomenological distillation provided by Jungian analyst John R. Haule.[2] It is a felt sense of an autonomous, invisible, impersonal field or force that seems to exist between the two lovers and to arise from their mutuality. The Third is to some extent cocreated by their union, but it is also impervious to deliberate manipulation by either partner, and cannot be reduced to them or to their relationship. It seems to exhibit its own transpersonal intelligence. Experiences of the Third occur in the here and now with intact ego boundaries, and with the exception of the Third itself, normal causal relationships among agents. Twenty-seven people (30%; 17 women [32% of women], 10 men [26% of men]) reported experiences of the

Third. The sense of the Third was variously described as a nameable entity, such as the Holy Ghost; a hallowed atmosphere that produced beatific sensations and emotions; and a beneficent state of mind, likened to a state of grace. The Third was always experienced very positively and with some degree of volition in terms of the participant's willingness to engage the state.

Past lives. Twenty people (22%) felt they were transported back in time and space as other individuals in past-life experiences. They seemed to "see" or experience themselves moving through scenes belonging to previous eras and different locations. Fairly complete biographical details about the past-life personalities were available. These experiences were usually disturbing because the events of those lives had unhappy outcomes. Participants frequently had no insight at the time of the experience into parallels with their present relationships, no matter how obvious these connections might be to third parties or in retrospect (a finding congruent with past-life regression therapy). Eleven women (21% of women) and 9 men (24% of men) had past-life experiences, including some believing they were accessing the lives of their direct lineal ancestors.

Out-of-body experiences. OBEs involve retaining an intact sense of ego in the here and now but having the personal sense of self and agency leave the spatial confines of the body, which is still identified as part of the self. Ego is experienced continuously, without any break at the time of dislocation. People in fact are startled to find themselves outside their bodies. Displacement lacks a sense of locomotion and is discerned through a realistic change in visual vantage point to a location outside, and usually above the body. Twenty-three (25%) participants (13 women [25% of women], 10 men [25% of men]) experienced leaving their bodies, most often after coitus.

One with nature. Seventeen individuals (19%; 12 women

[22% of women], 5 men [13% of men]) reported a sense of becoming one with all of creation. This diffuse state involved a limited melting of ego boundaries to become a part of the fabric of all nature, usually described as a blending with all the flora, fauna, and life forces of the terrestrial world. Individuals remain in the here and now with an observing and active self that feels blended with other creatures and natural forces so that the "separate" quality of or status of humanity apart from other living beings vanishes.

Visions. Visions here are limited to subjective, nonvolitional imagery superimposed on the here and now and experienced by someone with intact ego boundaries. Visions usually consisted of other beings appearing in the room located at a distance from the partner (and thus distinct from *trespasso*). At times they occurred with unusual vividness and intrusiveness in the mind's eye, but appeared to be distinct from the person's deliberate mentation though they did not overtake the psyche. Thirteen persons (14%) saw human or supernatural imagery interpreted variously as angels, demons, or deities. This appears to be a predominantly female response, with 12 women (25% of women), and only 1 man (3% of men) reporting visions.

Clairsentience. Closely related to past lives in terms of the information contained in the experience, though phenomenologically distinct, clairsentience refers to a sudden preternatural knowledge of "the truth." In clairsentience, a revelation that seems to come from nowhere arises fully developed without any apparent relationship to the passing events or any stimulus in the environment. People variously described this as "knowing everything," "realizing the truth," and having the "scales fall from their eyes." Typically the knowledge revealed concerns previously hidden dynamics of the lovers' relationship, and a sudden ability to comprehend exactly what is going on, however subtle or complex ("the true nature of things"), which is usually construed in a negative light ("it will never work"). Despite the fact that the revelation is typically saddening—indeed, often hopeless—people simultaneously sense an inner strength and resilience that enable them to make "the right decisions." Thirteen people (14%; 6 women [13% of women] and 7 men [18% of men]) reported clairsentience.

Unio mystica. Unio mystica is the nondual dissolution of time, space, and agency sensed as a complete identification with the absolute principle that represents All Being (usually described as God). It is a formless, dimensionless, infinite awareness typically suffused with light and ecstatic bliss as described in Western mysticism. It was reported by 11 individuals (12%; 7 women [13% of women] and 4 men [11% of men]).

Telepathy. Telepathy, the ability to access the unspoken thoughts and feelings of others, was reported by 9 individuals (10%; 4 women [8% of women] and 5 men [13% of men]). Respondents indicated that they had verified their telepathic insights with the person involved, who was usually the partner.

The Void. Impersonal nonduality or Void experiences constitute a nondual dissolution of time, space, and agency sensed as the primordial emptiness that underlies and also constitutes the cosmos. It is a formless, dimensionless, infinite awareness that may or may not be accompanied by light and bliss, as described in Eastern spiritual traditions. Nine persons (10%; 6 women [11% of women], 3 men [8% of men]) reported the Void.

Shapeshifting. Shapeshifting, as it is used here, refers to a form of possession, in which individuals in the here and now have an alteration in their sense of self so that the ego seems to be taken over by another, typically an animal, but sometimes a plant. Mentation is altered with such vividness that the body itself is also experienced as changing in form, sensation, and appearance. Nine people (10%; 6 women [11% of women], 3 men

[8% of men]) felt that they were involved in shapeshifting forms of possession.

Channeling. Channeling, as it is used here, refers to the sense of having the psyches, especially the emotional experiences of a nameless group of people, pour through the individual (similar to Grof's group identification or group consciousness).[3] Such experiences occur in the here and now without disruption of the ego but with a sense of identification with the group's experience and awareness. Channeling was reported by 8 people (9%; 5 women [9% of women], 3 men [8% of men]).

Transports. Transports describes spatial dislocation in which someone with intact ego functioning seems to be displaced to another location through a combination of altered visual imagery and somatic sensations of relative weightlessness (floating) or forward motion. During lovemaking, transports are typically accompanied by feelings of bliss. The experience of transport may be a female tendency. They were reported by 7 people (8%), of whom 6 were women (11% of women).

Magical connections to nature. Magical connections with entities in the natural world concern a sense of nonordinary relationship to plants, animals, and natural forces, especially an ability to participate in shared agency with those entities beyond the normal limitations of encapsulated egoic awareness. Plants and animals are experienced as having their own intelligence, which can now be entrained with that of the participant. Natural forces, especially the earth, may be perceived to be animate. Seven people (8%; 3 women [6% of women], 4 men [11% of men]) said they could communicate with animate, and participate in inanimate, entities in nature.

Trespasso. Six (7%; 4 women [8% of women], 2 men [5% of men]) experienced *trespasso,* an involuntary, here-and-now vision of another head, or a succession of heads (usually but not always human) superimposed on the lover's head. The hallucination, a recognized phenomenon in many traditions, typically does not extend below the partner's shoulders.

Deity possession. Five people (6%; 3 women [6% of women], 2 men [5% of men]) reported a sense of being possessed by divinities who overtook and displaced their psyches in the here and now. These forces were invisible, but they carried a distinct sense of supernatural personification identified with fierce archetypal beings, such as Kali, Pan, Dionysius, and the like.

Results of the Experiences

Respondents were asked whether they felt these experiences had affected them, and if so, how. Their answers were grouped into several general categories: spiritual awakening, personal growth, enhanced relationships, an expanded understanding of the nature of reality, the sacralization of sex, and personal healing.

Spiritual awakening. Forty people (44%; 23 women [43% of women], 17 men [43% of men]) reported a radical shift in their religious or spiritual beliefs as a result of their sexual experiences. Some self-identified atheists or agnostics prior to having a transcendent episode became convinced that Spirit (however understood) is a real force in the cosmos, and many of them took up spiritual vocations or adopted formal religious beliefs. Others converted from a previously held belief system to a new one.

Personal growth. The next most frequent outcome was personal growth, cited by 39 people (43%; 26 women [51% of women] and 13 men [34% of men]). Personal growth refers to positive changes in an individual's life or way of thinking as a result of a transcendent sexual experience. For many, this involved discovering unusual, even paranormal, capacities, such as the ability to sense subtle energies, or conducting intuitive diagnostics and healing through visualization and laying on of hands. For others, personal growth involved the strength and determination to make positive alterations in their lives, including changing professions, shedding limiting relationships, ceasing dysfunctional behavior, and discarding self-limiting beliefs, often despite formidable hindrances.

Enhanced relationships. A large proportion (23 or 25%; 12 women [23% of women], 11 men [29% of men]) reported significant improvements in their ability to relate to others. The primary relationship enhancement occurred with the partner, characterized by increased feelings of love and tolerance so that personal flaws or foibles no longer impeded a full and abiding appreciation of the person. It was as though lovers could "hold" a beatific yet unvarnished vision of the partner that included both negative and positive attributes in a loving way. Additionally, many of these respondents reported a "trickle-down" effect from the partnership that radiated increased tolerance and compassion to others. Participants said they were more loving in everyday transactions, a quality that was often related to greater self-acceptance.

Comprehending a greater reality. Sixteen persons (18%; 10 women [19% of women], 8 men [21% of men]) said their understanding of reality had changed drastically. This outcome category included a number of persons who were reluctant to ascribe a spiritual motive force to their experiences, but who frankly said they could not account for what had happened short of the supernatural. In the wake of their sexual episodes, they reported a sense of awe and mystery about the workings of the universe, regardless of attribution.

Sacralized sex. Twelve people (13%; 9 women [18% of women], 3 men [8% of men]) said that their experiences had convinced them that the act of sex was holy in and of itself.

This finding was usually associated with people who said their enculturation about sex had been repressive and negative, but it also included those with previously promiscuous attitudes about sex who determined to limit their relationships out of respect for what the act came to represent to them.

Healing. Finally, 8 people (9%; 5 females [9% of women], 3 males [8% of men]), including all 7 in the sample who reported histories of sexual abuse, said they had achieved dramatic levels of personal healing concerning sex and sexual issues. They reported an absence of pathologic symptoms, including vaginismus, dissociation, and numbness, as well as a greatly increased ability to enjoy sex, remain present and engaged, and have orgasms.

Relationships Among the Data

As much of the interview data merely indicated the presence of an experience rather than a measurable, continuous variable, traditional statistical analysis was unhelpful. Instead, a statistical technique called correspondence analysis, which deals specifically with dichotomous variables, was used to clarify relationships. Correspondence analysis is an exploratory technique related to principal components analysis, which finds a multidimensional representation of the association between the row and column categories of a two-way contingency table. This technique finds scores for the row and column categories on a small number of dimensions that account for the greatest proportion of the chi association between the row and column categories, just as principal components account for maximum variance. For graphic display, two or three dimensions are typically used to give a reduced rank approximation to the data. Correspondence analysis is designed to show how the data deviate from expectation when the row and column variables are independent in ways that permit patterns to emerge in large data sets that cannot be helpfully represented using association plot and mosaic display methods. It shows only the row and column categories in the two or three dimensions that account for the greatest proportion of deviation from independence.

While the results of this analysis are not predictive in the statistical sense, they nonetheless shed light on complex interrelationships among the data. The data set consisted of the demographic variables, the experiences, and the outcomes reported. In order to examine the relationships among the data, the correspondence procedure was used to create a two-dimensional scatter-plot scaling the input data based on differences and similarities among the participants and their reported experiences and outcomes. While the output from the correspondence analysis used for plotting the position of the variables does not directly translate to a simple statistic, eigenvalues comprising the multidimensionality within the selected variables were translated into two axes. The analysis produced three distinct groupings of the data.

The largest grouping was a cluster comprising experiences of the Void, *unio mystica,* and the Third with a demographic factor of frequency of experiences with one partner and an outcome of sacralizing sex. Such a grouping hints at subtle relationships among experiences having an unquestionably spiritual content in terms of their phenomenology. It also suggests that there may be some relationship between spiritual phenomenology and having transcendent experiences primarily within the context of a single relationship, as well as the inclination to believe that such experiences convey a hallowing of the sexual act.

The second cluster comprised kundalini, merging with the lover, and past lives with the greater frequency of enjoying transcendent experiences with a number of partners or being able to invite them to occur with some success, and an outcome of personal growth. This cluster suggests that with a greater ability to generate transcendent episodes, individuals have experiences whose content may be more related to relationship with the lover (over half the kundalini experiences involved both partners in some way) and less oriented to overt spirituality. It also suggests that these episodes do less to change belief systems and more to empower individuals to make positive changes in their lives. This is an intriguing association since these participants felt a greater ability to produce their transcendent sexual experiences themselves, which suggests a sense of greater personal power.

The third and last cluster of characteristics grouped channeling, shapeshifting, *trespasso,* deity possession, transports, and becoming one with creation with always having transcendent sex but no particular outcome. This grouping suggests that people who habitually have transcendent episodes are not as moved by these experiences to change in a particular way. This conclusion may not be too surprising since the experiences they tend to enjoy have no marked spiritual content and tend to take place with relatively less disruption in the dimensions affecting normal, waking consciousness.

Discussion

The objectives of this study were to identify and map the varieties of transcendent sexual experiences in a heuristic way.[4] Without belaboring those areas, it is clear that the data also suggest fruitful areas for future research.

Naturally it is impossible to generalize much about the sample, which was extremely biased for race, age, and education. Regarding demographic factors, there was nothing to suggest that heterosexual or homosexual, mainstream or specialized sex practices have anything to do with the ability to generate an altered state. Nor do there appear to be any significant differences concerning the demographics of the people who can have these experiences. In the first place, with the exception of kundalini, visions and transports, this small sample suggests that there are no major differences between male and female experiences of transcendent sex, indicating that physiological changes associated with differentials in arousal curves may not be causal. This is an interesting supposition, supported on the one hand by the fact that there was no discernible relationship between orgasm (male or female) and the altered states produced (with the possible exception of out-of-body experiences and past-life experiences, which showed some tendency to occur postcoitus). But on the other hand, it may also be somewhat mitigated by the indication that sustained high levels of arousal are necessary to induce these states since participants, on the whole, reported having sustained bouts of sex lasting hours or even days, which is also consistent with Taoist and Tantric practice.

It is likely that other factors, such as the capacity for absorption may play a large role in capacity for transcendent sex.[5] In the altered-state literature there is widespread speculation that certain types of developmental abnormalities and childhood trauma may predispose people to a capacity for adventitious nonordinary experiences. Additionally, the data presented in this study support the notion that the activation of primal psychological complexes sets up transcendent sex in some individuals.

It is surprising that religious belief and skill in contemplative practice seemed to have no relationship to the kind of experience individuals had. This finding runs counter to the imagery and interpretation characteristic of near-death experiences, which are idiosyncratic but generally congruent with broad cultural influences.[6] It also runs counter to the entire body of developmental theory, especially models associated with transpersonal psychology and contemplative paths, which postulate that people who have consolidated their development and ability to sustain certain states tend to access those levels in preference to ones that are either more or less complex.

It is also surprising that there were no strong relationships among the demographics of the individuals who had similar experiences, for instance, those who had channeling, shape-shifting, and possession experiences. The subtle associations with outcome and frequency indicated by the correlation analysis suggest further avenues of research, but they would not seem to account for predictive factors.

The relatively greater association of spiritual content with regularly occurring transcendent sex in a single relationship, compared to the two groups of relatively more frequent and more "ordinary" altered states, suggests an interesting but puzzling relationship: Why is it that people who enjoy transcendent sex more often tend to have experiences that maintain more of the normal dimensions of time, space, and agency?

It seems clear that sex is as much a trigger for altered states as other, more recognized means, such as meditation, trance dancing, psychedelics, etc., an argument I have put forward elsewhere.[7] I suspect that most of the full range of commonly recognized altered states can be produced under sexual conditions.

Finally, there are striking parallels between outcomes produced by these adventitious sexual experiences and those produced by near-death experiences, probably the best researched adventitiously occurring altered state in modern times.[8] The "little death" of orgasm metaphor aside, sex and death occur under completely different physiological conditions, with the possible exception of endorphin release, though brain chemistry during sex is not very well understood. It has been widely shown that near-death experiences occur under varying physiological conditions that are in no way predictive of either the extent of the NDE, nor of the most pronounced outcomes. Without overdrawing the connection, it seems that both these adventitious altered states: a) are typically interpreted as having at a minimum existential and metaphysical significance that is more often than not interpreted as coming from a source that can be described as Spirit; b) usually result in positive, life-enhancing personal change, regardless of their specific content; and c) tend to increase an individual's inclination to spirituality but outside the confines of most formal religious ideologies. The potential for the application of such knowledge is vast.

The Participants

The following table lists participants by pseudonym, sex, age, and occupation. The occupational descriptions are the ones given by the participants, not the categories created for them later in working with the data analysis. In a very few instances, participants requested that their occupation be disguised as they felt, that along with all the other demographic information requested, it might compromise their confidentiality.

PARTICIPANT	SEX	AGE	OCCUPATION
Adele	F	28	Student
Ann	F	44	Teacher
Ardrigh	F	34	Manager of conference services
Armand	M	37	Library assistant
Artemis	F	28	Music therapist and graduate student
Aurelia	F	53	Management consultant

Austin	M	24	Social services
Bengt	M	31	Director of a continuing education department
Betty	F	45	Organization development consultant
Blake	M	63	Retired
Blythe	F	43	Consultant
Carolyn	F	45	Spiritual healer
Cindy	F	41	Publishing
Clara	F	28	Teacher
Colleen	F	36	Graduate student
Cougar	M	49	Lawyer
Dee	F	26	Manager of a coffee roasting company
Dick	M	49	Executive director for a non-profit organization
Dion	M	63	Professor
Donald	M	27	Unemployed
Donna	F	27	Graduate student
Doris	F	55	Teacher
Doug	M	60	Psychologist
Eagle	F	47	Consultant in adult education
Elaine	F	45	Librarian
Elizabeth	F	54	Artist
Ellen	F	40	Marriage and family counselor
Esteban	M	38	Grant writer
Esther	F	46	Psychologist and educator
Eve	F	39	Graduate student
Francine	F	36	Maid service owner
Gertrude	F	26	Student
Gina	F	49	Counselor
Gloria	F	33	Store owner
Gordon	M	31	Biotech consultant
Gwen	F	46	Business executive
Hamilton	M	44	Radio station management consultant
Harold	M	55	Professor
Horst	M	42	Manager of logistics
Janice	F	29	Health insurance administrator
Jason	M	67	Social justice researcher
Jean	F	52	Therapist
Jill	F	32	Statistics instructor
John	M	65	Psychologist and teacher

Jorge	M	29	Assistant professor
Kali	F	40	Psychologist
Katherine	F	43	Organization development executive
Keiko	M	43	Advertising program manager
Keith	M	61	Physician
Kim	F	43	Sales manager
Kirill	M	46	Physicist
Kristen	F	34	Organization development consultant and teacher
Kyle	M	29	Conference organizer and writer
Laura	F	56	Documentary film maker and author
Lea	F	69	Teacher
Leona	F	34	Counselor and massage therapist
Lilah	F	45	Graduate student
Lucky	F	50	Special education teacher
Lynn	F	41	Trainer
Margot	F	43	Sex counselor
Marta	F	51	Writer
Martin	M	48	Artist
Matthew	M	58	Business consultant and author
Maureen	F	30	Business coaching
Max	M	50	Inventor and entrepreneur
Mike	M	53	Professor
Ming	F	29	Writer and editor
Muntu	M	53	Body worker
Nanette	F	38	Body worker and graduate student
Natasha	F	28	Graduate student
Nell	F	44	Housewife and counselor
Norberto	M	50	Trainer and organization development consultant
Norman	M	24	Writer
Opal	F	49	Computer business manager
Pascal	M	41	Management consultant
Paul	M	47	Musician and nonprofit health-care executive
Rachel	F	35	Graphic designer and technical writer
Ranier	M	27	Graduate student
Reginald	M	37	Association executive and writer/producer
Rhonda	F	29	Broker's assistant
Richard	M	48	Psychic and counselor

Roland	M	38	Professor
Sabu	F	43	Acupuncturist
Sandra	F	31	First-line supervisor
Shaka	M	54	Investment management consultant and lawyer
Steven	M	59	Lawyer and writer
Suzette	F	50	Healthcare administrator
Terry	F	55	Writer and organization development consultant
Vivian	F	49	Hypnotherapist and internet entrepreneur
Yolanda	F	45	Hairdresser
Zebediah	M	39	Teacher and counselor

Endnotes

Introduction: Discovering Transcendent Sex

1. Kovacs (1989, p. 9). English, like most modern languages, has no word for people who engage in ritual acts of sacred sex, reducing translators of ancient languages to inappropriate circumlocutions suggesting a low-status occupation quite at variance with these individuals' roles in their societies (see, for instance, Roberts [1992]).
2. The religions associated with tribal and clan-based societies (usually referred to today as "indigenous"), in contrast to the religions associated with civilization, generally did not concentrate authority but continued to honor distributed individual experience and to recognize sex as a legitimate avenue to spiritual power.
3. Especially in Nyaya, Yoga and Vedanta Hinduism. Classic Sanskrit literature emphasizes the need for the suppression of sexual desire in order to reach salvation. Desires or attachments are the major barriers to spiritual enlightenment, and sex is considered one of the greatest of these. Sanskrit texts on sex, such as the *Kama Sutra*, are not, as many people think, guides for mystical lovemaking so much as practical handbooks for the average householder. Significantly, strong carnal desires are considered unseemly, and by middle age, respectable people should largely be free of sexual urges (Kakar, 1994). Although Hinduism incorporates yogic practices that utilize the body as an instrument in reaching enlightenment, most practices emphasize increasing control over the body as a sign of spiritual attainment. A number of them are essentially ascetic. They incorporate austerities, especially the prohibition of sex. The austerities found in Hinduism are also found in Hinayana and Mahayana Buddhism, as well as Jainism (Pagels, 1979).

4. Tannahill (1980); Faure (1998); Van Gulik (1974).
5. White (2000); van Gulik (1974); Parrinder (1996); Tannahill (1980).
6. Van Gulik (1974); Faure (1998).
7. Eskildsen (1998); Saso (1997); Parrinder (1996).
8. By the time of Jesus, there were disagreements among different religious groups about sex. Sexual practices not leading to procreation (for instance, acts or positions that might inhibit conception, or remaining married to an infertile woman) were undesirable, if not actually forbidden. The Essenes practiced restraint (a few extremist groups were celibate), while the Pharisees enjoyed sexual pleasure within the restrictions their religious law permitted (Pagels, 1979; Tannahill, 1980). About 1200 C.E., when Kabbalic Judaism gained ground in some areas, traditional male seekers were adjured to aspire to Shekinah, the feminine personification of God's presence, represented in the earliest Kabbalistic records as God's daughter whom he gives to the world as its wife (Hoffman, 1992; Ariel, 1988). Shekinah is more broadly understood to be the feminine aspect of God as Divine Mother and protector of the world. The language of many of these texts graphically describes how the sexual union of the celestial King and Queen sustains the cosmos (Waite, 1960).
9. For Hasidic Jews, the modern-day sect most closely aligned with Kabbalism, sex outside the Sabbath and certain other days of sanctification should be avoided, and men are adjured not to linger in sensuality (Schacter-Shalomi, 1991).
10. The aspostle Paul surpassed this stance, recommending celibacy for serious spiritual seekers, even in marriage (I Corinthians 7:1–35). The majority of orthodox Christians in the first and second centuries (continuing to the present day) interpreted the Genesis story as a moral tale in which Adam and Eve were separated from God in the Garden of Eden by temptation leading to carnal knowledge. Elaine Pagels in *Adam, Eve, and the Serpent* traces the enduring repression of sexuality in the Judeo-Christian tradition back to the first four centuries of the Common Era.
11. He promoted the idea that during sex, irrational passions and desires displace God, reason enough to discourage sex for spiritual seekers. Responding to his and St. Paul's injunctions, some pious couples married for social, political or economic reasons but remained virgins. Sex for reasons other than procreation was sinful; so was lust, the mere thought of sex (Pagels, 1988; see also Murray, 1991; Ware 1997; Louth, 1997; Tripp, 1997; Weisner-Hanks, 2000; Brown, 1988).
12. In the Gnostic Gospels, Jewish Pseudepigrapha, Christian Apocrypha, and the Dead Sea Scrolls, God retains both male and female attributes, for instance. The sacred feminine is variously part of the original dual-sexed Creator, or the Divine Mother; or the Holy Spirit who, with God the Father, engendered Jesus; or Sophia, divine Wisdom who enlightened the

Creator (see, for instance, the Apochryphon of John, Gospel of Philip and Gospel of the Hebrews). Augustine's opposition to Gnosticism and sex, and his influence over what became Roman orthodox Christianity, set the tone for Western Europe and the countries colonized by Western European nations. However, Gnostic ideas continued to crop up, as did mystical sexual experiences, even among the orthodox. The mixing of spiritual and sexual imagery can be found in the writings of any number of Christian mystics.

13. Mohammed's astonishing sexual prowess and virility was at first considered a sign of his spiritual attainment, but later Moslem scholars were embarrassed by the stories (cf., Parrinder, 1996). Even some mystics recommended celibacy as a spiritual path (notably Ibn'Arabi whose influence on Sufism continues; see, for example, Schimmel, 1997). However, other mystics take a different path like the Baul contemplatives who liken the spiritual relationship between Allah and Mohammed, between Allah and the spiritual seeker, and between the seeker and his or her teacher to the love between a man and a woman "whose body is the temple of Allah and within whom is the unwritten Qu'ran" (McDaniel, 1989, p. 164. This is a reference to the belief that the Qu'ran contains thirty sections, but that there are ten remaining sections, unwritten ones that may be found in the experience of the fakirs.) One Baul mystic, Ali Rajah, writes that ritual practice cannot be performed without a woman.

14. For instance, the female and male principles of yin and yang have never disappeared from Taoist thought and have been incorporated into other Eastern traditions. They are abstract spiritual forces that interpenetrate all of manifest creation, together forming the Tao. Explicit depictions of the *yoni* (vagina) and *lingam* (penis) are among the most numerous sacred objects found in contemporary Indian religion. These symbols represent many levels of spiritual meaning current in Hinduism and Buddhism both, ranging from the celebration of human lovemaking to the arrival of the individual soul into the World Soul (Atman) or nirvana, and also the presence of nirvana in the world of life and death. Male and female aspects of God are still present in mainstream Western religions as well. The Bible's Song of Solomon is an ecstatic and frankly erotic celebration of sexual love in a text sacred to Jews, Christians and Moslems (for an interesting contemporary interpretation seeking to redeem this heritage, see Carr, 2003). The rabbinical teachings consider sex within marriage to be a holy act, and Jews are still expected to enjoy sex regularly as a blessed responsibility of conjugal life. The mystical union of Jesus and the Church as the Bride of Christ in Christianity clearly has sexual overtones. The Qu'ran, with its explicit descriptions of physical delights, is a much more sexually oriented holy book than the Bible (see, for example, 2:25, 3:15, 4:57). In fact, Islam considers human sexuality a natural and healthy drive in men and women

alike, with the Qu'ran condemning those who take vows of celibacy for spiritual purposes (57:27), a practice also sanctioned in other Islamic literature. Mohammed's sexual prowess was considered evidence of his supernatural capabilities by early Moslems. And in Islam, marital sex, as in Judaism, has a spiritual significance. The mystical branches of all these religions are even more frankly sexual, even if only metaphorically.

15. Publications include Wade (1999, 2000a, 2000b, 2001).

16. Although my study was a purposive rather than a representative sample, informal observations suggested that these numbers are probably about accurate, perhaps even somewhat conservative. In a study of 536 women, 86 (16.1%) seemed to have some sort of nonordinary experience during sex (Scantling and Browder, 1993).

17. Sexual altered states of course also occur during masturbation (e.g., Bonheim, 1997 and arguably much of the Tantric literature), and such instances were uncovered in the course of this study. Virtually all of the masturbation literature suggests involvement with a fantasized other. Such cases were, however, outside the scope of this research. In this study sexual contact with nonhuman partners was adventitious and outside any intentional invitation to lovemaking.

18. These findings do not exclude the influence of hormonal brain chemistry changes associated with arousal or high emotion that could be triggering the experience in either sex.

19. In all likelihood, this would be not be true for esoteric spiritual practices, such as Vajrayana Buddhism, Tantra and perhaps Taoist sex that combine sexual and meditative techniques.

1. Fireworks, Energy, and Light: Experiencing the Body Electric

1. See, for example, van Gulik (1974) and Tannahill (1980). Sexual intercourse is a spiritual practice that permits lovers to achieve yin-yang harmony. Classic texts on the art of making love usually begin with remarks about the cosmic significance of sexual intercourse and then go on to detail the recommended techniques and positions to bring it about. The original texts dating from the Han dynasty (206 B.C.E.–24C.E.) Are no longer extant, but it is believed that substantial portions of them are preserved in the Japanese *I-shin-po* and later Chinese texts, such as the *Fang-nei-chi* and *Chi'i-pien*. The most complete English-language discussion is found in van Gulik (1974). Modern Taoist books contain much the same kind of information (e.g., Wang, 1986; Reid, 1989).

2. "Crazy wisdom" has a revered place in some Eastern traditions. See, for example, the research on non-Westernized Bengali saints (McDaniel, 1989) whose divine madness included the violation of some of the most basic tenets of Hinduism. The fundamental philosophy of Vajrayana sexual spirituality, which contains many elements of earlier indigenous religions, is very similar to that of Tantra.

3. See, for instance, Tantraloka-Ahnika, 3.

4. Sex is often one of the first attributes associated with a deity, and among the earliest recorded creation myths are stories in which the Creator forms the two sexes out of his or her own hermaphroditic body. In the Norse cultures, for instance, this Divine Hermaphrodite is a giant called Ymir, from whose body the cosmos was made, along with the first man and woman. In China, the Great Original was a woman, T'ai Yuan, roughly equivalent to Mother Nature, who combined the principles of masculinity and femininity (yang and yin) in her being, embodying the harmonious essence of Nature itself (the perfect Tao). She not only created human beings in both sexes, but also arranged the workings of the universe according to the principles of yin and yang. In the first version of the creation story given in the Bible, God is represented as encompassing male and female principles and blessing the sexual union of humanity: So God created [hu]man[kind] in his own image . . . male and female he created them. And God blessed them, and God said unto them, Be fruitful and multiply, and replenish the earth. . . . (Genesis 1:27–8). Interestingly, there may indeed be some reason to associate hermaphrodism with heightened spiritual gifts, a connection still recognized in Native American and Eastern cultures, among others where transgendered individuals have enjoyed institutionalized spiritual roles for centuries. One contemporary study suggests that such individuals, without any training or knowledge of these cultures, may demonstrate unusually high levels of the paranormal, healing, and creative abilities associated with adepts (Sell, 2001).

5. They also are associated with altered states occurring in nonreligious contexts, such as during holotropic breathwork and network chiropractic.

6. A spate of popular books has come out in recent years concerning nonvolitional kundalini openings and shamanic initiations, both of which are characterized by unusual percepts and sensations (e.g., Hufford, 1982; Wolf, 1991; Adler, 1995).

7. Stanislav and Christina Grof were instrumental in creating the Spiritual Emergence Network (SEN) in 1980, a nonprofit information and referral service designed as an alternative to the services usually presented to people experiencing nonordinary states of consciousness (being drugged and locked in a mental ward). Their book, *Spiritual Emergency: When Personal Transformation Becomes a Crisis*, is a classic.

2. The Good Gods and Grace:
It Was a Religious Experience

1. Judges 13:3–25; Luke 1.
2. 1 Kings 19:5–18; Matthew 28:2–9.
3. See, for example, Moody (1975, 1977) and Ring (1980, 1984).
4. Ring (1980, pp. 63–66).
5. Barks (1987, p. 4). The reference is to Matthew 18:20, where Jesus says, "For where two or three are gathered together in my name, there am I in the midst of them."
6. Zimmerman and McCandless describe the Third as both "a distinctive state of awareness associated with the transcendent dimension of [a] relationship" and "something unconditional and ultimately mysterious that is not of the ordinary world" (1998, p. 114), yet they emphasize the material help the Presence provides.
7. Acts 9:1–22.

3. The Spirit of Gaia:
Supernatural Connections with Earthly Life

1. See, for example, classic sources, such as Eliade (1951/1974), Kalweit (1988), and Walsh (1990) as well as Devereux (1992) and Wolf (1991).
2. Grof (1985, 1998) reports that modern-day subjects ingesting hallucinogens have experiences of phylogenetic evolution, in which they undergo identification with a Darwinian progression of species, including that of single-celled organisms, coelenterates, mollusks, etc. that do not appear in indigenous spirituality. He and his subjects interpret these experiences as reliving their phylogenetic biological development as well as their ontogenetic past lives extending back to the origin of life on earth. Notably, many of these experiences tend to occur during sex, according to Grof, though his subjects were reporting mainly on sexual activity involving hallucinogens. None of the respondents in this book reported any sense of an evolutionary schema of life-forms. Given some of the current revision of biological evolutionary theory, Grof's and his subjects' Darwinian interpretations do not contribute to validity claims so much as they raise questions about the degree of enculturation factoring into these accounts.
3. Wolf (1991, p. 192).
4. See, for instance, Frazer (1951) and Fenandez-Armesto (2002).

4. The Many Faces of Love:
The Partner in Transformation,
Transfiguration and Transcendence

1. Exodus 34:29; Matthew 17:2, Mark 9:2; Matthew 9:28.
2. Lewis (1946, p. 30).
3. Lewis (1946, p. 107).
4. See, for example, Grof (1975, pp. 175–179) and Maurer (1994, p. 459).

5. By Love Possessed:
Shapeshifting, Channeling, and Possession

1. For overviews, see for example, Eliade (1951/1974), Walsh (1990), and Kalweit (1988). There is suggestive evidence that the ritual use of psychoactive plants was part of these sacred ceremonies, promoting the conjunction between human and animal spirits during altered states. Ayahuasca and ibogaine, for instance, typically engender altered states characterized by animal imagery.
2. See, for example, Wolf (1991), Walsh (1990), Eliade (1951/1974), and Kalweit (1988).
3. Stanislav Grof's research (1975) of people on psychoactive substances, especially LSD, is useful here. He makes clear distinctions between individuals who experience a symbolic animal transformation and those who experience a genuine identification with an animal. In the former, persons usually interpret their shapeshifting to be a symbolic message from their unconscious (or from a divine source, such as their Higher Self or Spirit) concerning personality or life issues. Sexual shapeshifting seems to resemble these more symbolic representations. However, in genuine animal identification, according to Grof, individuals reject any metaphorical interpretation of their experience, insisting they truly *were* the animal. Such persons may demonstrate a detailed knowledge of the animal's anatomic characteristics, habits, eating and mating patterns that greatly exceeds their education in biology and would likely only be known by specialists.
4. Although other scholars have suggested that it means "bare" as in naked, citing references to warriors advancing without body armor, artwork showing naked warriors, and references to nude ritual trance dancing before battles.
5. For instance, in the Icelandic sagas, *Egils Saga Skallagrimssonar* and *Hrolf's Saga*.

6. *Eirik the Red and Other Icelandic Sagas* (Jones, 1988, p. 313).
7. See, for example, *Ynglingasaga* (6), *Hrafnsmál* (*The History of Harald Hair-fair* [18] in the *Heimskringla*.
8. Hastings (1991).
9. Grof (1988).
10. An excellent recent reference is Bache (2000).
11. In fact, this seems historically to have been the function of orgies (Young, 1964; Partridge, 1960).
12. As noted, in the first version of the creation story given in the Bible (Genesis 1:27–8), God is represented as a divine hermaphrodite, a common treatment in many early religious systems, including Hinduism, Taoism, and Greek and Norse mythology, for just a few examples.
13. See, for instance, Tannahill (1980), Carr (2003), and McKnee (2002).

6. Breaking Away:
Cosmic Journeys That Leave the Body Behind

1. According to Malidoma Soma, a Dagar shaman.
2. Of course, it is entirely possible that the intensity of the pleasurable sensations reported during transcendent sex could pose a threat to the ego by overwhelming it with delightful excitation, and that the psyche preserves itself using the same mechanisms against dissolution in bliss as against shattering from pain.
3. The literature on OBEs is extensive, and indeed, it has become such a regularly studied phenomenon that it would be impossible to list even a representative sample of citations here other than general texts acknowledging the scope of this literature, such as Gregory (1987).
4. Gabbard and Twemlow using a questionnaire to study of OBEs (1984) found that 3% of all respondents reporting OBEs said that they occurred during orgasm in contrast to my participants who typically said their OBEs followed orgasm. The difference may be an artifact of the wording of their questionnaire.
5. Sexual visions may represent a relatively light altered state, perhaps similar to hypnogogia or Grof's abstract and aesthetic states (1975, 1985, 1988, 1998). Hypnogogia is neither as rationally lucid as waking consciousness, nor as psychodynamically "unconscious" as the dreams produced during REM sleep. It combines the features of both: realistic images and ideas associated in nonrational or magical ways. Unlike hypnogogia, though, the blissful visions of transcendent sex seem completely unrelated to top-of-mind concerns or environmental cues. Transcendent sex may activate

some of the same neural processing, but it seems to place the experience in more imaginal ambits. Grof's abstract and aesthetic experiences consist of visual, and to a lesser extent, auditory hallucinations in which the objects or sounds in the environment seem to change forms. Synesthesia is marked, as is heightened emotional tone. Grof regards these as threshold experiences. It is quite possible that the sexual transports, especially those occurring on the terrestrial plane, may indeed be precursors to more full-blown past-life experiences (see Chapter 8).

7. Time Travel and Revealed Truths: Falling into Past Lives

1. Joshua 10:12–13.
2. For instance, the experiments that show a retroactive ability to influence the present from the future in parapsychology. See, for example, Radin (1996) and Wolf (1998).
3. The sense of time appears to be correlated to brain-wave activity; as beta patterns slow down, so does the sense of time, although the ability to act in time does not. Familiar examples come from athletes who are "in the zone," that is, able to see the ball and other players moving as if in slow motion while they themselves are able to act quickly and perfectly to catch the ball and make a play. People whose attention is suddenly focused, for instance, if they are in a car accident, often see events happening as if in slow motion, but are usually unable to do more than watch.
4. This view is the basis for most regression therapy, which may or may not involve past lives. It seems that distancing events from the self by attributing them to a former self and cloaking them in the trappings of another time and place offers an effective way for individuals to work with ego-threatening material. Regression therapy is efficacious in working with problems that are resistant to more traditional forms of therapy, such as somatic complaints, primal complexes, and obsessive or perseverative behaviors, including addictions.
5. Ian Stevenson's research attempting to verify past lives (1975–80, 1980, 1987, 1997) reported by children in normal states represents an important literature for such claims.
6. See, for instance, Grof (1975, 1988), Netherton and Shiffrin (1978), Woolger (1988) and Wambach (1981).
7. See, for instance, Bache (2000), Grof (1975, 1988), and Ring (1998).
8. These include not only Hinduism, Buddhism, Shintoism, and Taoism, but also Jainism, Zoroastrianism, Sikhism, mystical forms of Christianity and

Judaism, and indigenous traditions in Europe, North and South America, Polynesia, and Africa (see, for instance, Bache [1990] Christie-Murray [1981], Head and Cranston [1985], Ten Dam [1990], and Winkler [1982]).

8. Being in Nothingness: Sex and Nirvana

1. The concept of *shevirah* dates back to the sixteenth-century tradition of Isaac Luria. The expression is not used in Kabbalah as it used here; rather the Shattering of the Vessels signaled the showering of the sacred shards and sparks of splendor into the gross world of impurity. The sparks of splendor are now inextricably mixed with the *kelipot*, the shells or husks of impurity that arose during the creation of the universe. According to the tradition, each person has a responsibility to heal the *kelipot* encountered in daily life to restore divine order. These restorative acts are called *tikkun*, and some of them include mystical sexual union. See, for example. Scholem (1974) and Hoffman (1992).

2. In actuality, these are only the broadest and most rudimentary designations. Various Hindu and Buddhist sects have different names for the end-state they recognize, and they may also stipulate gradations of this state or otherwise make distinctions about its momentary realization as opposed to consolidation in it as an ongoing state of awareness. Such distinctions are too numerous and technical to be treated within the scope of this book.

3. Taoism and Buddhism are nontheistic; Hinduism is the exception in that proper realization of mind will result in the aspirant's becoming one with Brahman-Atman. Some forms of Hinduism, like bhakti yoga, are ecstatic and relationally based, but the deconstruction of illusion can be broadly ascribed to the majority of Hindu spiritual paths.

4. Kena Upanishad, 3.

5. Rendered by translator John C. H. Wu as, "Tao can be talked about, but not the Eternal Tao" in Lao Tzu (1989, p. 3).

6. Attributed to Chuang Tzu, "author" of the eponymous work, who, like Lao Tzu, may not have been an individual; rather these "identities" may stand for collections of Taoist writings compiled by different authors at different times. Quoted in Needham (1956, p. 85).

7. Bhagavad-Gita, IX, 16.

8. The Thunder: Perfect Mind 19.9–15a.

9. The Gospel of Thomas 37.24a–35.

10. Kaplan (1976, p. 105).

11. Brihadaranyaka Upanishad, III, 4.2.

12. Mundaka Upanishad, I, 2.2.

13. Kapleau (1989, p. 239).

14. Chang (1959, p. 45). Emphasis in the original.
15. Quoted in Huxley (1945, p. 189).
16. Wilber (1979, p. 62). Emphasis in the original.
17. Quoted in Kapleau (1989, p. 311).
18. Quoted in Wilber (1979, p. 62).
19. Many of these transformative effects are thought to occur in the spiritual plane rather than in the material world, such as the elimination of karma or the release from certain types of reincarnation.

9. Divine Union: One with God

1. Oneness is also recognized in the Eastern traditions that are based on relationship and devotion as noted in the previous chapter, such as bhakti yoga. Eastern traditions were treated in the previous chapter more or less owing to their emphasis on the deconstruction of illusion prevalent in Buddhism and Hinduism, broadly speaking. This chapter emphasizes relational forms of unitive experiences long associated with Western theistic spirituality.

2. Technically, Jewish mysticism is unique in that its highest goal is not union with God, according to most sources (although there is some dispute; see, for instance, Idel [1988] on Abraham Abulafia and *unio mystica*). The word *yihhud* (union) is not used in referring to the aspirant's search for God; instead it describes the theurgic act in which the different *sefirot* (emanations or energy essences of God) are united among themselves. The highest form of human mystical achievement is the communion with the *sefirot*, not *Ein-Sof* (the absolute and eternal perfection of no distinctions, no differentiations; see Scholem [1974] for comparative descriptions). *Devekut* results in a sense of beatitude, intimacy and union, but it does not entirely eliminate the separation between creature and Creator for all that it produces an ecstatic, complete and transformative kind of consciousness (see for example, Ariel [1988] and Scholem [1974]). Moreover, according to some authorities (e.g., Scholem), only rare individuals, such as Enoch and Elijah, were able to achieve eternal *devekut. Devekut* is not a monolithic event. Rather it is characterized by stages, one of which, interestingly enough, is called *zivvug* (copulation) in which the (male) mystic sublimates his natural eroticism in order to channel it for sacred union with Shekinah, the feminine manifestation of Spirit (Ariel, 1988).

3. As in other traditions, Sufism recognizes additional states of consolidation, so *fana* is not necessarily the ultimate. For example, *baqa* (survival) connotes the return of the mystic after the absorption of *fana* to resume a more perfected way of being in the world.

4. Some researchers consider Eastern and Western impersonal and theistic

states more or less equivalent and interchangeable. See, for instance, Grof (1975).

5. Most kabbalistic texts, such as the *Zohar* and *The Book of Splendor*, are filled with highly detailed, explicit erotic imagery. This literature both affirms that sexual intercourse in marriage is one of the most powerful spiritual practices for transformation and that the cosmos itself is a balanced interplay between divine masculine and feminine forces drawn together by sexual attraction (a view represented in Hinduism and Taoism, as well). Some Kabbalistic writings suggest that lovers participate directly in the divine during the act of copulation. Likewise, in Christianity, the New Testament is full of references comparing Christ to a bridegroom and Christians and the Church to a bride, a metaphor literally enacted when female renunciates undergo a wedding ceremony in the Roman Catholic Church to become "brides of Christ." The Gnostic gospels also contain imagery of a divine sexual couple, with Sophia as the feminine counterpart of God similar to Shekinah in the Kabbalah. Saints like Teresa of Avila were known for their loverlike yearning for union with God. Islam also has many legendary saints and mystics who pursued God as the Beloved, including Rabiah (a woman often compared with Teresa), Abu Yazid Bistami, Husain ibn Mansur (the martyr better known as al-Hallaj), and the frankly erotic contemplative Hafiz and his followers. Indeed, many of the varieties of Sufism have stemmed from the range of ecstatic revelations of the suitors of God.

6. Quoted in Huxley (1945, p. 276).

7. Armstrong (1993, p. 218).

8. Quoted in Huxley (1945, p. 129).

9. In addition to innumerable associations of God with Light in the Bible, for instance, the Ishraqi tradition in Sufism is named for Suhrawardi, a mystic who became known as Sheik al-Ishraq, which means the Master of Illumination, from his personal experiences of God. Even contemporary near-death accounts of individuals going into the Light (not merely encountering a Being of Light) resemble unitive experiences.

10. See for instance, Nasr (1991).

11. Quoted in Huxley (1945, p. 12).

12. The Gospel of Philip, 53.14a.

13. John 10:30.

14. John 17:21.

15. de Caussade (1975/1861, p. 41).

16. E.g., Ariel (1988, p. 62).

17. Quoted in Armstrong (1993, p. 226).

18. Frager and Fadiman (1998), Armstrong (1994).

19. Quoted in Huxley (1945, p. 11).

20. Galatians 2:20.

21. Translation courtesy of the Rev. Rosemarie Anderson.
22. Teresa of Avila (1979, p. 89).
23. Goleman (1988, p. 65).
24. Teresa of Avila (1979, p. 89).

10. Why Didn't Anyone Tell Us About This Before? The Dark Side of Transcendent Sex

1. Probably owing to the way the recruiting query was phrased and to the newness of the research. It is likely that with time, more negative experiences will surface as the phenomenon of involuntary, spontaneous altered-state sex becomes more publicized, as they did in the history of near-death studies.

2. Laura's warning was not about her own experience or her partners' as she indicates, but about others she had met through professional counseling contacts, making her conclusion more of an inference. It is uncertain whether these alleged addicts were having ordinary or nonordinary sex. Nevertheless, her observation is highly plausible and was certainly borne out by participants in the study.

3. A full treatment of these dynamics is beyond the scope of this book. Folk wisdom has long held that people fall in love with their parents: women marry men who are like their fathers; and men, their mothers. It might be argued on fairly sound psychological grounds that fusion with a lover recapitulates a total reconciliation with the caregiver most central to a person's sense of psychological well-being, whether for good or bad. Popular books about the negative types of fusion, sometimes called addictive relationships, treat compelling attractions in which the individual unconsciously seeks a partner who represents the pathological aspects of the parent (for example, Howard M. Halpern's *How to Break Your Addiction to a Person,* Susan Forward's *Obsessive Love,* Robin Norwood's *Women Who Love Too Much,* and Stanton Peele's *Love and Addiction*). These relationships are usually characterized by a kind of merging associated with dysfunctional dependency. Conversely, people also bond with mates who embody the best and most self-affirming aspects of a parent, and such fusion can be extremely beneficial. The fact that the majority of the histories in this book are specific to a particular relationship suggests that some sexual liaisons do indeed meet deeper and more primal needs than others. This conclusion in no way diminishes the power of those connections, nor does it discount their very real spiritual aspects. In fact, in the field of transpersonal psychology, a number of different modalities suggest that there is a nexus

between primal and spiritual issues, and that some of the most exalted experiences affect individuals on multiple levels. See, for example, the work of Carl Jung, Roberto Assagioli, Stanislav Grof, Michael Washburn, et alia.

4. In a condition well documented as "thin boundaries" (Hartmann, 1991).

5. See, for instance, Ring (1992).

11. Grace and Practice: Facilitating Transcendent Sex

1. Ferrer (2002) suggests that all transpersonal events, including these, are better understood not as experiences in which an expansion of individual consciousness permits access to transpersonal knowledge (as is sometimes implied in contemplative forms), but as the emergence of transpersonal knowledge in the locus of the individual in a way that demands the participation of his or her consciousness. Thus the "experience" is no longer an individual, subjective event, but rather the participation of an individual consciousness in a multilocal, transpersonal, epistemic event. In many of these sexual accounts, the multilocal nature of the transpersonal event—in, through, and with the lover as well as the self—is evident. The event is neither in the person nor outside of him or her, but in and *between* both lovers; thus it is already apprehended as multilocal. As the lovers seek participation in each other they naturally effectuate an enveloping. Haule's Third (1990), for instance, is a numinous field that effortlessly enfolds and interpenetrates the lovers. Thus the lovers' experience seems less dualistic, less contrived and in some ways less remarkable than many sanctioned spiritual practices because it is merely the expansion of the mundane into the transcendent in the natural course of quotidian activity, not an event requiring special conditions apart from ordinary life. In this it resembles some mindfulness contemplative forms, though cause-and-effect appears to be more left to grace than the lover's ability to achieve a certain mental control. In some sense, lovers in this study do not feel that they or their partners control their experience, but that it originates outside themselves.

2. A small study of transcendent sex among mainstream Christians suggested that a precedent of interpersonal difficulties and forgiveness was a predisposing factor; see McKnee (2002).

3. Scantling and Browder identified different clusters of absorption they associate with the ability to have what they call "supersex" (1993).

12. Fruits of Transcendent Sex:
Lovemaking and the Spiritual Path

1. See, for example, Ring (1998, 1992, 1984), Flynn (1986), Atwater (1988), Grey (1985), Sutherland (1992, 1993), and Tiberi (1993).

Appendix: The Research Study

1. Wade (2000b).
2. Haule (1990).
3. Grof (1975, 1985).
4. Wade (2000b).
5. Scantling and Browder (1993), Hartmann (1991).
6. See, for example, Murphy (2001), Knoblauch, Schmied, and Schnettler (2001), Zaleski (1987).
7. Wade (2000b).
8. For a recent overview summarizing a vast body of literature, see Ring and Valerino (1998).

References

Adler, J. *Arching Backward: The Mystical Initiation of a Contemporary Woman.* Rochester, VT: Inner Traditions, 1995.

Ariel, D. S. *The Mystic Quest: An Introduction to Jewish Mysticism.* New York: Schocken, 1988.

Armstrong, K. *A History of God: The 4,000-Year Quest of Judaism, Christianity and Islam.* New York: Knopf/Ballantine, 1993.

Atwater, P. M. H. *Coming Back to Life: The After-Effects of Near-Death Experiences.* New York: Dodd, Mead, 1988.

Bache, C. M. *Lifecycles: Reincarnation and the Web of Life.* New York: Paragon, 1990.

Bache, C. M. *Dark Night, Early Dawn: Steps to a Deep Ecology of Mind.* Albany, NY: State University of New York Press, 2000.

Barks, C., trans. *Rumi: We Are Three.* Athens, GA: Maypop, 1987.

Benoit, H. *The Supreme Doctrine.* New York: Viking, 1959.

Bonheim, J. *Aphrodite's Daughters: Women's Sexual Stories and the Journey of the Soul.* New York: Simon & Schuster, 1997.

Brown, P. *The Body and Society: Men, Women and Sexual Renunciation in Early Christianity.* New York: Columbia University Press, 1998.

Carr, D. M. *The Erotic Word: Sexuality, Spirituality, and the Bible.* New York: Oxford University Press, 2003.

Chang, G. C. C. *The Practice of Zen.* New York: Harper & Row, 1959.

Christie-Murray, D. *Reincarnation: Ancient Beliefs and Modern Evidence.* Garden City Park, NY: Avery, 1998.

De Caussade, J-P. *Abandonment to Divine Providence.* Trans. J. Beevers. Garden City, NY: Doubleday, 1975/1861.

Devereux, P. *Shamanism and the Mystery Lines: Ley Lines, Spirit Paths, Shapeshifting & Out-of-Body Travel.* London: Quantum, 1992.

Eliade, M. *Shamanism: Archaic Techniques of Ecstasy.* Trans. W. R. Trask. Princeton, NJ: Princeton University Press, 1974/1951.

Eskildsen, S. *Asceticism in Early Taoist Religion.* Albany, NY: State University of New York Press, 1998.

305

Faure, B. *The Red Thread: Buddhist Approaches to Sexuality.* Princeton, NJ: Princeton University Press, 1998.

Fernandez-Armesto, F. *Near a Thousand Tables: A History of Food.* New York: Free Press, 2002.

Ferrer, J. *Revisioning Transpersonal Theory: A Participatory Vision of Human Spirituality.* Albany, NY: State University of New York Press, 2002.

Flynn, C. P. *After the Beyond: Human Transformation and the Near-Death Experience.* Englewood Cliffs, NJ: Prentice-Hall, 1986.

Forward, S. with Buck, C. *Obsessive Love: When It Hurts Too Much to Let Go.* New York: Bantam, 1991.

Frager, R., and Fadiman, J. *Personality & Personal Growth.* 4th ed. New York: Longman, 1998.

Frazer, J. G. *The Golden Bough.* New York: Macmillan, 1951.

Gabbard, G. and Twemlow, S. W. *With the Eyes of the Mind: An Empirical Analysis of Out-of-Body States.* New York: Praeger, 1984.

Goleman, D. *The Meditative Mind: The Varieties of Meditative Experience.* Los Angeles: Tarcher, 1988.

Gregory, R. L., ed. *The Oxford Companion to the Mind.* New York: Oxford University Press, 1987.

Grey, M. *Return from Death: An Exploration of the Near-Death Experience.* London: Arcana, 1985.

Grof, S.. *Realms of the Human Unconscious: Observations from LSD Research.* New York: Viking, 1975.

Grof, S. *Beyond the Brain: Birth, Death and Transcendence in Psychotherapy.* Albany, NY: State University of New York Press, 1985.

Grof, S. *The Adventure of Self-Discovery: I. Dimensions of Consciousness, II. New Perspectives in Psychotherapy.* Albany, NY: State University of New York Press, 1988.

Grof, S. *The Cosmic Game: Explorations of the Frontiers of Human Consciousness.* Albany, NY: State University of New York Press, 1998.

Grof, S., and Grof, C., eds. *Spiritual Emergency: When Personal Transformation Becomes a Crisis.* New York: Tarcher/Putnam, 1989.

Halpern, H. M. *Cutting Loose: An Adult Guide to Coming to Terms with Your Parents.* New York: Bantam, 1977.

Halpern, H. M. *How to Break Your Addiction to a Person.* New York: Bantam, 1978.

Hastings, A. *With the Tongues of Men and Angels: A Study of Channeling.* Fort Worth, TX: Holt, Rinehart and Winston, 1991.

Haule, J. R. *Divine Madness: Archetypes of Romantic Love.* Boston: Shambhala, 1990.

Head, J., and Cranston, S. L., eds. *Reincarnation: An East-West Anthology.* 5th ed. Wheaton, IL: Theosophical, 1985.

Hoffman, E. *The Way of Splendor: Jewish Mysticism and Modern Psychology.* Northvale, NJ: Aronson, 1992.

Hoffman, V. J. "Islamic perspectives on the human body: Legal, social and spiritual considerations." In *Embodiment, Morality, and Medicine*, edited by L. S. Cahill and M. A. Farley, 37–55. Boston: Kluwer, 1995.

Hufford, D. J. *The Terror That Comes in the Night: An Experience-Centered Study of Supernatural Assault Traditions*. Philadelphia: University of Pennsylvania Press, 1982.

Huxley, A. *The Perennial Philosophy*. New York: Harper, 1945.

Idel, M. *Studies in Ecstatic Kabbalah*. Albany, NY: State University of New York Press, 1988.

Jones, G. trans. *Eirik the Red and Other Icelandic Sagas*. Oxford: Oxford University Press, 1988/1961.

Kakar, S. "Ramakrishna and the mystical experience." *Annual of Psychoanalysis*, 1994, 20: 215–234.

Kalweit, H. *Dreamtime & Inner Space: The World of the Shaman*, trans. W. Wunsche. Boston: Shambhala, 1988.

Kaplan, A. trans. *Rabbi Nachman's Wisdom*. Brooklyn, NY: Author, 1976.

Kapleau, P. *The Three Pillars of Zen*. New York: Anchor/Doubleday, 1989.

Knoblauch, H., Schmied, I., and Schnettler, B. "Different kinds of near-death experience: A report on a survey of near-death experiences in Germany." *Journal of Near-Death Studies* 20 (1) (2001): 15–30.

Kovacks, M. G. ed. and trans. *The Epic of Gilgamesh*. Stanford, CA: Stanford University Press, 1989.

Lewis, C. S. *The Great Divorce*. New York: Collier, 1946.

McDaniel, J. *The Madness of the Saints: Ecstatic Religion in Bengal*. Chicago: University of Chicago Press, 1989.

McKnee, C. M. "Profound sexual and spiritual encounters among practicing Christians: A phenomenological analysis." *Journal of Psychology and Theology* 30 (3) (2002): 234–44.

Maurer, H. *Sex: An Oral History*. New York: Viking, 1994.

Moody, R. A. *Life After Life*. Covington, GA: Mockingbird, 1975.

Moody, R. A. *Reflections on Life after Life*. San Francisco: Cameron, 1977.

Murphy, T. "Near-death experiences in Thailand." *Journal of Near-Death Studies* 19 (3) (2001): 139–160.

Murray, J. "Sexuality and spirituality: The intersection of medieval theology and medicine." *Fides et historia* 23 (1991): 200–26.

Nasr, S. H. "God." In *Islamic Spirituality Foundations* (vol. 1), ed. by S. H. Nasr: 311–323. New York: Crossroad, 1991.

Needham, J. *Science and Civilisation in China* (vol. 2). Cambridge, UK: Cambridge University Press, 1956.

Netherton, M., and Shiffrin, N. *Past Lives Therapy*. New York: Morrow, 1978.

Pagels, E. *The Gnostic Gospels*. New York: Random House/Vintage, 1979.

Pagels, E. *Adam, Eve, and the Serpent*. New York: Random House, 1988.

Parrinder, G. *Sexual Morality in the World's Religions*. Oxford: Oneworld, 1996.

Partridge, B.. *A History of Orgies*. New York: Bonanza, 1960.

Peele, S. with Brodsky, A. *Love and Addiction*. New York: Signet, 1976.

Radin, D. I. "Respeption." Paper presented at Tucson II: Toward a science of consciousness. Tucson, Arizona, April 8–13, 1996.

Reid, D. P. *The Tao of Health, Sex and Longevity: A Modern Practical Guide to the Ancient Way*. New York: Fireside, 1989.

Ring, K. *Life at Death: Scientific Investigation of the Near-Death Experience*. New York: Coward, McCann & Geoghegan, 1980.

Ring, K. *Heading Toward Omega: In Search of the Meaning of the Near-Death Experience*. New York: Morrow, 1984.

Ring, K. *The Omega Project: Near-Death Experiences, UFO Encounters and Mind at Large*. New York: Morrow, 1992.

Ring, K., and Valarino, E. E. *Lessons from the Light: What We Can Learn from the Near-Death Experience*. New York: Plenum, 1998.

Roberts, N. *Whores in History: Prostitution in Western Society*. London: Grafton, 1992.

Saso, M. "The Taoist body and cosmic prayer." In *Religion and the Body*, ed. by S. Coakley: 231–247. Cambridge, England: Cambridge University Press, 1997.

Scantling, S., and Browder, S. *Ordinary Women, Extraordinary Sex: Every Woman's Guide to Pleasure and Beyond*. New York: Dutton, 1993.

Schacter-Shalomi, Z. M. *Spiritual Intimacy: A Study of Counseling in Hasidism*. Northvale, NJ: Jason Aronson, 1991.

Schimmel, A. " 'I take off the dress of the body': Eros in Sufi literature." In *Religion and the Body*, ed . by S. Coakley: 262–288. Cambridge, England: Cambridge University Press, 1997.

Scholem, G. *Kabbalah*. New York: Dorset, 1974.

Sell, I. M. "Third gender: A qualitative study of the experience of individuals who identify as being neither man nor woman." Ph.D. diss., Institute of Transpersonal Psychology, Palo Alto, CA, 2001.

Soma, M. Audiocasette. "Indigenous Views of Intimacy and Sex." Pacific Grove, CA: Oral Tradition Archives.

Stevenson, I. *Cases of the Reincarnation Type* (Vols. 1–3). Charlottesville, VA: University Press of Virginia, 1975–1980.

Stevenson, I. *Twenty Cases Suggestive of Reincarnation*, rev. ed. Charlottesville, VA: University Press of Virginia, 1980.

Stevenson, I. *Children Who Remember Previous Lives: A Question of Reincarnation*. Charlottesville, VA: University Press of Virginia, 1987.

Stevenson, I. *Where Reincarnation and Biology Intersect*. Westport, CT: Praeger, 1997.

Sturlason, S. *Heimskringla or the Lives of the Norse Kings*, ed. by E. Monson and trans. by A. H. Smith. New York: Dover, 1990/1932.

Sturlason, S. *The Poetic Edda*, second ed., rev. Trans. by L. M. Hollander. Austin: University of Texas Press.

Sutherland, C. *Transformed by the Light: Life after Near-Death Experiences*. New York: Bantam, 1992.

Sutherland, C. *Within the Light*. New York: Bantam, 1993.

Tannahill, R. *Sex in History*. New York: Stein and Day, 1980.

Tart, C. T., and Jones, L. Initial list of subsystem characteristics of some major emotional states. Unpublished manuscript, 1997.

Ten Dam, H. *Exploring Reincarnation*. Trans. By A. E. J. Wils. London: Penguin, 1990.

Teresa of Avila. *The Interior Castle*. Trans. By K. Kavanaugh and O. Rodriguez. New York: Paulist Press, 1979.

Thorsson, O., ed. *The Sagas of Icelanders: A Selection*. New York: Viking Penguin, 2000.

Tiberi, E. "Extrasomatic emotions." *Journal of Near-Death Studies 11*(3) (1993): 149–170.

Tzu, Lao. *Tao Te Ching*. Trans. by J. C. H. Wu. Boston: Shambhala, 1989.

Van Gulik, R. H. *Sexual Life in Ancient China: A Preliminary Survey of Chinese Sex and Society from ca. 1500 B.C. till 1644 A.D.* Leiden, Netherlands: E. J. Brill, 1974.

Wade, J. "Meeting God in the flesh: Spirituality in sexual intimacy." *ReVision 21*(2) (1998): 35–41.

Wade, J. "The love that dares not speak its name." In *Transpersonal Knowing: Exploring the Horizon of Consciousness*, ed. by T. Hart, P. L. Nelson, and K. Puhakka: 271–302. Albany, NY: State University of New York Press, 2000a.

Wade, J. "Mapping the courses of heavenly bodies: The varieties of transcendent sexual experience." *Journal of Transpersonal Psychology 23*(2) (2000b): 103–122.

Wade, J. Dangerous liaisons: Sex and spiritual emancipation. *ReVision 24*(2) (2001): 42–50.

Waite, A. E. *The Holy Kabbalah: A Study of the Secret Tradition in Israel as Unfolded by Sons of the Doctrine for the Benefit of the Elect Dispersed Through the Lands and Ages of the Greater Exile*. New Hyde Park, NY: University Books, 1960.

Walsh, R. *The Spirit of Shamanism*. New York: Tarcher/Perigee, 1990.

Wambach, H. *Life Before Life*. New York: Bantam, 1981.

Wang, S. T. *The Tao of Sexology: The Book of Infinite Wisdom*. San Francisco: Tao Publishing, 1986.

Ware, K. " 'My helper and my enemy': The body in Greek Christianity." In *Religion and the Body*, ed. by S. Coakley: 90–110. Cambridge, England: Cambridge University Press, 1997.

White, D. G., ed. *Tantra in Practice*. Princeton, NJ: Princeton University Press, 2000.

Wilber, K. *No Boundary: Eastern and Western Approaches to Personal Growth*. Boston: Shambhala, 1979.

Wiesner-Hanks, M. E. *Christianity and Sexuality in the Early Modern World: Regulating Desire, Reforming Practice.* London: Routledge, 2000.

Winkler, G. *The Soul of the Matter: A Psychological and Philosophical Study of the Jewish Perspective on the Odyssey of the Human Soul before, during, and after "Life."* New York: Judaica Press, 1982.

Wolf, F. A. *The Eagle's Quest: A Physicist's Search for Truth in the Heart of the Shamanic World.* New York: Summit, 1991.

Wolf, F. A. The timing of conscious experience: A causality-violating, two-valued, transactional interpretation of subjective antedating and spatial-temporal projection. Paper presented at Tucson III: Toward a science of consciousness. Tucson, Arizona, April 27–May 2, 1998.

Woolger, R. J. *Other lives, Other Selves: A Jungian Psychotherapist Discovers Past Lives.* New York: Bantam, 1988.

Young, W. *Eros Denied: Sex in Western Society.* New York: Grove, 1964.

Zaleski, C. *Otherworld Journeys: Accounts of Near-Death Experience in Medieval and Modern Times.* New York: Oxford University Press, 1987.

Zimmerman, J., and McCandless, J. *Flesh and Spirit: The Mystery of Intimate Relationship.* Las Vegas: Bramble, 1998.

Acknowledgments

I WISH TO DEMONSTRATE my gratitude to those who helped me develop this book. When I began working on it, the subject matter was sufficiently controversial and challenging that most of the responses I received were curious, doubting, or outright discouraging. It was a real joy to find those occasional individuals who were supportive, and my greatest hope is that learning how their work has transformed others will, in some way, repay their kindness. I can never adequately express my gratitude to the lovers who confided their sacred, weird, and sometimes frightening experiences to me, making it possible to share them with the world.

There are a number of others I wish to thank. I owe the deepest gratitude to Kenneth Ring, whose model of appreciative inquiry, continuous inspiration, and critical reading of this manuscript have been beyond price. I would also like to thank my dear friend Jorge Ferrer, whose work began to parallel my own and whose original exploration brought many new resources and ideas to my attention. Charley Tart was instrumental in sharing his encyclopedic knowledge of the limitations of the research on altered states associated with everyday activities, like sex. Stan Grof, whose work represented the most extensive, if largely unpublished, contemporary research on adventitious sexual altered states, was of immense help, especially in providing an early forum for presentation to other scholars. William Braud and Rosemarie Anderson at the Institute of Transpersonal Psychology were most encouraging of my early efforts. Ken Wilber and the stunning array of talent he assembled in his Integral Institute provided an interested group who contributed to this work in innumerable ways. Thanks also to Rhea White, who was the catalyst for getting the English version of this book published. Finally, thanks are due to my dear friend Kaisa Puhakka and her coauthors Tobin Hart and Peter Nelson, whose request first sparked my formal inquiry into what had previously been completely private experiences.

Index

abstinence, 6, 228
accepting whatever happens, 251–52
agape, 57
agnosticism, 15, 26, 105, 164, 254, 259
al-Hallaj (Sufi mystic), 189
Allen, Woody, viii
altered states:
  ancient deities, possession by, 104–10
  animal possession, 94–101
  dark side of transcendent sex, *see* dark side of transcendent sex
  defined, 204
  deliberate pursuit of, 37
  destabilizing effect of, 37–38
  enlightenment, *see* enlightenment
  goodness of relationship unrelated to, 231–32
  learning how to stop, 230–31
  out-of-body experiences, *see* out-of-body experiences
  past-life experiences, *see* past-life experiences
  shapeshifting, 94–101
  union with God, *see* union with God (*unio mystica*)
amrita, 37
Amrit Desai, Yogi, 209

ancient deities:
  possession by, 104–10
  sacred ceremonies, 69–70
  visitation by, 43–49
angels, 41–43
animals:
  possession, 94–101
  religious rituals to bring about possession by, 95, 100
  spiritual connection with, 61–68
Ansari of Herat, Sufi, 185
Aristotle, viii
asceticism, 5, 6
astral body, 117
astral projection, 112
atheism, 15, 26, 254, 259
Augustine, Saint, 6, 185
awakening, 170, 189
awe:
  enlightenment and, 166

bears:
  berserkers, 100–01
  possession by, 96, 97–98
berserkers, 100–01
Bhagwan Shree Rajneesh, 209
birds of prey, possession by, 94, 99
Bistami, Abu Yazid, 188
blissful emotions, 29, 37, 53, 112

313

Dr. Jenny Wade invites adult men and women to contribute to her ongoing research on spontaneous altered states that occur during sex, whether alone or with a partner. She welcomes reports of what happened to you if:

You are over the age of 21

You have had a sexual experience in which your sense of your body, yourself, your surroundings, relations with objects or others, or the passage of time have seemed to have changed from your normal, waking sense of reality

You were not using drugs of any kind

You were not practicing Tantra, Taoist sex, or meditation at the time

Your confidentiality is strictly protected. To submit an experience, or learn more about such experiences, go to Dr. Wade's internet address for this project:

www.TranscendentSex.org

Lightning Source UK Ltd.
Milton Keynes UK
UKHW011906060520
362886UK00001B/317